The Wayfarers

*Journeying through
a Century of Change*

Virginia Ames

The Wayfarers: Journeying through a Century of Change
Copyright© 2014 Virginia Wade Ames

Library of Congress Control Number: 2014908657

ISBN: 978-1-4993878-6-5

BIOGRAPHY & AUTOBIOGRAPHY / Personal Memoirs
TRAVEL / Essay

QUANTITY PURCHASES: Companies, professional groups, clubs, and
other organizations may qualify for special terms when ordering quanti-
ties of this title. For information e-mail VWA@flordemayoarts.com.

This book is printed in the United States of America.

The
Wayfarers

*Journeying through
a Century of Change*

Virginia Wade Ames

Dedication

Dedicated to the memory of my husband, Robert Hyde Ames,
and to our daughters Lucy, Martha, and Mary

Bob Ames in his Tucson retirement, 1980s

Lucy Dunbar Ames, age 4, pastel portrait

Martha Hyde Ames, age 4, pastel portrait

Mary Elizabeth Ames, age 6, pastel portrait

Contents

Foreword

In the mid-nineteenth century, my husband's grandmother, Sarah
Lucy Hyde Ames, read a suggestion in *The New York Times* that
everyone should describe what life was like during their time, personal remembrances that one might not find in history books. This
inspired her to record recollections from her childhood in Manhattan
and on into her maturity. She wrote of her father taking her to see
a menagerie of animals on 42nd Street in New York, brought there
by P.T. Barnum. Sarah and her father walked to 42nd Street—what
is now Times Square—on sidewalks made of wooden planks. As was
the custom, her father walked on the outside to protect his daughter
from dirty water that residents might throw into the streets from the

windows above. She also recalled that sheep grazed in the fields of Morningside Heights.

Sarah's daughter, Catharine McEwen Ames, carried on her mother's tradition, describing her memories of life in St. Paul, Minnesota, when she was young. She walked to school in moccasins, where her classmates were both Anglos and Native Americans. One day, while leaning on the picket fence of her home, she watched a parade passing by. She saw Grover Cleveland at the head of the parade. He was campaigning in the Twin Cities during his race to become the President of the United States.

The stories of these two women inspired me to write what life was like in the twentieth century, since I was privileged to experience most of it. I was born and grew up in the Deep South and spent my college years and early married life in Cincinnati, Ohio. Years later, after Pearl Harbor, the Navy ordered my husband to duty in Washington, D.C. When peace came and Bob was discharged from the Navy, we remained in the metropolitan area for almost four decades, our residence across the Potomac in Alexandria, Virginia.

There are few today who do not know that the Russians sent the first satellite into orbit around Earth, but can anyone today *feel* both the wonder and the anxiety that we felt as we huddled close together in the dark of the Cold War watching Sputnik on its silent pass over our nation's Capital City?

Later, when our astronauts landed safely on the moon, I felt like I was jumping lightly up and down with them as they bounced out of the capsule and floated across the moon's surface. I trained my eyes on the video that the astronauts were taking of the earth from space, dizzy with disorientation for a moment. Where was I? What could this mean for our future?

So many powerful happenings influenced my life. We felt tension in our country about the war in Europe, but when my brother-in-law called to say, "The Japanese have just attacked Pearl Harbor!"

I picked up my one-year-old baby with a foolish thought that I could protect her from this kind of world.

Many such memories came alive in conversations with my daughter Mary as we drove a twenty-year-old Dodge Wayfarer from Washington, D.C., to the State of Washington. This "epic journey" took place during the month of October 1970. Our reflections on that journey reached across the century that brought more change to humankind than all the combined years since our ancestors came down from the trees and walked tall in the grassy plains of Africa.

An Important
Note to the Reader

Throughout the text of Part One you will find numbered "Note" references. These correspond to their explanations of the times after this trip took place, which are found in Part Two, "How It All Turned Out." Photographs and artwork referenced within the text of each chapter are included at the end of the chapters with their captions.

A caveat: Memory can be tricky, and though I have been accused of being an elephant in that regard, I apologize if happenings or the names of individuals related in this writing differ from others' perceived "facts." I have fact-checked to the best of my ability and striven to be as truthful as possible, yet the most significant contributions provided within these pages are a recounting of what life was like for me and those closest to me in an attempt to show how regular people lived through, dealt with, and felt the impact of our shared history.

PART ONE

A composite of the historical buildings in
Old Town Alexandria–original silkscreen
print on cloth by Virginia Ames

CHAPTER I

October 19, 1970
Odometer: 27,076

Location: Somewhere
south of St. Louis, Missouri
Trip meter: 1,076

The Lonely Road, original watercolor by V. W. Ames

What's Past Is Prologue

My twenty-three-year-old daughter, Mary, and I took turns driving a 1950 Dodge Wayfarer over a deteriorated dual highway south of St. Louis. The car, affectionately dubbed "Betsy" by her former owner, was, despite her twenty years, well-engineered and solidly built. She absorbed bumps easily. The car, in fact, was a lot like the two of us, flawed yet reliable, unfashionable but intriguing. For whatever reason, she turned heads.

Though rain clouds hung low over the rolling Missouri farmland, our spirits were high. Since leaving St. Louis earlier in the morning, we'd seen few signs of life except for lonesome farmhouses and the occasional silo on the far horizon. The road, damaged by winter frosts,

17

had been halfheartedly repaired with patches of asphalt. Uncut grass and weeds grew high in the median. Every few miles, in places too barren even for weeds to take root, hard-packed tire tracks left evidence of drivers desperate to turn back the way they had come.

"Mams," Mary called out from her place behind the wheel as we passed under a bridge. "Keep your eye out for police cars. They hide in places like those. Not that I'm speeding."

We were climbing a long, steep hill when our engine faltered several times. There was no doubt about it. We both felt the repeated hesitation of the motor. The engine sputtered and then cut out entirely moments after we reached the brink of the hill and started to roll down the other side. Mary turned Betsy to the safety of the shoulder on her left and secured the emergency brake. After gaining our composure, we spied an old filling station on the opposite lane of the old dual highway that we hoped was still serving cars.

"If you'll watch for oncoming cars," Mary said, "I'll let Betsy roll down to the bottom of the hill. She is so heavy I'm sure she will gain the momentum needed to cross over to that garage. If we can't make it I'll just pull off the highway wherever I can. Ready?"

"No cars coming!" I shouted.

Mary released the brake and the car picked up enough momentum to cross the median, creep across the opposite lane, and stop on the broken apron of the filling station. We sat for a moment to let our pulses return to normal and figure out what to do next. Near the old building were two equally ancient gasoline pumps. They stood tall, topped with a large glass container through which the fuel could be seen as it was pumped. I told Mary I thought that pump had gone the way of the Model T Ford.

A young man—maybe in his twenties—appeared. He wore dirty overalls. Grease covered his hands and spotted his face. A shock of black hair stuck up like rough-cut hay coated with oil. He blended in perfectly with his surroundings. He looked us over carefully but was so silent I wondered if he might be mute.

"Our engine cut out back on that hill and we saw your garage," I finally said. "We were wondering if you could help."

"Sure ... I could really help two ladies like you. Just roll 'er in here." He opened the creaking double door, and the three of us pushed the car onto the dirt floor of his shop and over the lift.

Mary and I flashed a glance at each other. Without a word we got back into the car, seeking whatever protection we could find from this stranger and his penetrating gaze. Soon enough, we knew we had made a mistake. Without warning, the man raised the car on the lift, took a quick look underneath, and departed—leaving us stranded a few feet in midair. We saw him dial the telephone in his makeshift office and heard him say, "Hey, Joe. What ya' doin'? Get on over here. I got a couple of good-looking women in my garage."

Mary and I threw open the car doors and slid down to the floor. If we had to abandon the car, so what? At least we would be free to escape on foot. Bob had said Betsy wasn't worth fretting over if she gave us trouble.

The mechanic's buddy—we could tell from the part of the conversation we heard—would not be joining him. Thank Heaven! At least the odds were in our favor. Mary seemed calm but I was still imagining the worst.

The mechanic returned, whistling to himself and grinning. Unaffected by our imminent escape, he proceeded to lower the lift, remove Betsy's carburetor, and examine it like a medical student. "Here's your problem," he proudly announced.

We were not so sure.

He put the part in a vise on a workbench and motioned to us. "Come on over here. I want to show you a little something."

We leaned our heads in close to better see the carburetor's moving parts, expecting to see something stuck, rusted, clogged, or broken. The mechanic pressed his finger down on a lever, causing gasoline to spurt out through a small tube and into another cavity. "Sexy little thing, isn't it?" he said, his mouth curling up at the edge.

19

I stepped back, away from him, and spoke with a calm I did not feel. "Well, the carburetor appears to be working fine. If you'll re-install it and tell us what we owe, we won't take up any more of your time." We went outside, putting as much distance as possible between us and that offensive young man.

When he was through and I'd paid him, Mary hurried into the driver's seat. I closed my purse tight, jumped in the passenger side, and slammed the door behind me.

"Whew!" Mary whistled as the engine actually turned over. Miraculously, it kept running, despite her heavy foot on the accelerator.

As we bounced across the median and turned south again, I sighed. "At least we got away without having to pay that creep for a carburetor we didn't need."

We still didn't know what the problem might be, but as uneventful miles between us and that disconcerting mechanic increased, we felt assured that Betsy would not let us down—or leave us in a dubious situation. After such a bonding, we had truly become a threesome.

CHAPTER 2

October 8, 1970
Odometer: about 26,000

Location: Alexandria, Virginia
Trip meter: Zero

The Car Buff
Succumbs to a
Woman in Distress

Bob Ames, the "car buff," with Pappy Blood
(Kaye Sanborn's father, Albert Blood)
and Bob's 1936 Rolls Royce

W hen Mary heard that her father had bought yet another old car—not an antique one, officially speaking, but still "old"— she came up to our house on Seminary Hill from her apartment in downtown Alexandria to see it.

Bob removed his tweed cap and scratched his forehead, "I really didn't want the car. It was just too good a deal to pass up."

Mary laughed. It was not like him to buy anything on impulse, especially a car.

"I guess Emma caught me in a weak moment," he said.

Emma, an acquaintance from church, was former owner of the 1950 Dodge Wayfarer that now belonged to us. Over the years she had grown fond of her automobile and had named it Betsy, as if the car were her close companion.

When Emma reached eighty, her doctor told her to stop driving. For two decades the car had been parked in front of Emma's apartment and used only to take her to church each week or to the grocery store at the corner. Once in a while Emma and Betsy may have ventured elsewhere, but never far from home. Every six months, despite the scant mileage driven, Emma took the car religiously to her local garage for an oil change.

Shaking her head with vigor, Emma had declared that she would never sell her car to just *anyone*, not even to the Episcopal minister who coveted it. When the cleric test drove it, Emma told Bob, "He put the brake on too hard." The vegetable man made her an offer too, but she refused him because she was sure he'd soil Betsy's immaculate upholstery.

Emma knew that Bob owned two antique automobiles, so she asked one day if I'd bring him by to see her car. Maybe he could help her find the right buyer.

Bob frowned. "I know very little about the Dodge brand of automobiles, especially the older ones. It sounds as if Emma really needs help, so I'm willing to try if you want me to."

We found Betsy parked in her usual spot, a streamlined chrome ornament shining on the hood, but the paint was pitted and dulled from having lived too long in the sun, humidity, and winter road salt of Northern Virginia. Emma urged Bob to get behind the wheel and drive Betsy around the block. He obliged, and I watched his interest grow as he shifted through the gears.

"Ginny," he said, "this car has fluid drive."

Bob was a living car encyclopedia. He knew how automobile manufacturers had experimented over the decades, trying to develop innovative gearing systems, including this one—a kind of hybrid between standard shift and automatic. I had never heard of fluid drive before. Bob was amazed at how smoothly Betsy shifted, for an old girl, and how her motor purred.

During his test drive, Bob decided to take the car onto the Shirley Highway and really open her up. But before he did that, he checked the gauges. Gas tank full. Odometer–26,000 miles. He couldn't believe it. The car had been driven only an average of 1,300 miles a year. I didn't realize it then, but looking back, I think that must have been the moment he fell for Betsy. She was exotic and experienced, but still had plenty of good years ahead of her.

We had pulled the car into its parking place and were about to say farewell to Emma when Bob blurted out, "How about this? I'll give you $50 more than your best offer."

I was stunned. Bob and Emma talked for a minute in low tones. Then he got out his checkbook, penned a few lines, and the car was ours—just like that.

As she waved goodbye, a $250 check in her hand, Emma called out, "Oh, I forgot to tell you. Don't drive Betsy more than forty-five miles an hour. She doesn't like to go faster than that. But you won't have a bit of trouble if you stay under forty-five."

We entered Orleans Place, the quiet cul-de-sac where we had lived for seven years. It was a relatively new neighborhood of individually designed homes built in the early 1960s on a portion of a hundred-acre estate that, until then, had been largely untouched since Civil War days. Our neighborhood was sandwiched between the sprawling campus of the Virginia Theological Seminary on one side and the modern Alexandria Hospital on the other. It was located on a hill known simply as Seminary Hill, or the Hill, about three miles west of historic downtown Alexandria.

How strange our motorcade must have looked to the neighbors, with me at the wheel of our shiny Ford Galaxy followed by Bob driving old Betsy. Bob slipped the Wayfarer between his 1936 Rolls Royce and a 1955 MG roadster that he and Mary owned together. He leaned against Betsy and surveyed the scene. "This place looks like someone's trying to start an antique car museum." He paused and sighed. "I really don't know what made me buy Betsy."

Listening for the second time to this admission, I asked, "If you don't want the car, why don't you give it to Lucy and Mike? With their two small children they could probably use another car."

Bob's face lit up. "Perfect."

Lucy is the eldest of our three girls: Lucy, Martha, and Mary. Lucy, who is older than youngest Mary by seven years, graduated from Stanford University in 1962. While we were building our "new" home in Alexandria, Lucy and Mike, a young Westerner she had met at university, were married. He had since become a doctor, and they'd settled in Seattle, Washington, his hometown—3,000 miles from ours—where they had bought a home and started their family. Our granddaughter was now three years old and our grandson was one. Dr. Mike used one of their pre-kid cars to commute to his long day of work downtown, and Lucy used the other—a small BMW roadster—to haul the children on her daily errands or to the park. I was concerned for their safety.

We dialed Lucy and told her about Betsy. "If you want the car, she's yours. Would you be embarrassed to drive such an old car?"

"Not at all, Mom," she said. "I'd be happy to have it, *if* you can get it here."

Bob, who would have jumped at the chance for a cross-country road trip, was too busy at work to leave. But Mary was due two weeks of vacation time from her first year as a reporter with the local newspaper, the *Alexandria Journal*. She volunteered to go with me and share the driving. What a joy it would be to have nine or ten days together on an adventure across the continent!

Mary began immediately to make plans for the trip. "Since it's so late in the fall, maybe we ought to take the warmer southern route. I know you'd like to spend the first night with your sister in Cincinnati. Then we could head south through Missouri. Dad has relatives somewhere near St. Louis, doesn't he?"

24

"Yes, the Pope family: your dad's niece Marcia and her husband, Fred, an Episcopal minister."

"If there is time, it would be neat to dip southwest to Tucson to see Muffin and meet some of her amazing friends, those brilliant scholars like the one who was the first geologist to set foot on Antarctica with Admiral Byrd's expedition. It will be great to know what her life is now like in her adopted desert home."

Martha, our middle daughter, is known as Muffin, or Muff for short. After graduating from Brown University in 1967, Muff had gone to Tucson, Arizona, to continue her studies in geology and tree-ring dating at the University of Arizona. She became so interested in her work and so enamored with the beauty of the rich Sonoran Desert environment that she decided to make Tucson her home.

I ran the itinerary past Bob, then told Mary that I agreed heartily with her suggested route. Bob's only condition was that he would have Betsy thoroughly road tested by his trusted mechanic and the points and plugs replaced before we set off. If the mechanic had any hesitation about whether the car could make the trip, we wouldn't go.

"I've never seen a twenty-year-old car so well maintained," the mechanic told Bob. "Give her a paint job and you'd think she was new."

Two days later, when Bob kissed us goodbye, he said, "Don't forget how little I gave Emma for this car. If it gives you any trouble, just get rid of her and fly home."

25

Vaucluse — a Virginia Homestead

"Vaucluse"—one of the first Fairfax homes

CHAPTER 3

Thursday, October 15, 1970
Odometer reading at trip
departure: 26,000 miles

Location: Alexandria, Virginia,
to Wheeling, West Virginia
Trip meter: We set the trip
meter at *Zero* before
departing Alexandria.

Two Families, Three Centuries

It was after noon when we finally got on the road. Mary steered Betsy out of our gravel driveway and onto the firm pavement of Orleans Place. In the rearview mirror I saw Bob still standing, as I knew he would until we were out of sight. We waved another farewell.

Mary and I were in a jubilant, holiday mood, with lunch in our bellies and a car full of presents for friends and relatives along the way. I did have a momentary tightness in my throat on leaving home. How dear to my heart this parcel of land had become, this *pied a terre* that Bob and I had chosen in our middle years on which to build our dream home.

27

Memories of its birth flooded in. I had urged the developer to call the neighborhood Vaucluse, to preserve the old name of the land I had seen on an early deed, and he had not only consented but asked me to name the streets of his development as well. Here we were, in a mature oak forest, and I felt that one of my best-ever contributions to preservation was seeing that the developer cut *only* the trees necessary for the home footprints. With the woods preserved, the neighborhood of Vaucluse has an integrity that few new developments, built on scraped land, can enjoy. Knowing my penchant for art, the developer also asked me to design the decorative fireplace tiles in another home he was building. This really endorsed my artwork as professional, rather than just a hobby.

"Whoever originally named this land Vaucluse," Mary theorized, "must have been influenced by some Frenchman, just as Thomas Jefferson was."

"That would have been the Fairfax family in the early 1800s."

From Orleans Place we turned onto Gaillard Street, both names I had conceived in keeping with the French theme of our community. Gaillard meant "gay blade" (or perhaps "cool dude" in another parlance), which I romantically derived from a story about a young Confederate soldier who reportedly became the Ghost of Vaucluse. It also happened to be the name of an old flame from my Mobile High School days.

We turned west on Seminary Road and passed a large oasis of open property still known as the Andrews' estate, though the Andrews family had not lived there for many years. The twenty or thirty acres were the remainder of a larger parcel that had been eaten away at its edges by a new hospital and our housing development. Visible through the trees was the old frame house where the hospital administrator and his family now lived. It was dignified by age and sparkling with a fresh coat of white paint. The estate's old guest cottage, a cozy little WWI-era prefab that supposedly had been moved from Fort Belvoir, was no longer there. Our family had rented it in

1962 while our Orleans Place house was being built, but it ultimately went under the blade of development. During its existence, it had become known on Seminary Hill as The Cottage.

"You know, Mamsie, when we lived in The Cottage, I used to look out my bedroom window at that big house and wonder what the family was like that lived in such a huge home."

I smiled at Mary's term of endearment. Mary—and Muff—still frequently address me as Mamsie, as they have done ever since reading *Five Little Peppers and How They Grew* when they were young. I thought about the additional title bestowed upon me in recent years. I'd been affectionately dubbed Oma Ginny by my first grandchild, Clo, in Seattle, as she was born in Germany.

"Well, I don't know for sure, but they left some interesting clues. You know that book I've talked about, *Confessions of a Poor Relation?*"

"Yes."

"That was written by Mrs. Andrews. Her maiden name was Marietta Minnigerode. She was very well-connected and entertained many prominent people in that house. I can tell you all sorts of stories from her book, but the one I like the best isn't one of hers. I heard it from the former caretaker of the property, who visited with me at The Cottage from time to time to talk about the old days."

"What story is that?"

"Do you remember that old pine tree out in the meadow between The Cottage and Seminary Road?"

"Yeah, you called it 'The Woodrow Wilson Tree'?" [Image 3.1]

I nodded. "Do you know how it got its name?"

"I just thought someone admired that president."

"There's more to it than that. Evidently President Wilson's wife was a good friend of Marietta Andrews. According to Mr. Howard, the caretaker, the First Lady had come to tea on the day the pine tree sapling was to be planted. When Mr. Wilson arrived to pick up his wife, he asked to be driven across the field to watch the planting from the comfort of his limousine."

"You mean President Wilson was driven across the same field in front of The Cottage that Dad and I used to mow with our old push-it lawnmower?"

"That's right, if you believe Mr. Howard's story ... and I do. No telling who else might have walked across that field or stayed at The Cottage. Madame Andrews was hostess to a remarkable array of people. I wish I had known her."

"You'd need a time machine. If I remember from American history class, President Wilson was elected the year you were born, Mams."

"1914 ... right you are."

The Wayfarer had reached U.S. Route 50, and Mary was preoccupied with making the turn west. I consulted the map. "When Dad drives to Cincinnati he stays on Route 50 all the way, but I would rather avoid the mountains in West Virginia at night. What do you think of going north to the Pennsylvania Turnpike, crossing the river into Ohio at Wheeling, and then turning south to catch Route 50 again?" Mary agreed to the extended detour and volunteered to keep driving until she was tired.

"Now, about the history of Vaucluse. Could you start from the beginning so I can follow better? I'm your math girl, remember? History wasn't my strong suit. Besides, it's much more interesting when you know there won't be a test."

I turned to her with a smile and renewed enthusiasm.

"My love of the land on Seminary Hill is kind of an obsession. I've been delving to learn the fascinating history of colonial Virginia ... especially our local part ... back to the early 1600s. Soon after 1607 when Jamestown was founded by the English, King James the First granted a patent of land, thousands of acres, to Thomas, Lord Fairfax, Earl of Cameron. The holdings were consolidated around a colonial mansion named Belvoir that the Fairfax family built on the southwest shore of the Potomac River near the present-day town of Alexandria. The family became so dominant that the name persists throughout the area."

"Seems it's everywhere ... Fairfax County ... the City of Fairfax ..."

"Well, there was another loyal subject of the king who was granted just as much land as Lord Fairfax, though you may never have heard his name."

"Who was that?"

"Sir John Peyton."

"Right, that's a new one on me. Not the guy that *Peyton Place* was named after, is he?"

I laughed. "Not likely."

"So there were two families that settled Northern Virginia?" Mary asked more seriously. "Hmm. Sounds to me as though the king had something more than generosity in mind in giving away all that land. He must have figured a little competition would get the colony established faster and its natural resources flowing back to England sooner."

"That competition must have worked. Both men, of course, divided the land among their heirs about 200 years after the land grants. One of John Peyton's heirs, Valentine Peyton, sold 100 acres to a Thomas Fairfax, apparently a direct heir of the original Thomas Lord Fairfax. Land records still accessible in the Fairfax County courthouse reveal that in the 1830s Valentine Peyton sold approximately 100 of his acres to Thomas Fairfax, a descendent of the Thomas Lord Fairfax who got his land by royal grant. That was the 100-acre tract on Seminary Hill of which our neighborhood is a part."

"Okay, I'm with you so far," Mary said.

"The significance of that for us is that it was the first connection of the land with the Andrews family. You see, Mrs. Andrews was a descendant of Valentine Peyton."

"But he sold the land to the Fairfaxes. How did it get back into the Peyton family?"

"Well, it took another seventy-one years, which, as you probably know, were some of the most fascinating and tumultuous years in our young nation's history. For now, though, I'll skip forward to the time the Andrews acquired their estate."

"Good. I'm reaching my limit for absorbing historical facts."

I laughed and went on, cutting the story short. "According to Marietta Andrews' book, in the early 1900s, her husband, Eliphalet Fraser Andrews, in order to please his wife, bought what was left of the 100-acre tract from the Fairfaxes to get it back to a Peyton descendent. They built a large Victorian-style home on their land ... the same large, white house visible from your old bedroom at The Cottage.

"Eliphalet Andrews was a son of a wealthy Ohio merchant and a newcomer to the nation's capital. He was an artist and teacher at the Corcoran School of Art and Marietta was one of his students. They fell in love and were married. Some years later, after they had reared two children to adulthood and had lost their daughter, Mary Lord, Marietta built the guest cottage in her memory."

We grew silent thinking of the happy days we had spent in that cottage. After a while Mary said, "I loved my earlier years in Virginia Heights, before we moved to The Cottage. So many friends to play with ... and nice adults as well. We felt safe in our little community under the oak trees."

"It is a pity we outgrew those little post-war ramblers. My challenge was where to move with our growing family. There was undeveloped acreage along Seminary Road, right within the City of Alexandria, with a forest of huge trees and fields of wildflowers. When a sign appeared on that property announcing that a developer was offering home sites for sale, I persuaded your father to inquire about building there. We purchased the first lot. Over a period of three centuries only two families had owned the land on which our house would be built. That was 1961 and real estate was selling fast. We immediately sold our little Virginia Heights house in Fairfax County, before our new one was built. The developer, who had purchased The Cottage along with about half of the Andrews land, rented it to us for lodging during construction."

I interrupted myself to see how far we'd gotten along U.S. Route 50. After all, I was supposed to be the navigator when Mary was driving and vice versa. We'd gone about eighty miles, so it was time for me to alert her that Virginia State Route 79 North would be appearing soon. Our goal was to reach the Laurel Mountain entrance to the Pennsylvania Turnpike and find a suitable motel not too long after dark for a quick overnight stay in order to arrive in Cincinnati at a reasonable hour the following day.

"I'll hurry every chance I get," Mary teased. "But go ahead with your story. Listening to it doesn't slow me down."

"Let's see, where was I?"

"I think we were about to build our new house on Orleans Place."

"Well, it took a long time to build, and when we finally moved in, I could hardly wait to tackle the garden ... to plant azaleas in the dappled light of our oak and dogwood trees. As I turned over the soil exposing the stones, it occurred to me that if these stones could talk they would tell us of the people who hunted this land in moccasin feet, who crossed it on horseback and in carriages, and later in motorcars. These stones would tell the history of America in microcosm. [Image 3.2]

"It pleased me to imagine George Washington riding through our woods. General Braddock, with a young Washington by his side, could have explored this land during the French and Indian War, before the two marched together to Fort Duquesne. During his youth as a surveyor, Washington would surely have ridden his horse up the southeast slope of our hill on his way from Mount Vernon to survey the diamond square of land that was to become the nation's Capital City. Although a corner of that original square south of the Potomac never became a part of D.C., it did become Arlington County, Virginia.

"It is also possible, though pure conjecture, that the young Robert E. Lee explored The Hill when he was living in Old Town Alexandria with his widowed mother. It's a fact that he attended school down in the town."

Mary looked quizzical. "When was it in this scheme of things that the Theological Seminary was built and the whole area became known as Seminary Hill? I know it was before the Civil War. Was it even before Thomas Fairfax bought the 100 acres from Valentine Peyton?"

"It was in 1823, seven years before Thomas Fairfax arrived on the scene. The Episcopal Church needed a place to train young men to become ministers, so they founded the Virginia Theological Seminary on a huge plot of land atop the hill and built a bell tower at the highest point. It was such a landmark that the campus and the neighborhood around became known as Seminary Hill, or simply 'The Hill.' The name persists to this day.

"Francis Scott Key, the composer of our national anthem, was one of the founding members of the Seminary, and many other illustrious men have been associated with it as well. Myth has it that Phillips Brooks, a student at the Seminary, composed the Christmas carol, 'O Little Town of Bethlehem,' while looking down at the twinkling lights of Alexandria from Aspinwall Hall. A certain Dr. Joseph Packard, who was an early member of the faculty, roomed at Mount Vernon as a young professor during a period after George Washington's death when the plantation was used as a boarding house. From Mount Vernon, Dr. Packard rode his horse eight miles through dense woods to teach at the Seminary each day."

"Remember my friend Anne Harvey from high school?" Mary asked. "Her dad was a professor and associate dean of the Seminary in the 1960s, and they lived in that huge brick house on Seminary Road with the hexagonal bay window."

"Sure, I remember Anne and her endearing family."

"They told me their house had been used as a hospital during the Civil War. It was full of hiding places. We even found a secret passageway that had been boarded up."

"I'm not surprised," I said. "After Manassas, the Union Army was no longer so sure of an easy victory over the Confederates. They took over the entire Seminary, buildings and grounds. They summarily evicted everyone: staff, faculty, and students. Dr. Packard's autobiography says they had no idea when they vacated that it would be four long years before they returned to find little of their homes and possessions. The Union army used the Seminary buildings as they pleased, including that hospital for the Union wounded."

"Anne Harvey's dad told me that General George McClellan exercised his troops over and over on the Seminary quadrangle, to the consternation of President Lincoln, who was anxious for McClellan to take his troops into battle. Lincoln, at the height of frustration, supposedly said, 'If General McClellan does not want to use the army, I would like to borrow it for a time.'"

"There are some rare photographic images of those exercises on the Seminary grounds, thanks to photographer Matthew Brady, who must have known about Lincoln's feelings and took pictures of the troops. [Image 3.3]

"I want to tell you some other things I learned from Packard's autobiography. When he was evicted from his home he had no place to go and no job to support his family. He found residence in one place after another with sympathetic Episcopalians. For a while he lived in the District of Columbia with Dr. Miller, a physician of high regard. Packard would stand on the Capitol steps, sadly gazing across the Potomac at the Seminary tower in the distance. Eventually, Packard moved his family to Alexandria, which by now was under martial law. Once after this move, he needed medical help from Dr. Miller, so he crossed the Potomac in a boat. When he returned to the boat, it had been seized, and he had to use influence to return to Alexandria. Upon entering the city, he was arrested. The Yankees feared he was a spy. After three hours of interrogation, the Provost-Marshal sent him under guard to the Fairfax courthouse eleven miles away. Along the way he was transferred to a coach filled with a guard of Union cavalrymen to prevent Mosby's Raiders from rescuing him. Packard was forced to spend the night on the courthouse floor, a soldier on either side of him. One of Packard's influential friends went to the Secretary of War to plead his case, and the order to arrest him was immediately countermanded.

"Northern Virginia must have been in awful confusion at that time, with communications being slow or erratic. There was an incident that still amazes me. In late July of 1861 when the Union generals did not consider the Confederacy much of a threat to their troops, the two forces met for their first engagement at a vital railroad junction near Manassas, Virginia. Many important Washingtonians, including some congressmen and their families, had filled their coaches with picnic baskets and traveled the twenty-five miles south and west to Manassas, expecting to be entertained by the spectacle of a one-sided contest. However, after a long day of heavy fighting, the Union troops retreated north in wild disarray. The terrified spectators, unable to escape fast enough, bogged down at Bull Run, slowing the Union army's retreat. The Confederate soldiers were too exhausted to pursue, but the battle put an end to any notion that the war's outcome would be decided quickly.

"The Capital City was now considered vulnerable and the government hastened to fortify its defenses by completing a circular string of sixty forts on the highest promontories surrounding Washington ... two of them on the Fairfax family's acres, Fort Ward and Fort Worth. Between these two forts the Federal Army destroyed all the trees, which might have provided cover for Confederate soldiers. The Union troops dug trenches and piled the earth into breastworks. In the process, the original brick Fairfax homestead was destroyed."

"You know, Mom, when we kids used to go exploring in the woods around The Cottage, we'd come upon mounds of earth that were obviously part of those Civil War defenses. We could almost always count on finding some relic there. We found mini-balls that were used in rifles and sometimes something more personal, like a rusted belt buckle or snuff box. As we pocketed our treasure, we wondered if it might have belonged to some soldier who died there."

"It's unlikely," I replied. "To my knowledge, no major battle, like Manassas or Antietam in Maryland, was waged on The Hill. But Robert E. Lee's cousin, Cassius Lee, was a member of the board of both the Seminary and the adjacent Episcopal High School and was deeply concerned that the ancient oaks shading the grounds of these institutions might be destroyed just as the trees on the Fairfax land had been. So he appealed to his friend, President Lincoln, to use his influence with the army. The ancient oaks were saved and to this day provide shade over the grounds of both schools. Today these campuses cover the equivalent of eight city blocks and are home to what I think are the only old growth oaks in the region.

"And Mary, remember this heartrending story? When the Civil War broke out, Madame Fairfax had been living with her daughter and three grandchildren. The men in the family must have been away joining with the Confederate forces. A young Confederate soldier, stationed eleven miles from Vaucluse in Fairfax City, was in love with the granddaughter, Constance Cary. One night when he slipped through Union lines in an attempt to visit his sweetheart, he was fatally shot by a federal picket. It is said that the shot that killed this romantic young man was the only wartime death on the 'Holy Hill.'"

"Mams, I had friends at Hammond High School who declared that they had seen the Ghost of Vaucluse on a moonlit night wandering in the ravine below The Cottage where he was shot."

"He may be the most famous of all the Ghosts of Virginia."

"You made a believer out of me, Mams, when you told me about the night when I was thirteen and we were living in The Cottage. You woke up hearing me talking in my sleep, as if I were carrying on a conversation with someone. And some nights you would hear sounds, but when you got up to see what was causing them, there would be nothing. Could I, youngest of three girls, like the Fairfaxes, have been the one the soldier's ghost might have mistaken for the Cary girl?"

"Can't say it was the ghost ... and can't say it wasn't," I said. "After wartime fighting started in Northern Virginia, General Pierre Beauregard offered to take Madame Fairfax and her progeny south under his protection. It was said that Beauregard liked to associate with fine people, and this story suggests that he did, for his offer was probably beyond the scope of his military duties.

"And the legends go on. Before Madame Fairfax left her home on The Hill, she is said to have put the family silver in a wooden box and with the help of a Negro servant buried it near her house. When she returned after the war, the house and the woods were obliterated and Madame Fairfax couldn't even tell where they had been. She and her servant spent all day trying to locate where they had buried the box. As the sun went down, the old man's spade hit a soft spot in the earth. He had found the silver and rescued it 'down to the last teaspoon.'

"There is an amazing sequel to this Civil War tale that connects your dad's abiding interest in classic automobiles and mine in the history of the Seminary Hill land from which the plot for our home was carved."

"I don't remember this one ..."

"You do know that your dad and I are members of the local Rolls Royce Owners Club so that he can 'kick tires' with other *aficionados* ... that is, share enthusiasm for those fine old engines and one-of-a-kind pre-World War II chassis."

"And also help him locate a knowledgeable mechanic and some rare old parts!"

"One RROC member, Miles Cary, who owned an antique Rolls, invited the club for lunch at his home in the rolling Maryland hills.

While people were arriving and greeting one another, your dad said to our host, 'Miles, we are building a house over in Alexandria on what is often referred to as the Fairfax-Cary property. We were wondering if you are related to these Carys.'

"Miles replied with a gentle, affirmative nod, and he listened politely to the story that had so intrigued your dad and me … of how Madame Fairfax and the old Black servant hid the silver, and when she and her loyal servant returned years later after the war, they found the place totally destroyed, including their home. And how they searched all day for where the silver might be, until the old man's spade hit the soft spot. Miles looked at me and said, 'Would you like to see the silver?' I must have gasped when he pointed to the dining room sideboard. For there, in plain sight, was a highly polished tea service … the most beautiful I had ever seen … the very set that had belonged to Madame Fairfax 100 years earlier."

"More amazing than finding the silver is the fact that the Union Army didn't uncover it when they tore up the land for the breastworks," Mary observed.

Glancing at the speedometer—suddenly concerned that she was making Betsy hurry along at fifty-two miles per hour when the car's former owner had warned us not to exceed forty-five—she inhaled. "Mams, do you think I'm breaking Betsy in too fast?" We were climbing a steep, winding road to the Pennsylvania Turnpike. As if on cue, the car suddenly hesitated and then jerked forward.

"Did you feel that?" Mary queried. "What do you think it was?"

"Maybe it's some problem with the gas line or a loose wire …"

The repeated succession of jerking movements felt like a fish nibbling at a line, releasing and then pulling again. Betsy hesitated a few more times before we reached the plateau and the Laurel Mountain toll booth. But she kept going, and there we were on the turnpike, heading west.

We talked it over and decided if the engine problem was caused by poor quality gas, we might be able to solve it by filling the tank and mixing the old stuff with some higher octane. "But let's call Dad, too, in case he has a suggestion."

We pulled off the turnpike at the first service plaza. As Mary filled the tank, I called home to describe the "nibbling" to Bob. He said, "It sounds like a fuel line problem to me. Why don't you start with the simplest repair first, by replacing the old gas cap. Maybe it doesn't seat tightly and causes a suction problem in the fuel line."

We could not act on Bob's suggestion right there, since the service station did not have a parts department, but we decided to stop at a real garage in the next large town. Meanwhile, it made us feel better to have a fresh tank of high-test gas and a plan. Since everything was going well, I enjoyed the passing scene. Our attitude on the turnpike continued high, and the fall foliage was a spectacle of brilliant orange, red, and russet in the long light of evening.

Next day, zooming smoothly along on the turnpike, I went back to the story of Seminary Hill. "Captain Walter Karig was another one of the interesting people who lived on The Hill. There was a documentary series on television in the early 1950s, called *Victory At Sea*, for which Captain Karig wrote some of the scripts. And, rumor has it, Mary, that he was one of the ghost writers for Carolyn Keene's Nancy Drew teenage mystery series. It was in his backyard that Muff got her first pony-back riding lessons from Captain Karig's daughter Patty, who had created a riding school under the oaks.

"Then there was Jessica Mitford, the English author who wrote *The American Way of Death* during her short stay on The Hill. The scuttlebutt on her was that her family was under a cloud because prior to World War II they had been openly sympathetic to Germany.

"Living for a time on Seminary Road was another fascinating woman, a liberal political activist and author, Virginia Durr. I never knew her, but in my mind she is a true hero. Virginia and her husband had lived in Montgomery, Alabama, during the tense time after Rosa Parks defied the Jim Crow law that required Negro people to sit in the rear of public buses. In the face of widespread public opinion, which, contrary to her own, endorsed discrimination of all kinds based on race, Virginia and her husband believed in Rosa Parks' cause, paid her bail to release her from jail, and employed her when no one else in Montgomery would.

"Virginia Durr was the sister of Josephine Foster, the first wife of Supreme Court Justice Hugo Black, so it may be that his wife had a liberal bent too. At any rate, the sisters' father had been a minister in a Protestant church in Alabama, and because he preached the truth as he understood it and admitted he did not believe that Jonah could have survived in the belly of a whale, he was fired by his fundamentalist superiors and cast out by the church. He must have had a profound influence on Virginia Durr, because she backed up her belief in justice and fair play with action throughout the civil unrest of the 1950s and '60s."

"She must have been a force to be reckoned with," Mary said. "By the time I came along, it was easier to take action like she did, but it's never easy to go against the crowd."

Mary steered Betsy across the narrow panhandle of West Virginia that sticks northward between Pennsylvania and Ohio. Descending from the hills, we saw the capital city of Wheeling. What a relief to be somewhere populated enough to have a modern garage! On the outskirts of the city, we spotted a brick building that looked promising, with multiple repair bays within. We pulled in and told the lady at the service desk our problem and asked if they had a new gas cap to fit our old car. In a few minutes, a mechanic in blue overalls went out to the car and looked it over. He came into the waiting area and asked if we were the owners of the antique green Dodge. "Wow," he said, "you ladies are a long way from home."

"And we have to get to Cincinnati tonight," I said. "We're hoping a new gas cap will fix the problem we've been having."

"Are you sure it's not something more serious? I could run a check on the engine. It'd only take about an hour and you'd be on your way if everything checks out."

"I don't think that's necessary because we had that done before we left. And the engine doesn't quit. It just skips a beat when we're going uphill, as if it's not getting an even flow of gas. My husband suggested we try the simplest solution first by replacing the gas cap."

"Okay. That's a good idea. The fuel line may not be getting the suction it needs. I'll see what I have that fits."

The mechanic smiled and left. The next time we saw him, he had some shiny metal objects in his hand and was walking from the parts department toward the car, still outside right where we'd left it. He opened the small door to the gas tank, unscrewed the old cap, and tried several new ones until he found one that fit. Then he got in the driver's seat and started the engine, listening.

He re-entered the office. "That should do it," he said triumphantly. "The engine runs great." With thanks to him, we asked what we owed. He leaned toward the receptionist and told us to settle up with her, tipped his cap, and left.

The lady at the counter gave us a handwritten bill for three dollars, which we paid in cash. "We get in plenty of old trucks, but not old cars like that one," she said, adding, "'specially not driven by women." We thanked her and smiled, keeping to ourselves how far we expected Betsy to take us.

Mary and I agreed that I'd take over the driving while she looked for signs to US Route 40 and the Ohio River Bridge. Ahead of us, we spotted an old stone archway with steel cables hanging from both sides. In no time, we crossed the old bridge into Ohio.

3.1 *Woodrow Wilson Tree*, quick sketch
from the front porch of "The Cottage,"
by Virginia Ames

3.2 Ginny's azalea garden, Orleans Place,
Vaucluse neighborhood (1963-1983)

3.3 Union soldiers at Aspinwall Hall on the
Virginia Theological Seminary grounds, photo by Matthew Brady

Confederate uniform cap
(original sketch by MABurgess)

CHAPTER 4

Thursday, October 15, 1970
Odometer at Wheeling: 26,296

Wheeling, West Virginia,
to Cincinnati, Ohio
Trip meter at Wheeling: 296

Bomb Shelters,
Whistle-Blowers,
and Ghosts

A fter crossing the bridge, we turned south and followed the Ohio River along its western bank. Seventy miles downstream we passed Blennerhassett Island, the site where Aaron Burr colluded with a wealthy Irish aristocrat named Harman Blennerhassett to raise their own army in defiance of the principles of our young American Republic. They failed in their rebellion meant to create a nation of their own.

I imagined what it must have been like living in those days of mixed allegiances and the constant threat of war on our young, untried nation. It must have been similar to the tension created by Russia during the years of the Cold War. During Kennedy's administration, the nation was filled with hope and enthusiasm for a youthful president. There was a sense of pride in many of us, as though we all somehow shared in the elegance Jackie Kennedy brought to the White House. Then Vietnam divided the country, widened the gap between generations, and created disillusionment with our way of life. Our nation was thrown further off balance by the social change that accompanied the civil rights strife. The late President John Kennedy had averted the threat of attack by Soviet missiles based in Cuba, but fear and distrust of the Russians remained high.

As I ponder that period of time, one basic fact emerges out of the chaos. America searched its soul and voted for civil rights legislation. For a while many Americans regained their sense of fair play, more like the country I believe I was born into, a nation of people who, by and large, espoused the cause of the underdog. [Note 1 – Patriotism]

I remember particularly the insecurity we felt in 1965, three years after the Cuban Missile Crisis and after we'd finally moved from the Andrews Cottage into our new house in Vaucluse. During this Cold War period, our neighbors, the Sibthorps, like many other Americans, were so fearful of nuclear threats that they built a bomb shelter in their basement, believing it could save them should an atomic bomb be dropped on nearby Washington. They were the only people we knew who had actually built a bomb shelter. My good friend Edith Sibthorp was a spry but delicate woman. Her husband, George, was of Scottish background, a military man, tall and handsome, conservative and strong-willed. George informed me one day that he would like *me* to be the person designated to share the shelter with his wife, should he not be home at the time of the warning.

"Do you remember the Sibthorps and their bomb shelter?" I asked Mary.

"Of course ... when I was walking home from school during those early years, I'd look up at the sky to see if anyone was dropping a bomb. But George was a little far out, wasn't he?"

"I guess you had already left for college when he called and invited me to be the one to occupy the shelter with Edith. 'There's only room for two people,' he said. 'And I want you to take my place if the warning comes in the daytime and I can't get home from The Pentagon in time. There's a bicycle that you and Edith could take turns pumping to generate electricity for light, and there is food and water to last you for weeks.'

"Since all three of you girls were away by then, and Dad would probably also be at work, I began to consider his offer seriously. Then George said, 'You will need a gun and know how to shoot.'

"'Why?' I asked.

"'Naturally the neighbors will fight to take your place. You will have to shoot to stop them.'

"That was too much. The whole idea suddenly went from interesting to impossible. 'Well, no thank you,' I said. 'Find someone else to be with your wife.'"

"Good thing you turned him down," said Mary. "I can't imagine getting to the point that we'd be toting guns on Seminary Hill, though things only got worse during the Vietnam War."

I told Mary, "Thinking about other Seminary Hill characters, I am reminded of another quite different member of our Seminary Hill and Immanuel Church community, Mary Walton Livingston, who played a part in the downfall of President Richard Nixon. She was kind of a beautiful anomaly, a native Virginian with Fairfax ancestry who fought for justice and fairness for all citizens and was outraged by dishonesty. She was a small woman who packed a big punch. Do you remember Mrs. Livingston and the time she blew the whistle on Nixon?"

"I never got the full scoop on that. What actually happened?"

"In 1969, she had a position in the National Archives in Washington. Up until then, charitable gifts of papers to the government, libraries, and universities were tax deductible. But on December 30, 1969, Congress eliminated this deduction, retroactive to July 25,

1969. President Nixon missed this July deadline and falsified the date of the donation of his vice presidential papers to the Archives in order to receive the benefit of a deduction. Her position with the Archives gave Mary Walton responsibility for receiving gifts such as Nixon's papers. Upon examining them, she noticed the alteration. She made a point of disclosing the discrepancy and did not stop until the falsification was made public. This was before there were protections for government whistle-blowers. She was moved to a less politically sensitive post at the Archives, but not before she'd become a hero to the many people who learned of her courage."

"I remember admiring her even before that incident," Mary said. "My own political ideas had become very liberal by then, pretty much in line with Mrs. Livingston's, so she served as a sort of gauge for me. I noticed how, even though she was treated almost as an outcast by some of her neighbors, she persisted anyway, and that made me realize I could be persistent too."

"You have to imagine the fear we had all lived with for so long. It made people slow to question authority. Almost no one did during the Eisenhower years." I paused, trying to remember what changed things.

"In September of 1959, when President Eisenhower's two terms were almost over, we got our first glimmer of hope since the dawn of the Cold War in the late 1940s. And it came from the most unexpected source. Soviet Premier Nikita Khrushchev announced he was coming to the U.S. He was the first Russian leader to do that. For nearly two weeks, his visit dominated the news. Up until then, the Soviet Embassy had stood like a fortress in the middle of Washington. But, for his visit, the embassy was opened for a reception. Eisenhower wanted to reduce the tensions between our countries and encouraged official friendliness, but not by the highest echelons of the military forces. Junior officers and government officials were urged to attend.

"The Gridiron Club had hired your dad as publisher of *The Army, Navy, Air Force Journal* until they could sell the property. The privately owned 'journal' had flourished until the editor/publisher died. It was prized by military families because it gave them personal news they appreciated ... such as who among their military associates had, in their terms, 'matched, hatched, or dispatched.' Despite some misgivings, Dad felt compelled to attend this groundbreaking Russian Embassy event representing *The Journal*. It is next to impossible now to imagine how difficult that decision was. We were still gun-shy from the horrible effect on some of our close friends due to Congressman Joseph McCarthy's interrogations, black listings, and purges five years earlier. Many, including us, had a lingering fear that we might be accused of being friendly to Communists and lose our jobs or ruin our reputations. Dad was so tense that, when offered a Russian cigarette that evening at the embassy, he took up smoking again after seven years of abstinence. I drank a large quantity of vodka and ate far more than my share of caviar before I began to relax. With this visit, the whole country seemed to loosen ... well, until the shoe-banging incident by Khrushchev at the UN."

South of Belpre, Ohio, we stopped to stretch at the place where the river road joined Route 50 toward Cincinnati. One hundred miles to go. Light from the afternoon sun grew hazy as we headed west across southern Ohio. Mary commented about how smoothly the car was now running, but we decided we would have the motor checked anyway once we were in Cincinnati.

"It's funny," she said, "but as wonderful as it was to be in a spacious new house during my latter high school years, I remember our time in The Cottage as a joyous adventure."

"Well, living there was probably one of the happiest periods of my life too. It's true that we rented the place only because our old home sold more quickly than we'd expected and it was conveniently close to our new building site. The added advantage was that you and Muffin could walk to your new high school. When Lucy graduated from college in May of 1962, The Cottage had a makeshift back room where she stayed until she and Mike were married the following January. So, the whole family was able to be back together for a time. That was special in itself.

"Dad and I had been told that this guest house, The Cottage, was a Sears Roebuck prefabricated one, assembled on the site sometime after World War I. Marietta Andrews had named it 'Good Intent' in memory of her granddaughter. Before we arrived, it had been neglected, but it was solid except for that back room. The insulation would have suited a winter in Alaska, and the steam heating system made The Cottage very cozy on the coldest nights. [Image 4.1]

"When we moved in, we had to fight our way through a sea of tall grasses to reach the brick pad at its front entrance. Each weekend, with his push mower, Dad arduously trimmed the grasses farther and farther from the house. Eventually, we looked out over a vast lawn of bluegrass worthy of the Fairfax estate that had once been there."

"I mowed that field quite a few times myself and it was huge," Mary interjected.

"You might remember what happened when little rain fell that summer and the lawn browned off in patches. As the grass died, a pattern of brown rectangles and squares appeared on the lawn."

"I do remember the excitement when we realized that those squares might indicate the foundation of a building."

"When it turned out to be the foundation of the original Fairfax house that had been destroyed during the Civil War, we were stunned. The brick pilings had been lying a few inches below the ground, undiscovered for all that time. As far as we know, not a soul had located the site of the Fairfax home until your father did … and we were straddling it!

"Muffin, then sixteen, suggested that we use a few bricks from that foundation in our new house. 'Maybe they will attract the Confederate ghost to visit us after we leave The Cottage,' she'd said laughing. I thought it was a delightful idea. So we dug up three of the bricks and incorporated them into the fireplace hearth in the library at our new house on Orleans Place. But the ghost couldn't be so easily tricked. He never visited us there."

"That's a shame. I liked the idea of his hanging around."

"One friend of mine, Billie Miller from Immanuel-on-the-Hill Church, had lived with her husband in The Cottage some time before we did. She said the ghost of Vaucluse visited her many times there. She always knew when the ghost was present because her little dog grew excited and his fur stood up. 'One time,' she said, 'a college friend was staying with us. At breakfast she angrily announced that she was leaving immediately. Scowling at my husband, she said a *man* had entered her bedroom in the middle of the night and frightened her. I reassured her it was only the ghost,' Billie said, 'but she left anyway.'

"Billie also told us that the ghost had caused trouble for the Andrews when they were living in their Victorian frame house across the ravine from The Cottage during World War II."

"I don't have any recollection of that story at all," Mary said.

"As I remember it, early in the war when the officials in Washington were concerned about the possibility of an air attack, an air raid warden on his rounds reported to Marietta and Eliphalet Andrews that some of their blackout curtains had not been lowered, allowing light to escape and providing a potential target for enemy planes. The Andrews insisted that they had closed the curtains themselves. Billie was convinced it was the work of the ghost, but I thought it would have been uncharacteristic of such a kind ghost to endanger others like that.

"Do you remember, after listening to all those stories, how you and Muffin would hear strange noises in the middle of the night, like heavy footsteps down the hall and the rattling of chains?"

"I'm sure our imaginations went wild, especially after you said you heard me talking to someone in my sleep. But my only actual

memory of the ghost was the night I had a girls' slumber party at
The Cottage. We were all in our pajamas, telling scary stories in the
living room. Somebody screamed. The rest of us turned around and
saw a Confederate soldier peering through the window. Then he disappeared into the darkness. We were still screaming, jumping up and
down and clinging to each other, when Dad bounced into the room
holding up a broomstick with a Confederate cap balanced on top."

"I'm not sure if I heard about that one, but I wouldn't put it past
your dad to pull a trick like that."

A glance at our mileage and the highway signs reminded me
we were not far from the exit to Hyde Park, the Cincinnati suburb
where my sister lived and our destination for the night. I was still
absorbed in thinking, though, of other ghost stories I'd heard about
the many haunted houses in the Virginia countryside. "It's too bad
we never attracted a real ghost to our house," I said. "All the best
homes have them, you know."

Mary knew I was teasing, but she also knew that she was in for
one last tale before we left the highway and had to start searching
for street signs.

"John Marshall, the first Chief Justice of the United States, was
from Fauquier County ... only another twenty miles or so west of
Manassas," I began, hoping I could recall the details of this, my favorite ghost story, as I went along. "He had several children and he built
each of them a home not far from his own. Your dad's maiden aunt,
your Great Aunt Rina, bought a country house called Plowshares
during the Depression that was built on eleven acres carved from one
of the Marshall home sites. In time, Rina, a proud New Englander,
was accepted by the equally proud Marshall family. Later, after she
was no longer able to care for her country property, Aunt Rina moved
to an apartment in Georgetown. One evening, she invited Dad and
me to join her for dinner at the Arts Club there. A Miss Alice Marshall stopped by our table and sat down, as if she were going to stay.
As soon as the introductions were over, Miss Alice looked at Bob and

me and said, 'I want to tell you a true story about the part of Virginia where your Aunt Rina used to live.'

"She paused for effect. 'You may know that we Marshalls go home every year for a horse show in Upperville. One particular year, I had planned to attend but wasn't sure where to stay. My cousin still lived there in a lovely old home with floor-to-ceiling French doors and, of course, it had a haunted room. She invited me to stay in her home and I accepted, but I told her I refused to sleep in the ghost room by myself. When I arrived, I found that not only was I to stay in the haunted room, but my cousin had been called away and I would be staying in the ghost room by myself. Naturally I didn't like that one bit, but I went to bed, determined not to be afraid. Not long after I had blown out the lamp, I heard a heavy tromp, tromp, tromp down the hall. It got louder and I became so frightened I couldn't move. In no time, the sound was in my room. Terrified, I pulled the sheets over my head. The bed started to move, and I knew it was the ghost. I wanted to die right then and there. I finally summoned the courage … I don't know how … to open my eyes. And what I saw was not a ghost, but two giant eyeballs staring back at me. You see, the hired hand had left the gate open and a cow had wandered out of its pen, into the house through the floor-length windows, and all the way into the haunted room.'

"With that, Miss Alice stood up, said goodbye, and left."

I had become so distracted telling my tale of Alice Marshall's ghost that I missed the exit to Hyde Park.

4.1 *The Cottage, Seminary Hill, Alexandria,*
oil painting by Catharine McEwen Ames, 1963, at age 86

CHAPTER 5

Thursday, October 15, 1970
Odometer at Cincinnati: 26,576

Near Cincinnati, Ohio
Trip meter at Cincinnati: 576

The "new" Cincinnati Union Station
built in the 1930s, reflecting Art Deco in its design
(original sketch by MABurgess)

The Clean City
of the West

Having missed the first exit from U.S. Route 50 into Cincinnati, we decided to take the next one. There was so much new development on the outskirts of Cincinnati I couldn't get my bearings. Hoping to shore up Mary's confidence in my sense of direction in my once-familiar town, I told her that Blue Ash Airport must be somewhere near us—and to keep an eye out for it. Daredevil flyers from World War I used to put on air shows in their biplanes at that airport for breathless spectators on the ground. Around 1920, when he was ten years old and enamored with flight, these flying aces thrilled her dad.

"Your dad's mother, Bessy, could not have imagined how far her son rode his bicycle out to the Blue Ash Airport to witness the dare-

devil air shows. And, of course, he never told her about the near ac-
cident he had on his way back home, because he never told her how
far he had gone. While riding down the winding road into the river
valley, his bicycle chain flew off, so he had no brakes. At the speed he
was going, he had no choice but to ride it out, his fear increasing as
he gained momentum. Fortunately, he stayed on his bike all the way
down the hill, finally coming to a stop after reaching level ground
and dragging his feet until the soles of his shoes practically wore off."

"Was this the airfield where Dad learned to fly?" Mary queried.

"No, not here. He learned to fly at Lunken Airport. They called it
'Sunken Lunken' because it was in a flat bottomland valley between
two of Cincinnati's seven hills, to the south of here.

"Did I ever tell you why he quit flying? He was on a solo flight
in a light Piper Cub when a thermal carried him above 10,000 feet.
It was a pretty hazardous situation. He had a devil-of-a-time getting it eventually back to the ground. When he got home safely, he
announced to me that he'd never fly again. It had been one of those
soul-searching incidents when, as a young 'male immortal,' he suddenly faced his own mortality. 'With one child, Gin,' he told me, 'you
might be able to find another husband, but with two children, remar-
riage would be iffy.'"

"A sobering thought for me, as I've really got the itch to learn to
fly myself," Mary reflected, but I went on.

"Being here in my old stompin' grounds and thinking of Sunken
Lunken sure jogs recollections of my college days at UC. Before I
ever knew your dad, when I was chairman of the rush committee
of Chi Omega, I had to find an interesting venue for the rush party.
Imagine how, back in 1934, airplane flight was so new and exciting that I wanted to use that as our party theme. It turned out to
be quite a coup when I was able to rent a vacant hangar at Lunken
for the catered luncheon. My sorority sisters and rushees were completely awestruck ... so few of them knew anything about flight."

"Mom, do you recall the first time you ever *saw* an airplane?"

"Do I recall?! It is more vivid than yesterday in my mind ... though I was only about five or six. I remember looking up into the blue sky and seeing a little double-winged plane, with smoke streaming out the tail, actually writing out the letters, L U C K Y S T R I K E. I don't think I even knew what that meant at the time.

"Men home from the World War were exercising their new flying skills. Barnstormers, as they were called, were like air acrobats, doing unheard-of maneuvers in midair ... loop-de-loops, barrel rolls, flying under bridges. What crazy loons they were! Our dear Washington friend, Coe Lanpher, who is a lot older than Bob and me, was once one of those wild fliers. After a few Dubonnets on the rocks at a dinner party, he told us about his 'Iron Cross Award' while serving in the World War I Air Corps. The 'Iron Cross,' he admitted sheepishly, was received for 'bringing down more *American* planes than anyone else in the Corps!' In those days, aircraft were so rickety and flight speed so slow that Coe had apparently come out of multiple crashes and mishaps unscathed."

By now we were in total darkness. It took forever to find any road I recognized, even with Mary's help reading out the street signs. Because the heart of Cincinnati is next to the Ohio River, I kept tending downhill until, suddenly, we reached a major intersection with a traffic light that I finally recognized.

"Eureka! Spring Grove Avenue. Familiar territory at last! It will be late when we arrive, but I know the way from here." We released our breath simultaneously, and tension left our bodies with an audible whistle. We were approaching Ivorydale on the right. "That's the home of Procter & Gamble," I said. Mary nodded her head in recognition of the household brand name.

To anyone who believes that one or two individuals cannot make a significant difference in the world, I would offer the case of William Procter, a candle maker from England, and James Gamble, a soap maker from Ireland, both of whom immigrated to America and on to Cincinnati in the early nineteenth century. When the two happened to marry sisters, the girls' father convinced his new sons-in-law to merge their separate business ventures. In 1837, each partner pledged $3,596.47 to fund their joint enterprise and the Procter & Gamble Company was born.

"They used to call Cincinnati the Queen City of the West," I mused. "It should have been called the *Clean* City of the West."

We passed Spring Grove Cemetery on our right, its area so vast we saw nothing more than darkness ahead, which jogged another recollection.

"When your dad was a young boy, he and one of his foolhardy little pals decided to explore the storm sewer that runs under that cemetery, not having the slightest idea where they'd come out."

"That doesn't surprise me a bit. Did they get lost?" Mary wondered.

"They tramped on and on, shoulders stooped, for a fairly long distance. Uneasy, they considered returning to the place where they had entered the drain pipe. They decided it might be safer to keep going forward. Your father admitted they were glad to see the light at the end of the tunnel, literally."

"Don't you think it's amazing, Mom, that boys survive to manhood?" [Image 5.1]

At that moment the bright lights of a political campaign signboard lit up the interior of our car. A judge, it said, was soliciting votes in a forthcoming election. It reminded me that David Stewart Porter, my husband's childhood friend with whom he explored the world above and below ground, had grown up to become a respected U.S. federal judge in the United States District Court for the Southern District of Ohio. He was nominated by President Lyndon B. Johnson and confirmed by Congress in 1966. We laughed out loud. Mary knew Dave Porter only as a gray-haired man with an imposing title. The image of him trespassing through a sewer pipe was too funny for words.

We were following the valley where Mill Creek eventually joins the Ohio River. In the 1800s, a manmade canal flowed for miles through this valley. Along the canal banks, horses used to pull barges loaded with commercial goods. When the railroads came, canals were no longer used for transport, although the tracks sometimes followed the abandoned canals. Sometime in the 1930s, about the same time that I was finishing my degree at the University of Cincinnati and Bob had gone off to Chicago to seek work, the C.H.&D. (Cincinnati, Hamilton, and Dayton) Railroad was operating in one of these canal corridors.

Being in a place can spark deep recollections. "When your dad was a boy in the 1920s," I told Mary, "there was a canal down there in the Mill Creek Valley. In winter, the kids ice skated on it. Your father tells how he and his friends would go down there early in winter when the ice had just formed. They'd take a running start and skate across, listening to the sagging thin ice crack under their blades, just to see if they could make it to the other side without falling through."

"Yes, he's boasted to me more than once about those escapades," Mary said, "and once took us to skate on a low place at Episcopal High School that they flooded in the winter. He seemed to think it was cheating to skate on an artificial pond where you couldn't drown if you fell through the ice."

After traveling west past Ivorydale and the cemetery, we made a sharp left turn toward the river. I looked back over my shoulder. Dingy brick houses bumped into each other, climbing the hillside toward the Clifton neighborhood. I pointed out the buildings to Mary.

"There used to be a speakeasy in one of those tenements during Prohibition, and I remember sneaking into it with a date when I was seventeen years old and not yet in college. My date was a college boy, which was exciting enough, but he also had a Pierce-Arrow automobile, and that was the best. I felt very sophisticated. But when I realized we were going to a speakeasy, I was terrified. The owner slid open a peephole in the door and then let us in. It was a sleazy-looking place, filled with college students drinking awful-tasting, home-brewed beer from tin cans. I couldn't wait to leave. The very next night the joint was raided. The police took the girls home to their parents and, I suppose, they hustled the boys to the police station, if only to give them a scare. Among the students caught in that raid was a nephew of the dean of women at the university. When I enrolled the following year, I got to know her well. One day she told me she was certain her nephew did not drink 'because he was always so thirsty in the morning.' It was all I could do to keep from laughing at her innocence."

Mary and I rolled on toward the Ohio River. Betsy, apparently content that we had brought enough trouble on ourselves by missing our turn, ran like a top. I knew coming up on our right was the magnificent Art Deco-style Union Station that had been built outside the city to consolidate the many rail lines previously served by five stations.

"In 1933, two years after my father's job brought us to Cincinnati and one year after I entered college," I explained, "Union Station was built just over there. It was a great time in Cincinnati. We had the most amazing city manager, Clarence A. Dykstra, a forward-looking man who had the guts to support the construction of this new Art Deco building in the middle of the Depression.

"As the station was being built, the Depression worsened and money was so tight the city contemplated abandoning the project. Because they had already contracted for custom features and furnishings that suited the Art Deco style, such as red and tan leather-covered settees rather than the conventional wooden benches, the financial officials concluded that it would cost as much to abandon the project as to finish it and decided to proceed. As a result, Cincinnati got not only a new train station but an architectural wonder as well.

"In the station was a small theatre where a talented director, Owen Phillips, produced and staged plays. When the space was no longer available, Phillips moved his company to Virginia. People came from their farms and rural homes seeking entertainment, and they paid with hams and chickens in lieu of cash. The theatre became known as the famous Barter Theatre.

"At the outbreak of World War II, when Lucy was a baby and we were living in Clifton, Union Station became a major transfer point for soldiers traveling to debarkation points on the East and West Coasts. Thousands of troops marched through the spacious waiting area with its high, vaulted ceiling.

"One day at the height of World War II, we were in the station awaiting the arrival of a friend. Three-year-old Lucy broke away from my hand and ran into the midst of a group of soldiers exclaiming, 'Hi, soldier boys.' This was all the excuse they needed to break ranks. Some of them knelt down, grinning and saying hello to the small stranger; some teased her gently or pulled her pigtails. You could almost tell which of them had baby sisters or daughters of their own by the way they showed their affection.

"In the more recent 1950s and '60s, trains have fallen victim to the sudden expansion of the interstate highway system and to the airlines. Today, only about two passenger trains a day pass through this terminal." [Note 2 – Cincinnati Union Station]

Mary and I completed our unintended circle around the city, then went through the heart of downtown and headed back to Hyde Park on the northeast side.

"I wonder what those two English authors, the Trollopes, would say now if they could see Cincinnati's modern skyline." I was thinking of the insulting word-picture Frances Trollope and her son Anthony had painted in the early 1800s, after visiting the city and returning to England.

"Why?" Mary asked. "Did they say it was backward?"

"Did they ever! In her book, *Domestic Manners of the Americans*, published in 1832, Frances Trollope referred to Cincinnati as the 'Pork Capital,' and I don't think she was referring only to the fact that pigs were sold here."

Mary grinned.

"Her characterization might not have been terribly far from the truth," I continued, "but, to this day, some Cincinnatians still bristle at the mention of the Trollopes. I suspect that Mrs. Trollope fell into the habit of the English upper classes at the time. Apparently, it restored their sense of superiority to deride the rougher lifestyle of the inhabitants of their former colonies."

From downtown Cincinnati, I easily found my way onto Columbia Parkway and headed east, paralleling the river. On our left rose Mt. Adams, a hill that was still being reached by an incline street car carrier during the time we lived on nearby Clifton Hill. I pointed out to Mary where the rails had been.

"At the top, opposite the former station house, the famous Rookwood Pottery Works still stands. The bud vase in our living room was a wedding gift from there. On the last day that the incline streetcar operated in 1944, just before we moved from Cincinnati to Louisville, Kentucky, we took Lucy for a ride so that someday she could tell her children and grandchildren about it."

I steered Betsy north onto Delta Avenue and headed to the house on Hayward Avenue in Hyde Park where my sister Mary Louise (whom we affectionately called Mamie Lou) and brother-in-law Harry Kasson had lived for years and raised their children, Hank and Cynthia. It was a middle-class neighborhood, on the nicer side of middle, like ours in Alexandria, so I wondered once again what the neighbors would think of our old car. It really did have that embarrassing old rounded shape of 1950—so dated and different from the sleek angular car designs of 1970.

On the way we passed Linwood Road, where Lucy was born just one year before the Japanese pulled the country into World War II, a time when our lives—like those of everyone around us—took on an entirely different perspective and feeling.

5.1   1915 studio photo of the William Henry Ames Family taken at Coney Island, Cincinnati;
young Malcolm McEwen Ames with his dad in front seat, Elizabeth Atwater Butler Ames
and young Robert Hyde Ames in rear

Gustav Eckstein's canaries on his cup of coffee

CHAPTER 6

Friday, October 16, 1970
Odometer at Cincinnati: 26,626

In Cincinnati
Trip meter at Cincinnati: 626

Cruising through Time in Cincinnati

The next morning we followed the aroma of coffee down to the din-ing room. The table set for the four of us sparkled with Mamie Lou's colorful china and well-polished silver. Harry came through the kitchen door with four servings of his famous breakfast of Kas-son's Eggs Benedict.

"Mary, this is how we celebrated happy days when your dad and I and Mary Lou and Harry were young married couples living near each other in Cincinnati," I reminisced, savoring our early-morning feast.

Everyone was smiling as we placed our napkins on the table and rose to go outside. When we crossed a well-trimmed grass lawn to-ward Betsy, parked in the drive, Harry's smile melted. Dark furrows creased his brow. For a few moments eyes were fixed on Betsy, but I was aware of a shiny 1970 Lincoln at the house across the street, and as though to upstage Betsy, a well-restored vintage Packard rolled down our street and out of sight. Harry was looking again at our old car.

When he learned of Betsy's trouble on the climb to the Pennsylvania Turnpike, he was skeptical about Betsy's ability to make it to Seattle and tried to dissuade us from the trip. He replaced an old rotten floorboard under the rug on the passenger's side, mumbling that his mechanic ought to inspect our car. This is exactly what we had hoped he would do. We drove to his shop. His mechanic put a filter on the fuel line and advised us to buy a rebuilt fuel pump in the event we should need one, declaring a part for a twenty-year-old automobile would be hard to find anywhere in the United States, except in a large city. He located a fuel pump and we purchased it from him. Harry was still not convinced that we should continue this adventure.

Mary and I devoted the rest of the day to nostalgia. She went with me to visit favorite old haunts. We cruised Clifton Avenue and saw the church where Bob and I were married, with Mamie Lou in the wedding party. [Images 6.1, 6.2]

Further down Clifton we saw the grammar school Bob had attended. Turning back up the hill on the left was the campus of the University of Cincinnati, from which both of us graduated. On the right, even further up the hill, we saw Hughes High School where Bob received most of his secondary education.

"Where else in this country could anyone receive all of his education within a mile along one street?" Mary commented.

"Another bemusing memory is when our family moved temporarily into an apartment down a side of Clifton Hill. My sister and I had not yet enrolled in the university but were enjoying our last summer of freedom, sunbathing face down in the backyard of the apartment. Little did we know that directly above us on Clifton Avenue was the

SAE Fraternity house, perched on the edge of the steep embankment behind the apartments, offering a perfect view of us sunbathing! Suddenly, a chorus of male voices began singing to a familiar oompa tune, 'See the little angels, asc-end up, asc-end up ...'" This brought Mary tears of laughter when she heard how we scrambled as fast as we could to get inside and out of view.

I told Mary about how, soon after my marriage in 1936, I heard on the radio that King Edward VIII of England would soon make an announcement. Near this intersection, at Clifton and Ludlow Avenues, I had pulled the car into a parking place to listen more attentively to the radio. I heard the King of England himself saying he was going to abdicate the throne in order to marry the woman he loved. I sat entranced, tears filling my eyes. As a new bride myself, I felt this poignancy acutely. For a man to do anything as earthshaking as abandoning his kingdom for love was a model of marital romance I could now understand. Oh, if we could all love that deeply!

It was time to return to the Kassons', so we headed east. Rolling down from Clifton we saw to the left the University of Cincinnati College of Medicine. We could see the windows of the laboratory of Dr. Gustav Eckstein, Associate Professor of Physiology, for whom I had served as secretary for two-and-a-half stimulating years during my early married life.

"Oh, Mary, there's Dr. Eckstein's lab! On the other side of those windows is a very large laboratory where I worked. There in that spacious room were thirty-four canaries flying free, his behavioral subjects as well as his pets, with various roosting places on the exposed pipes high above the wall of windows. Once, a cleaning woman left open a window and all the birds flew away. When Dr. Eckstein returned to his lab, he was devastated at the loss of his feathered friends. He sat down at the grand piano and played the music that was so familiar to the canaries. Every one of them flew back through the window and back to their roosts!"

Mary turned to face me. "It's no wonder you hated to leave that job. On our last visit to Cincinnati, you introduced me to Dr. Eckstein ... during my sophomore year at Cornell. He shared his thoughts on how to write, and his ideas have served me well in my own writing. I've brought a copy of his recently published book, *The Body Has a Head*, thinking we might read it along the way."

"What an inspired idea, Mary! Let's call him before we leave Cincy."

Returning to my sister's house, we saw on our left the original Graeter's Ice Cream Parlor amongst the shops we passed at Hyde Park Square.

I turned to Mary, "Early in her career ... it must have been in the 1930s, when we first moved to Cincinnati ... Regina Graeter hosted a gathering of the ladies of the Methodist Society. Your grandmother was a part of her inner circle when Mrs. Graeter shared her ice cream and candy confections that later became famous. Although it was her husband, Charlie, from Bavaria who began making ice cream in a market at the base of Sycamore Hill, it was Regina who expanded the business after her husband died young. Now their ice cream is popular way beyond Cincinnati."

That evening, Mary Lou and Harry took us to Cold Springs Country Club for dinner. When a bountiful meal was spread on the table before us, I reflected, "Remember when food was rationed in World War II and we were issued those little tokens that allowed us to buy a stingy amount of meat and dairy products? Our friend Katie Dunn had no more rationed tokens than any of the rest of us, even though her father owned the company that held the government contract to produce millions of tokens."

When it was time to order dessert, Harry recalled how during those days restaurants had anything you might crave. Restaurants could get anything that Joe Citizen could not. FDR saw to it that the restaurants stayed in business. With a war on his hands, he had to rid the country of the last vestiges of the Depression. Harry flashed a smile toward Mary. "Before your dad joined the Navy, the four of us had dinner at a good restaurant down on Eastern Avenue. Mamie Lou told the waitress, 'For dessert I want the blueberry pie with whipped cream ... without the blueberry pie.' The savvy waitress laughed and brought Mary Lou a great big bowl of whipped cream. And Mary Lou didn't have to use her precious red tokens for the whipped cream that she loved."

The whipped cream incident brought back more thoughts of those times, and I began musing aloud with a rush, "In retrospect, it's amazing to me how FDR inherited the Depression, singlehandedly pulled us out of that, then handled World War II with the same skill. He captured our hearts and got our attention from the beginning with his famous inaugural address, saying, 'So, first of all, let me assert my firm belief that the only thing we have to fear is fear itself.' His innovative 'New Deal,' in response to the nation's poverty during the Depression, both shocked and relieved us at the same time. It was unprecedented. Government had never stepped in like that before. What a heroic rescue to get talented, unemployed people off the streets and into creative jobs like the national writers' project, the CCC, and the artists' project! Today, because of this program, we have murals in public buildings painted by famous artists, as well as hiking trails all over the country.

"Remember, Mamie Lou, how his fireside chats in 1933 gave us calming confidence that his new programs would help us through the hard times? They certainly did! Our kids can't imagine in these good economic times how scary it was when there was a run on the banks and FDR had to close them and rescue the currency. FDR's New Deal inspired us to work together for the good of all, including the difficult feat of getting the Republicans and Democrats to agree on legislation."

"If only his conciliatory influence could persist!" Mary chimed in. "Now our representatives from both sides of the aisle seem to be poorer compromisers, preferring to promote their own political agendas rather than negotiate solutions for the benefit of the country or the greater good."

Thinking of how history goes, I continued, "It's interesting to me how, at the beginning of the Second World War, FDR was determined to keep America out of the conflict. It must have upset him that he could not always count on the press to 'tell it how it was,' or at least his version of reality. He put the press in its place by saying, 'Repetition does not transform a lie into a truth.'"

"The eternal struggle of journalism," Mary remarked from her experience.

"When Hitler began bombing England from the air, Winston Churchill begged for America's help, believing that if England were to fall, all of Europe would fall to Hitler as well. It was that brilliant American news reporter Edward R. Murrow, sharing Churchill's fear, who used his influence with FDR to get a response. Our allies needed planes and ships, munitions and supplies. America could produce them all. The president did listen to Murrow and created a program called 'Lend/Lease' in which the U.S. went into heavy production to fulfill the needs of England and other allies."

Thinking of those war years and their impact on our lives, Harry pensively resumed, "I heard Roosevelt when he reported on the radio that we had been attacked at Pearl Harbor. Our ships and hundreds of our sailors were lost—they had been sittin' ducks. The president had no choice but to declare war."

"I will never forget the sound of your voice, Harry, when you telephoned us that dreadful Sunday to say that we had been attacked."

Mary mused, "Most of my friends were not born then, but we know that Roosevelt called it 'a date that will live in infamy.'"

That evening Harry built a fire and we sat in its glow, thinking about old times and catching up on more news.

"Remember Eleanor Brill at the University of Cincinnati, Mary Lou, my big sister in Chi Omega Sorority? We lost touch for many years but found each other again, both married with children and living in the Washington area. We started getting our families together. She had married Merriman Smith, head of the United Press International in D.C., and he was the selected one who ended each press conference, after he thought that all of the important questions had been asked, by saying, 'Thank you, Mr. President.' He was one of those privileged newsmen included in the inner cadre of people who traveled with FDR wherever he went in his presidential plane. The press, including Merriman Smith, followed along in the plane provided for favored press corps. Eleanor invited Bob and me to many dinners at their home. She confided in me that Merriman enjoyed an audience to help him unwind when he came home from one of these trips.

"There was much he couldn't report, but plenty that he could share, particularly concerning the personality of FDR. It is understandable why Roosevelt would place so much confidence in Merriman, because their two personalities were similar in many ways. Both were candid and filled with confidence. As president, FDR gave us confidence by keeping the American public abreast of everything that was going on, especially in his fireside chats.

"There was intense competition between the pressmen traveling with FDR, and Merriman Smith was often the first one to get his story off to his paper after landing. In fact, later Smith was the first reporter to report Kennedy's assassination in 1963, which was the reason he received the Pulitzer Prize in 1964.

"President Johnson honored Merriman by giving him the nation's highest civilian award, the Medal of Freedom, in 1967.

"Merriman's son, Merriman Jr., had been killed in Vietnam the previous year when his helicopter crashed near Saigon. I have a hunch that may have motivated the president but don't really know for certain. I do know that he thought very highly of Merriman Sr. Eleanor was outraged at Johnson's attempt to use their son's death for political reasons by having him honored in a special ceremony; she raised such violent objection about this proposed spectacle that they never followed through on the ceremony."

"Whatever happened to Eleanor?" Mary Lou asked.

"Well, between her divorce from Merriman in 1966 and her son's death the following year, I know she was very despondent. She just disappeared out of my life."

For a long time I gazed at the flickering fire in the fireplace, ruminating about how suddenly a happy life can be disrupted due to forces beyond our control and turn sad, lonely, and difficult.

Suddenly I was aware of Mary Lou, Harry, and Mary in the room and returned my attention to the conversation. "I was thinking about how hard it was to break up our home in Cincinnati when Bob went off to the Navy to be trained as a commissioned officer. Lucy and I became basically homeless until Mother asked us to come to Louisville to help her with our dad, Mamie Lou, not knowing it would be his final days.

"When Dad's leukemia worsened so rapidly and he died so young, Mother quickly announced that she wanted to sell her Louisville house and return to Cincinnati because that city seemed more like home to her. Feeling homeless once again, I was overwhelmed by my desire to join Bob in Cambridge at the Naval Communications School at Harvard. I needed to be with him before he was sent to join the fleet in the Pacific. His whole graduating class was told that would be their next assignment.

"When the time drew near for us to leave for Cambridge, Mother, who remained in Cincinnati, said, 'You take our Oldsmobile, Gin, and go to Bob.' It was almost Christmas. I packed a sled and other gifts for Lucy and asked a friend, a Navy wife, if she and her little son would like to ride with us to Massachusetts to join her husband as well. Mother packed the car with meats and vegetables that we had canned while we were together. She held back tears as she waved us farewell on our journey to Cambridge.

"By evening we were in Painesville, Ohio, on the shores of Lake Erie. A light snow was falling. We stopped at the first motel we spied and found the lobby packed with travelers, mostly professional truck drivers who warned me that the ice on the highway made driving treacherous. I was determined to get the four of us to Cambridge for Christmas. The next morning, the sun was bright and we bravely headed east. Shortly after getting on the highway that hugged Lake Erie for some miles, we slid on black ice and finally came to a stop, facing west. Unnerved, I crept along until we got off the lakeshore highway at the first chance to return to our motel on well-salted city streets. Fortunately, my passenger had a friend in Painesville, a young man eager to help. He drove us to the train station, promising to arrange for shipping my car to me when space was available on the over-busy railroads. I told him I could never repay him for his kindness to us, and I hastened to add that there were canned vegetables and meats stored in the car. 'Don't let them freeze. Take that good food for your family.'

"Without a reservation, we climbed on the next train heading east, trying to hide Santa's gifts from the children. Once on board we found all the seats taken; people were standing in the aisles in both the coaches and Pullman cars. For a moment of panic, I felt that I was floating in a surreal world. No supportive dad alive to give me courage, no home to return to, no home I could imagine in the future with Bob off to war, not even a place to rest our weary heads that night. Lucy put her little hand in mine and my doubt melted away. Somehow, somewhere, I would make a home for the three of us, no matter what the future might bring. 'Let's go to the dining car and get some supper,' I pronounced with renewed bravado."

Mary wanted to know if dining cars on the trains were as well stocked as the restaurants were during the war.

"Fortunately this one was, and when we finally were ushered to a table, we sank into our chairs with relief. Our smiling waiter delighted the children with jokes, and to us he said he would try to arrange berths for the four of us that night. Securing a place to sleep seemed unlikely with so many passengers without reservations on board. But when he presented the check he told us quietly that he had secured an upper and lower berth together in the coach ahead. With deep gratitude, I thanked him and left a tip for that thoughtful man.

"When we arrived, your dad met us at the train station in downtown Boston and took us to our apartment. He had been lucky to find a place in Porter Square in Cambridge, but our quarters were drafty, cold, and ramshackle. Despite the fact that we paid extra for more heat, there was a quarter-inch of ice on the inside of all the windows, the tiny tub was so cold that I seldom used it, and I was driven to hold my hands around the light bulbs for extra warmth. But, at least Lucy and I had a roof over our heads and could see Bob when he was on leave. We stayed alive by eating fish from the wharf market because other foods were hard to come by.

"Aunt Rina provided a bright spot in our lives in Cambridge. She contacted a Hyde cousin, Ruth Hyde Hanford, who invited me and Lucy for Sunday dinner, a lovely chicken meal. After we finished, her husband took Lucy to a nearby park for her first sled ride. She was taught how to enjoy the snow by a dean of Harvard University!

"While the two were sledding, Ruth Hanford told me a story about the Hyde branch of the Ames family that I may never have told you, Mary. Your dad and Martha got their middle name from the Hydes. Ruth told me that when she was a child she visited a little friend's home, where she was entranced by Robert Louis Stevenson's book, *A Child's Garden of Verses*.

"Ruth said that she'd expressed regret to her friend's mother because she did not have this lovely book at her house. Her friend's mother then clutched the book and replied, 'Please, please don't tell your mother that we have a Stevenson book in our house.'

"To understand her dismay you have to know the Father Damien story. Father Damien was a Catholic priest who volunteered to live among the lepers on Molokai Island in Hawaii. 'At the same time,' Ruth had said, 'my uncle, the Congregational minister, Dr. Charles Hyde, was tending his parish in Honolulu and was also instrumental in creating a museum to preserve the culture of the Hawaiian people.

While there, he received a letter from a Presbyterian minister on the mainland who asked if it were true that the good Father Damien was living in sin with his housekeeper. Uncle Charlie responded to the letter in true Victorian fashion. In confidence he wrote that he had, indeed, heard this to be true. The foolish recipient of this confidence shared the letter with a local newspaper. The shocking news reached Robert Louis Stevenson, who suffered from ill health. Outraged, Stevenson wrote an open letter to the Reverend Hyde in defense of his hero, Father Damien.'"

"Yes, I remember that letter to Reverend Charles Hyde. It was used in my English textbook at Cornell as a perfect example of vitriolic writing," Mary interjected.

"Ruth went on to explain, 'It is family legend, though I suspect the truth of it, that not content with his letter, Robert Louis Stevenson named the evil character Hyde in his story, *The Strange Case of Dr. Jekyll and Mr. Hyde.* In any case, Stevenson became *persona non grata* in the family.'

"Ruth had a contemplative look as she bade us goodbye that day, and as we parted she said, 'You know, Uncle Charlie truly was a lovely man.'

"It was at about this time that your dad unexpectedly received orders from the Navy to proceed immediately to Washington, D.C., to report for duty by 5:00 p.m. the following day. A heavy snow fell in Cambridge the week Bob and the others were to graduate as communications officers. While he was being detached from duty at Harvard, I was shoveling snow from thirty feet of driveway so that we would be able to free the car in time to leave for Washington.

"Bob told me that all the men at Harvard who were about to go to sea asked him the same thing, 'Who do you know in Washington?' The truth is that he had applied for a Navy commission at the beginning of hostilities, but it was denied on the grounds that he was too old, thirty-two, and too thin. Undaunted, Bob went to Washington to add to his application the special skills he had that might be valuable to the service. He called on our old Cincinnati friend for guidance, Herbert Brown, then an aide to Admiral Frank Knox, Secretary of the Navy."

Mary Lou said, "I remember when Bob went to ask advice from Herb."

"Herb made it clear that he could not ask for special consideration for Bob from this office because that would be preferential treatment, but Herb *could* direct him on how to find the office where he might enhance his original application with added information about his hard-to-find skills and experience. So, Bob visited the office on his own behalf and reported that one of his skills was the ability to rewrite difficult scientific material, to make it understandable and useful to an intelligent layman.

"By the summer of 1944, loss of life had been so great that many new officers were commissioned and sent off for training, Bob among them."

Harry interjected, "You never did tell us why you were suddenly transferred to D.C."

"You know, Bob never discussed his work in Washington, for it was very hush-hush. After the war, when the code name *Nancy Hanks* was common knowledge, Bob finally told me about his work. The *Nancy* equipment, as it was popularly called, utilized a new, advanced technology that allowed them to send secret messages from ship to ship when the ships were in formation. But sending messages was not the only thing that this equipment was capable of, as the Navy suddenly realized. The *Nancy* equipment, a giant searchlight using special filters, could illuminate objects miles away at night with light that the enemy could not see, such as a shoreline seventeen miles distant from a ship or an airplane approaching in the night sky from far away. Before the *Nancy* equipment was developed, our fleet suffered the new kind of attack, by Japanese kamikazes. Somehow evading radar, these suicide bombardiers would appear out of the night sky prepared to fly their armed planes as dive-bombs into our ships. With the infrared *Nancy* gear they could be seen at a distance.

"The admirals in Washington ordered that the *Nancy* equipment, with instructions for using it, be rushed to the Pacific for immediate use, but when, in the heat of battle, the captains received the unfamiliar material marked 'Top Secret,' they threw it into the safe and did not use it. The instructions were so complicated they couldn't take time to decipher them. Bob's assignment in Washington was to simplify the *Nancy* instructions as soon as possible into a booklet that could be easily understood even by a young sailor. When the new instructions arrived in the Pacific, the sailors were able to understand them and put *Nancy* equipment into immediate use, saving ships and thousands of lives, which helped to turn the tide in the Pacific theater."

Getting back to the story of our move to Washington, D.C., I continued. "It was going to be hazardous for us to get to Washington by car because of wintry weather. And with wartime shortages our tires had little tread. Chains weren't available. Nevertheless, we set out for Washington in a snowstorm, with the deadline of 5:00 p.m. the next day, and didn't stop. By the time we reached Baltimore the sun was shining, and as we rolled into D.C., spring was in the air and in our spirits. The three of us would be together again at last.

"Our euphoria melted away all too soon, though, for quarters were almost impossible to find because of the thousands who moved to Washington for the war effort. Bless her heart; Aunt Rina rescued her homeless relatives once again. She invited Lucy and me to stay with her at her charming country farm in Fauquier County, Virginia, while Bob searched for lodging. Lucy and I would be with family, only an hour's drive from Bob.

"In the Valley of Virginia, near the little town of Hume, the view to the west of us contained the Appalachian Mountains, wide ridges in Virginia, and narrowing southward into Alabama and Georgia. These were the mountains where, as a young man, George Washington surveyed the Valley of Virginia and noted one particular short range whose silhouette looked like a boat floating in the valley. Indians had called the range Massanutten. When George reached the top of that range, he discovered it was truly shaped like a boat, actually a double ridge with a high valley completing the sense of a very large canoe. It was filled with trees and rich soil, and as George surveyed this beautiful hidden land he saw the perfect site to support hundreds of colonists as a potential safe haven in case of attack from the Indians or the French. In fact, this brilliant idea caused him to *exclude* the high Massanutten Valley in the survey maps he created.

"A few weeks after Lucy and I settled at Plowshares with Aunt Rina, Bob was finally successful in finding a temporary place in Lee Gardens Apartments in Arlington, Virginia, subletting from another Navy officer for a couple of months. We gathered in the courtyard of our building during evening time to get to know each other. This little community could have evolved only in the chaotic migrations of a war.

"Among our new friends were the Banes. Charlie was a member of the secret OSS that later became the CIA, and his wife, Eilene, and little daughter, Susan, became close friends. Another member of the group was a newcomer from Mt. Vernon, New York, where, Bob mentioned, he had been enrolled in high school in his senior year. The Mt. Vernonite excused herself for a moment and returned with her yearbook, where Bob and our new acquaintance were pictured side by side. Wartime Washington mixed people and made coincidences like that happen frequently.

"Others we enjoyed, Andy Holt and his lovely wife, were from Tennessee. Andy had a victory garden, like the one *our* dad always cultivated for Mother during the war, Mamie Lou. It flourished in a vacant plot nearby. Everybody pooled their meat tokens for a dinner, and Andy provided the salad, potatoes, and green vegetables. Andy was unbelievably likeable, and I'm not surprised to have learned that he retired from the Army as a major and became president of the University of Tennessee.

"Knowing that our contract on the apartment at Lee Gardens was coming to an end, Bob continued to put pressure on the manager of Park Fairfax to find a place for us in this Alexandria apartment complex covering a hillside where wartime housing had mushroomed. There were far more people waiting in line for an apartment than there were places available. The fact that we were expecting a second child convinced the manager that we were the most in need of a home and signed us up for a two-bedroom unit.

"Once we moved in, five-year-old Lucy became acquainted with the neighbors faster than I did. I heard her tell Mary Annis Jackson, who lived beneath us, 'We have a new game in our family. We're trying to see if Daddy can make money faster than Mommy can spend it!'

"When Mother, who by then had been dubbed 'Gran-gran' by Lucy and Cousin Hank, came to visit us, she was satisfied to sleep on a single bed in Lucy's little bedroom. One night she hurt her foot on a plastic toy and said to Lucy, 'Why didn't you pick up your toys and put them away? *Your* mother didn't treat *me* like that.'

"Lucy replied, 'Those were the Good Old Days, Gran-gran, and they will never come again. But I'm glad you had Mommy when you were young, so I could see you before you died.'"

Mary and I continued reminiscing about important family events with the Kassons through a few more after-dinner drinks—about their unforgettable wedding on the boat and how Harry, the camera buff, had taken such fabulous photos documenting our younger days. [Image 6.2a] We questioned them further. How were Mamie Lou's golf game and tournaments and her volunteer work at Children's Hospital? And we wanted to know about Gran-gran's independent apartment on Delta Avenue, Hank's recognition by the *Law Review,* and Cynthia's stand-up-comedian husband, Curt McIntyre, who we all agreed was bound to become a beloved college professor someday. [Images 6.3, 6.4, 6.5, 6.6] [Note 3 – The Kassons]

"Oh, Mamie Lou and Harry," I said, standing up stiffly and sharing hugs, "This has been so wonderful remembering old times with you and catching up on current family news too, but Mary and I better get some sleep if we want to leave early in the morning."

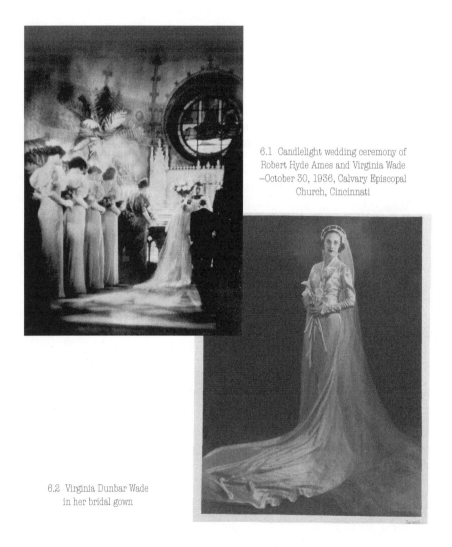

6.1 Candlelight wedding ceremony of Robert Hyde Ames and Virginia Wade —October 30, 1936, Calvary Episcopal Church, Cincinnati

6.2 Virginia Dunbar Wade in her bridal gown

6.2a Virginia Dunbar Wade—a
photographic portrait by Harry C. Kasson taken in the 1930s during
her college years

6.3 Mary Louise Wade and
Harry Kasson, married on his boat
Kismet, July 27, 1933

6.4 Hank Kasson, Mamie Lou's and Harry's
son as a beguiling youth, 1940s

6.5 Cynthia Brooks Kasson, Mamie Lou's and Harry's daughter, at her graduation

6.6 Cynthia Kasson, their grandmother Gran-gran (Pearl G. Wade), and cousin Martha Hyde Ames at her 1966 Cotillion

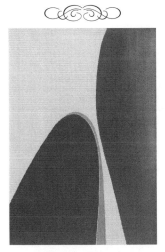

Beneath the St. Louis Arch–
original watercolor by Virginia Ames

CHAPTER 7

Saturday, October 17, 1970
Odometer reading
at Cincinnati: 26,651

Cincinnati, Ohio, to
St. Louis, Missouri
Trip meter reading
at Cincinnati: 651

All Experience
Is an Arch

The next morning, Harry and Mary Lou sent us off with their blessings, despite Harry's misgivings about our means of transport. But Betsy prevailed, purring through the flatlands.

Our route to St. Louis took us for some time through the blue sky, fall foliage, and red barns of southern Indiana. I told Mary, "This is the district that sent the Hamilton family, our neighbors in Vaucluse, to Washington, and Lee Hamilton as their representative in the House of Representatives. His wife, Nancy, is such a delightful person."

"Their kids too," Mary added. "Seems like for every public figure there is at least one invisible team member somewhere in the wings keeping things supported, sane, and balanced."

"Representative Hamilton has been chairman of important committees such as foreign affairs and intelligence. We recently watched
a Congressional investigation on TV in which Lee Hamilton was doing the questioning. With the dignity of a statesman rather than of
a politician, Hamilton avoided histrionics that might have helped
him politically and instead spoke with dispassion and fairness. I so
respect him. The Hamiltons are exciting neighbors."

Thinking about the Hamiltons and many members of Congress
who had been our friends, neighbors, or fellow church members at
Immanuel-on-the-Hill over the years got Mary and me reminiscing
about life in Alexandria again with gusto as the cornrows rolled by.

"Senator Nixon and his wife Pat lived in the Park Fairfax apartment building next to ours when I was pregnant with you. Though
we never saw Richard Nixon, I became acquainted with Pat over our
housewifely laundry chores, and I admired her from the beginning.
She created her own significant role as a senator's wife. Almost every
day, she dressed up and was available to take his constituents on
sightseeing tours of the nation's capital.

"Then *you* came into the world, Mary! Our third child. Two babies and a schoolgirl in that tiny apartment and we were bursting
at the seams, hungry for an adequate house, but there were few to
be had. One day in 1948, the *Washington Post* carried a story of a
builder, Ad Waterval, who would construct a dozen homes and have
them available in a matter of weeks. A model home was scheduled
to be on exhibit the following Sunday. Traveling west into Fairfax
County on the Leesburg Pike, we saw a sign for Virginia Heights. We
turned right on a new road that wound its way down a hill through a
forest of young oaks. Cars were parked throughout the new development of Virginia Heights and in the two cul-de-sacs that interrupted
the main street at different elevations. The setting was beautiful.

"The model home was a simple factory-engineered rectangle, its
prepackaged parts having arrived on the site and assembled there.
Mr. Waterval, designer and developer of the rural property, later

worked with the famous architect Edward Durell Stone to build the American Embassy structure in New Delhi, India. Here he sat in his model home, conferring with potential buyers, telling them of his plan to add custom details, including a porch or patio to add variety to each home design.

"If he thought a family would enhance the neighborhood, he said, 'Yes, I can have you a home in six weeks.' To those who did not match his expectations, he promised a house maybe within the year. We were lucky, because we made the grade and signed the contract that sunny Sunday. On that day, a fascinating community was created.

"When the time came to move, we loaded you kids into the car and drove the short distance to our new home. Two of our new neighbors were standing in the middle of the street, eager to find out who was moving in. Later we found ourselves just as curious.

"Among the new inhabitants of Virginia Heights were some truly amazing people. These included our friends for life, Sandy and Kaye Sanborn, and son, Jim, who was the same age as Muff. Sandy was a successful printmaker and watercolorist, and chief exhibits officer at the Library of Congress. Frequently, he would bring fascinating stories home from the Library to Kaye, your dad, and me that he would share over an informal supper. When a Bedouin shepherd, he told us, discovered a cave in Qumran, Israel, and brought out clay pots containing ancient scrolls, he showed them to anybody who might be able to understand their significance. As I remember, Sandy said that a man titled 'Metropolitan' brought some of the scrolls to the Library of Congress and to Sandy, in hopes that they could be properly identified and exhibited. Sandy was ecstatic that these scrolls might be of historical significance. As a matter of fact, this later proved to be true; they were identified to have biblical connection and thereafter were known as the 'Dead Sea Scrolls.'

"Kaye had been a concert pianist, who later did picture research for writers and historians. When the kids were young, she could always be counted on to partner with me on field trip adventures to the

85

Smithsonian or the National Zoo. When the Sanborns bought a set of swings for their yard in Virginia Heights, the kids in the neighborhood took over. At first Jim was content to watch from the sidelines. He leaned against one of the support posts and watched for hours to see how the others worked the swings. The next day, fully trained and emboldened, he scared his mother by standing up on the wooden seat and pumping so hard it looked like he might flip upside down. [Note 4 – Sanborns and Jim]

"Our French Canadian neighbors, the LaHeureuxs, were the first to add an addition to their home ... enough bedrooms for their six children. Our old friends from Cincinnati, Herb and Ada Brown, became neighbors again in Virginia. Ada was an artist, and Herb, now out of Admiral Knox's office, lived with their son and daughter on the cul-de-sac near the entrance to our woodsy village. Our contemporaries Norm and Bea Harper had Barbee, who became your closest neighborhood buddy. Bob Hankins, lawyer for an airline company, and his family rounded out our tightly knit community.

"Unfortunately, when Mr. Waterval developed our Virginia Heights home sites, he destroyed part of an ancient horse trail. This hit home for me when four Virginians on horseback approached our circle through a wooded horse trail and came to a stop, discovering a house in their path. This had been *their* woods and we were the invaders. We were reminded of this from time to time when foxes, deer, or rabbits passed through the yard. Arlington County and Fairfax County were both rapidly developed, as trees made way for more homes. From our front porch, we could look over the Arlington County rooftops, across the lowlands of the Potomac River, with a straight-line view of the Washington Monument. It was a beautiful view but had been acquired at a cost to others.

"Post-war basic services were slow in coming way out to Virginia Heights, and Herb Brown was particularly irritated at having no telephone. At last, Herb was in a position to go to bat for us, as he was the editor of the Kiplinger's Washington Editors magazine,

Changing Times. He told the telephone company that they had an obligation, as a *monopoly*, to give us service immediately. The word 'monopoly' struck a chord, and to our great surprise, within one day workmen invaded the community, stringing a telephone wire that connected all our homes.

"One line meant we were connected by phone to the outside world, but it also meant we were connected to each other. Being on a party line made for some interesting situations. With eleven households on the same line, we never knew who might be listening to our conversations. Sometimes I would pick up the receiver and there would be someone on the line. We'd just strike up a conversation with several neighbors at once, like in old movies. I found out some things strictly by chance that maybe I shouldn't have, like who was pregnant, or who was making eyes at someone else's wife at a cocktail party, or that someone had to go out west to Las Vegas for six weeks in order to have *a divorce*, which 'nice people' didn't do in those days. Fortunately, with progress, the neighborhood was able to get a private line to each household.

"We were extremely happy in Virginia Heights ... I with my azalea gardening and your dad joining his cronies for bridge in the evenings. On one memorable bridge group evening, a new guest was surprised to realize he had met Bob before, revealing yet another return in the circle of our lives. This man had been the young ensign who worked in the Navy office where Bob had gone to add to his application for a commission during the war. This was the man who had remembered him when, three years later, the Navy was desperately looking for someone to rewrite the *Nancy* instructions. Over the card table he said to your dad, 'Do you know how you got sent to Washington?' and proceeded to tell him how he had been instrumental in getting Bob's assignment to Washington.

"Other neighbors, the Cantrells from Texas, hosted square dances in their spacious basement. He was a gifted caller. Like family, they invited us to bring our children to sleep in their bedroom upstairs, while all the neighbors danced downstairs. Next door to them were the Johnstons, also hailing from Texas, who were in some high position in the federal government. Grandma Prickett babysat our young kids and led them in their bedtime prayers. [Note 5 – Virginia Heights]

"Although this was a wonderful neighborhood to join, we did face a few hurdles early on. As permanent residents of Virginia, your dad and I visited our registrar to sign up to vote. Mrs. O'Shaughnessy, an old-time Virginian who maintained the voter registration books, gave us quite a runaround. She protested that she would be out of town or otherwise 'unavailable' so often that it would be hard to accommodate us. We soon realized she was trying to exclude us. When we got together with neighbors, we found our experience was not unique. We had a feeling that Mrs. O'Shaughnessy wanted to disenfranchise all the newcomers, treating us like the enemy who had invaded her territory. We persisted until she ran out of excuses and finally had to register all of us.

"We newcomers 'bumped heads' against some of the locals another time when one of them wanted to expand his gravel pit closer to our neighborhood. When we protested on legal grounds, a member of the Board of Supervisors for Fairfax County responded, 'We got thirteen illegal gravel pits operating in Fairfax County. I do not know why we should be prejudiced against this one.'

"At our local elementary, Bailey's Crossroads School, we encountered even more challenges. The lavatory did not work, the basement smelled, a boy who was deemed unable to learn was given a broom to sweep the halls, and a fundamentalist teacher warned our children that they would go to hell for their sins. It was hard for me to believe that deterring voter registration, allowing illegal gravel pits, and a dysfunctional school could exist in Virginia, the home of Thomas Jefferson.

"When we met John Horne from church, head of the Small Business Administration under two presidents, and his wife at the first PTA gathering at the old Bailey's Elementary, we agreed that we

ALL EXPERIENCE IS AN ARCH

must get our children into another school immediately. The Horne family resolved the situation by moving into Alexandria, and we resolved it by sending our children to the Burgundy Farm Country Day School. Oh Mary, how that changed all of our lives for the better from there on, didn't it?"

Mary heartily agreed, saying how first grade at Burgundy, with Camay Brooks as her beloved teacher, opened up whole new horizons for her—and all of our family. [Note 6 – Burgundy]

I resumed thoughts of our time in Virginia Heights and Fairfax County. "In the woods behind our house we built a sandbox for Muffin, where she played alone. Mary, you were still a baby and Lucy was too old to be a playmate for either of you at that point. One morning when I was planting azaleas in the garden, I overheard Muffin talking as though to a pal. I listened, worried, because I had read that imaginary playmates were often invented by lonesome children. To my surprise, her 'friend' was none other than George Washington. I talked about this with your dad that evening at dinner, wondering if this could be serious. George Washington, he reminded me while laughing, is a real person to Muffin. 'She heard us say that George Washington had surveyed the line between our property in Fairfax County and Arlington County right up our driveway.' We had essentially introduced her to him, and he had been in her domain near her sandbox.

"Months later, while quietly reading, I heard someone slashing branches that lined our driveway. Outraged, I shouted to the stranger, 'Young man, what do you think you are *doing?*'

"'I am triangulating,' he replied.

"'You are also destroying my dogwood tree and my azaleas!'

"He looked ashamed and said, 'I have to open a pathway to use my surveying equipment. George Washington's instruments were not as precise as mine when he surveyed this boundary, so we have to redo it with our modern equipment.'

"In our little community, do you recall when you were very young, Mary, how we Virginia Heights parents developed that neat program to keep you children busy and happy during summer vacation? One of the parents took the kids on tours of the U.S. Capitol and museums on the National Mall. Ada Brown taught pottery and puppet-making. Kaye Sanborn amused all of you by teaching songs, accompanying them on the piano. Her husband, Herb, set up easels and each child enjoyed *plein air* painting. Marguerite LaHeureux taught conversational French with choruses of *Alouett-tah, Gentil Alouett-tah*, and you learned to swim in the LaHeureuxs' pool made by filling a surplus WWII pontoon boat with water. I directed you children in two different dramatic plays. We wrapped up the summer by performing a hilarious rendition of *The Three Little Pigs* with the wolf blowing the house down, then all the kids sang and staged an exhibit of their own creations. Mary, maybe you were too young to remember it all, but you were a worthy participant!

"We like to think that our neighborhood 'summer camp' influenced some of the children's futures. *Family Circle* magazine even featured it in one of their issues. Bob and I are sure that it contributed to you and your sisters graduating with honors from good colleges.

"It was during this time in the late '40s into the early '50s that your dad was working for Capitol Airlines in advertising, helping them create a new logo and presence in the world. He really loved this job, but it didn't pay very well, so when Mr. Kiplinger of *Changing Times* magazine approached your dad with an offer to be his circulation director, with a nice salary working under Boyce Morgan, he could hardly turn it down.

"While he was employed with Kiplinger we thought we were on Easy Street. Finally, he had a great job and was well regarded in his position, but you never know when the tides will turn. When Dewey and Truman were vying for the presidency, and as Election Day approached, your dad kept getting a hunch, against all the polls and odds, that Truman was going to win the election. It was so tight that the magazine staff had two different stories ready to run, depending on who should win.

"Kip, as staff affectionately called founder and head man Willard Kiplinger, kept saying, 'Bob, Dewey is a shoe-in. Don't worry about it.' On the day of the election, your dad had seen the multitudes of people at the voting polls and told Kiplinger one more time of his sense that Truman would be voted in, but Kip was still confident in Dewey's win. At Kiplinger's request, your dad put Dewey's face on the front page of the magazine galley, as did other periodicals, for release the next day. He came home, unable to eat, and barely able to sleep, until he got a phone call from Kiplinger at 3:00 a.m. asking, 'Bob, whose photo did you put on the front page?' He was desperately hoping that your dad had followed his own hunch. It was so devastating for Kiplinger to be wrong that he fired the general manager above Bob, Boyce Morgan ... who was a brilliant mathematician ... and the whole team below him too. Funny thing, twenty years later, after both Bob and Boyce had successful businesses, he got a call from Kiplinger, 'Bob, could I buy some of your time?' wanting him to return as a consultant, which he did. When Kiplinger asked whom he should hire as a general manager, your dad replied, 'The guy you fired twenty years ago,' and Kiplinger did just that. What goes around comes around, right, Mary?"

"What did Dad do after he got laid off from Kiplinger's in the early '50s?"

"Well, the airline your dad had worked for before Kiplinger had hired an ad agency to do all of their advertising, and they hired him because of his previous reputation with the airlines. It was not a job that your dad liked, and in fact this is when he started getting sick with tuberculosis. We suspect he was exposed to it by the elevator operator who worked in the agency's office building, who they later found out had it. He was working too many hours and bringing work home. He was stressed and frustrated.

"In the early 1950s, TB still threatened people around the world. Fortunately, not everyone who was exposed contracted the disease. The only cure at that time was bed rest, so your dad was sent to a sanatorium designed for this kind of disease, down in Charlottesville.

"At the beginning of his illness in 1953, the future was uncertain, and I faced it with three children. I had always been a homemaker, not a working woman, ever since Lucy was born. I was fortunate that Andy Gould, the vice president of *U.S. News and World Report*, one of your dad's business associates and a friend, offered me a position in his office, confident of my ability to learn on the job. I suddenly moved from housewife to executive secretary. Bob had known Andy through a professional group of circulation directors of publications, such as *U.S. News and World Report,* American Association for the Advancement of Science's *Science Magazine*, and Phi Beta Kappa's *The American Scholar*, who would meet regularly to discuss and share ideas to increase circulation.

"Life was tense in Washington when I entered the business arena. Joseph McCarthy's witch hunt for communists had many a loyal American fearing for his job. Silent were the owners and publishers of important magazines and journals, including *U.S. News and World Report*'s David Lawrence, the voice for conservative Americans. His own writers fumed that their employer remained silent. He had more cause than most to be silent; Lawrence had been a member of the communist party, a common thing among college students in the 1930s.

"McCarthy was singlehandedly trying many innocent Americans in a fabricated court, based on hearsay and with no evidence or due process, not allowing the accused to face the accuser or be defended, thus ruining the careers and the lives of many, creating an air of fear throughout the country. Finally in 1954, that renowned news reporter Edward R. Murrow was brave enough to expose McCarthy and his self-proclaimed power, which his senatorial position should not have given him, calling his bluff and ending his reign of terror.

"During your dad's illness, while I was working, I needed some-one to be at the house when you came home from school, even though twelve-year-old Lucy was there too. Gran-gran came from Cincinnati to be with you girls for six months, and when she returned to Cin-cinnati, I depended upon Lucy to look after you and Muff until I got home. One day, when I was driving home from work on a dark wintry evening, I recalled with horror that Lucy had not been due home af-ter school and Muffin was at a neighborhood birthday party, leaving you alone. I pulled into the driveway and raced into the house calling your name. You were only five years old. When you emerged from a dark closet, I hugged you and said, 'Oh, Mary, were you afraid?'

"'Yes,' you replied. 'I thought you were Mrs. Carver and I would have to entertain her because you weren't home.'"

Through the laughter, I asked Mary if she remembered this in-cident and she said, "Not really, but I do remember when Gertrude came to be with us."

"You're right … as a result of this incident, I employed Gertrude. She had worked for our neighbors, the LaHeureux family, until their six children had outgrown the need for such supervision.

"She was one of a kind, wasn't she? Gertrude was a perfect ex-ample of the folly of generalizing about Black people or any group. If I were to say they're all alike then I would miss some interesting personalities. Gertrude was one of these.

"Gertrude agreed to come to us in the early afternoon and do a few light chores before I came home to release her. She had a dogged fidelity to her job. She came every school day. She saw that you girls were safe and she did a few tasks that I requested, but in her *own* way. She would cook a vegetable or put a roast in the oven, but on one occasion I called Gertrude and told her that you had been invited to a party in the neighborhood and I wanted you to look neat, so I asked her to brush and braid your hair into two pigtails and to secure each with a pretty ribbon. Because she didn't believe this was one of her duties, Gertrude answered in a voice loud enough for all the office to hear, 'I'll scream if I have to.' I hung up the receiver, hoping for a positive outcome.

"On another occasion, I asked Gertrude if she would clean the oven, as there were no other chores that needed to be done. On returning home that evening, I went into the kitchen. Gertrude opened the oven door proudly to show me her good work and ordered me firmly, 'Now, you *keep* it that way!'

"I gasped, but I held my tongue. She had worked for our neighbor for years and had conscientiously tended the children. So I overlooked her idiosyncrasies and was glad I did, for I later learned she was a recovering alcoholic and she did not feel like being kind and courteous. Loyalty was as much as she could manage. She always kept our children from harm."

"Luvenia was totally different from Gertrude, wasn't she?"

"So true. When we lived in The Cottage, and then Orleans Place, Luvenia Christian helped me keep the places tidy. She would carpool a long distance once a week to keep the sparkle in our home. She told me that when she was eight years old, she had worked for Fairfax Harrison in his home in Fauquier County, Virginia. He was the son of the secretary to Confederate President Jefferson Davis, and an accomplished lawyer, businessman, and writer. Mainly, she washed the dishes for us because she was already past middle age, yet still capable and assured.

"One day as we sat together at the kitchen table, the usually mild-mannered Luvenia shared an experience with me that revealed how Blacks were still being treated. Luvenia's daughter Molly lived with her family in The Plains, Virginia. Molly was a respected schoolteacher who passed on the need for a higher education to her children. Molly's teenage son, like the white kids, drove his car with the roar of a cutout muffler. A policeman stopped him and gave him a ticket for the seldom-enforced, forbidden use of the noisy cutout. When the officer found out who the boy was, he apologized to Molly saying, 'I am so sorry. I didn't know he was *your* son.'

"Luvenia continued, 'On a snowy Christmas Eve, another member of my family was driving with a fresh Christmas tree hanging out the back of her car and was cited because the left rear tire touched the center stripe of the road. On Christmas Eve!' Luvenia told me these things without rancor, but she thought I needed to know.

"Luvenia had great respect for my mother's generation and would not sit at lunch with me when Mother was visiting from Ohio. She seemed pleased when Mother asked a favor of her. It was as though she was comfortable in reliving her youth.

"When she left us, she promised me she would always keep in touch through letters, and I have saved them all."

"I'd like to read them some day after we get back, Mams." [Note 7 – Luvenia]

"Okay, make a note. So back to your dad. When he had recovered and returned home to Virginia Heights, after a year in the sanatorium and with the help of some experimental drugs, I thought it wise to continue working for a while because we had no idea if he would relapse. Dad wasn't sure if he was up to full-time work, so he called on his old friend Boyce Morgan, who started giving him some part-time projects to get him back on his feet. After a few months, the National Press Club called your dad and asked if he would help them get their newly inherited *Army, Navy, Air Force Journal* back into profitable operations after its owner had passed and left his sweetheart in charge. Knowing this was only a temporary position for a year or so in order for the *Journal* to become solvent enough to sell, we were still left without security, so I kept working even though I longed to be homemaking with you girls. It turned out that this position helped get your dad back into the business market, and he had no trouble continuing to find lucrative jobs after that. One funny little perk your dad got with this position was an opportunity to attend a big event at the National Press Club. They put on a play, a sort of lampoon of the current men in 'Big Press' ... quite an affair in D.C. ... and your father got to be there, rubbing elbows with John Kennedy,

Richard Nixon, the Duke of Windsor, editors from *The New York Times*, and others. It was quite the party!"

We had covered lots of ground literally and figuratively, yet it seemed little time had passed when we crossed from Indiana into Missouri.

Reflecting on the previous evening's conversation with the Kassons, Mary asked, "Why didn't you and Dad return to live in Cincinnati after the war?"

"Well, Mare, after living in Washington," I confessed, "nowhere else had the same allure. Your dad surprised me by asking if I would like to bring up our family in Virginia. Alexandria really felt like being back home to me. Your dad reminded me with a teasing grin that we weren't yet free to leave the Washington area until he was discharged from the service.

"In a voice more accusatory than information seeking, I asked him whether he had requested his honorable discharge yet. His voice was serious when he answered, 'Yes, Gin, but it's complicated. I can't be discharged until I return all the top secret material the Navy issued to me that I used to create the *Nancy* instruction booklet. In the speed of creating the booklet, I used the literal cut-and-paste method to rephrase the booklet, so now there is no more *original* to return. The only way I can get out of the Navy now is to have the material declassified to *confidential*, and that will take the approval of the Joint Chiefs of Staff.' Fortunately, they finally approved.

"Mary, the idea of living in Northern Virginia pleased me to no end because it felt so right for us. Alexandria had everything to make it a delightful place to be ... a small town with a vibrant city nearby ... a town that clung to old Virginia traditions."

"Like the tradition of the punch at the gala ball in Gadsby's Tavern the year you were chair? You said the previous chairwoman gave you the old family recipe but withheld the right proportions, and everyone got plastered."

"That wasn't so funny at the time because I was responsible." I paused momentarily. "And that's another story worth telling ...

"Alexandria today is much more than just an historic old town. Mary, I would sure miss the Torpedo Factory Art Center if I did not live there anymore."

"But you can do art wherever you live, Mom."

"I know, but the Torpedo Factory is unique. Do you remember that the City of Alexandria bought the old building from the federal government? It had been used for making torpedoes in World War I and again in World War II. After they bought it, the city fathers did not know how to make use of the building. It was not easy to destroy because the engineers learned that the base was an eight-foot-thick concrete foundation. While they were arguing about how to transform the ugly building into something useful, a savvy, politically minded gal, Marian Van Landingham, proposed that it be used temporarily by the artists in town. At a hearing in city hall, each member of the art league presented an argument in favor of this temporary use. Our mayor, an airline pilot, thinking of places like Ghirardelli Square in San Francisco, favored the idea. But the merchants on lower King Street were violently opposed. 'Those artists will take all our business away from us!' Local residents of the fine Federal Period homes complained that Old Town would be 'full of hippies.' When Mayor Beatley heard this testimony he asked, 'Hippies like Virginia Ames?' Thankfully, the artists prevailed. The first year that we occupied the Torpedo Factory, five thousand visitors came to Alexandria to tour our new art center and local businesses fed on new foot traffic.

"The city restored the heating and cooling systems and built partitions for separate studios. They allowed us to have low rent if we agreed to have each studio provide a window for the curious public to watch us work. We had the duty of cleaning, painting, and furnishing our own studios. My partner, Clarinda Jennison, and I decorated furniture with faux finishes and made other creative items. That's where we produced the miles of wallpaper that we silkscreened with my bamboo and poppy print, which now bedecks our entrance hall and dining room at Orleans Place. But the most important use I made of our studio was to produce an authentic replica of a painted floor cloth that had been commissioned by the Society for the Preservation of Virginia Antiquities for installation in the John Marshall House Museum in Richmond. [Image 7.1]

"If I get the commission from the Library of Congress to replicate flags flown in the American Revolution to hang in their Great Hall during the upcoming Bicentennial, my Torpedo Factory studio will be seeing some large-scale fabric work soon." [Note 8 – Virginia's Art Career]

I thought for a moment about the meanings of some of the street names in Alexandria. The Torpedo Factory is at the bottom of King Street in Old Town, right on the Potomac River wharf. The streets of Old Town tell its history well. The main cross streets are King and Washington, a metaphor for the revolution itself. The monarchy died hard, for Queen, Duke, and Prince Streets survive in the center of town. The Fairfax and Peyton families survived in the naming of streets there too. The Fairfax estate name, Belvoir, survives in a street on Seminary Hill.

"Mary, I'll bet you'll remember Elizabeth Anne Campagna from your newspaper work. Up the street from the Torpedo Factory she presided over the YWCA like a benevolent dictator. She was possibly one of the greatest influences in social reform in the modern times of Alexandria. It was the 1960s, and she was determined that the YWCA actually serve for social change. Campagna, a Georgian with a deep-rooted sense of social justice, devoted one of the rooms in the YWCA to Head Start even while the merits of this new program were still being debated nationally. She also provided space for a support group for unwed mothers, a rare social service at that time.

"She deplored the fact that a large living room in the building was infrequently used, so she gave permission to a budding young sculptor to have an exhibition there. During the course of the open house, one of his pieces fell to the floor and was broken. The poor young artist sued the YWCA for the value of his broken sculpture, and Elizabeth Anne found herself in court. In the course of the trial, a lawyer asked her to answer a question yes or no. She demurred and the judge said, 'Mrs. Campagna, just answer the question, yes or no.' She said to the judge, 'Your honor, I swore to tell the truth, the whole truth, and nothing but the truth, and, Sir, the truth lies halfway between yes and no.'

"Campagna came to my home one day to tell me that the chairman of the annual Alexandria Christmas Walk, a fundraising festival sponsored by the YWCA, had quit her volunteer role in midstream. Campagna had created the Christmas Walk to help fund her new programs at the Y. She said to me, 'We are without a chairman. Virginia Ames, we need you. Will you take on the Christmas Walk?' I had been chairman of the festival ball the previous year. The banners created to hang over the doors of the participating merchants had been silk-screened in my studio, so I felt familiar enough to take on the unfinished job. Women who could afford to do so, as I now could, thanks to your dad's good health and flourishing businesses with WETA and Kiplinger, gave their time and talents to social services.

"As chairman of the Christmas Walk, I was responsible for all of its events, including the Grand Ball. For years, one Alexandria matron had prepared the special bourbon punch traditionally served. This particular year, she too reneged on her job and told me that she would give the recipe for the punch to her successor, who would be preparing the refreshments. She did give her all of the ingredients but failed to mention proportions. The punch that night was so strong that the happy dancers were smashed by 11:00 p.m. and the bourbon was all used up, while the other ingredients, sparkling water and ginger ale, had been hardly used in the punch. When I realized what had happened, I was quite worried for the safety of the partygoers. But by the close at 1:00 a.m., it was obvious that time had worn off the effects and everyone got home safely. I couldn't help wondering if, when George Washington celebrated his last birthday in this very place, the Gadsby's Tavern ballroom, they'd had as much fun as our group." [Image 7.2]

Mary said that she wished she had been at *that* party and continued, "I knew George Washington had said farewell to his troops from the steps at the entrance of Gadsby's, though I didn't know he celebrated his last birthday there. But, hey, I'm neglecting my job. I'm supposed to be keeping track of Betsy's oil consumption on this trip. I will check the oil in Granite City, the next little town we come to in Missouri."

We stopped at a small filling station there, and she noted that the odometer read 26,850.

"We have enough gas to make St. Louis safely. I suggest we fill up the tank in the city, where it will be cheaper. It will be time for an early supper there too."

I agreed and volunteered to drive for a while. As we left Granite City, we rolled down a steep incline at 64 mph, far exceeding our 45 mph limitation imposed by Emma. Suddenly, we were shocked out of our carefree mood by the lurching of the car—hesitating, moving forward, then hesitating again. Was this irritating recurrence because we were speeding or because the problem was now manifesting not only when going uphill but also when heading downhill?

We made it to East St. Louis in the afternoon. Betsy hesitated again as we rolled into Skelly's Garage on E Street. We were in the underskirts of an industrial town that would have looked depressing even under the best of circumstances. We were tired of trying to figure out what to do. The oil was okay, but at times, for reasons we did not understand, we could not go up a hill or sometimes downhill or over 45 mph without running the risk of the engine cutting out.

Our gloom was momentarily dispelled by two eager young mechanics anxious to fix the car for Mary. Before road testing her, they filled the tank and then opened up the Wayfarer at top speed on the highway, as if trying to blow out any trouble. Remarkably, the car was operable again. Had the mechanics' extravagance somehow solved our enigmatic problem?

In any case, we were glad to be getting closer to relatives who would welcome us into their home that night. Cheered by that thought, we began to enjoy the passing scenes of the city of St. Louis.

I am a part of all that I have met;
yet all experience is an arch where thro'
Gleams that untravell'd world whose margin fades
For ever and forever when I move.
(*Ulysses*, Alfred Lord Tennyson)
[Image 7.3]

The Arch came into view and appeared to grow larger as we got closer to that giant steel sculpture. This heroic structure matched the magnitude of Thomas Jefferson's vision when he purchased the Louisiana Territory—a decision he made though he found no precedent in our Constitution for such a purchase. The architect and furniture designer, Eero Saarinen, who won the commission to design the Arch, understood the historical significance of St. Louis as the gateway to the unexplored West. He understood the significance of the rivers as highways for the fur traders and the adventurous mountain men, most of whom bought their canoes and supplies in St. Louis before heading north on the Great Mississippi and west on the Missouri River. Saarinen knew that Lewis and Clark, sent by Jefferson on the Voyage of Discovery, made a map of their course through the uncharted areas from St. Louis to the Pacific. They had outfitted in St. Louis for this journey into the unknown. Once the territory between St. Louis and the Pacific opened for settlement, families in Conestoga wagons and wagon trains flooded through this gateway in search of opportunity west of the Mississippi, in search of their own "manifest destiny."

Manifest destiny, as far as I can tell, was an enunciation of a popular belief that the United States would eventually include Texas and the Pacific Northwest, and later California. John O'Sullivan, of the *New York Morning News*, had argued in 1845 that the United States had the right "to claim the whole of Oregon. And that claim by the right of our manifest destiny to overspread and to possess the whole of the continent which Providence has given us for the development of the great experiment of liberty and federated self-government entrusted to us." Such verbal bravado of those times! The Arch expresses it in a far more dignified way.

Leaving the Arch behind, we fortified ourselves with a good meal and headed for our destination, Ferguson, a suburb northwest of St. Louis where we were to stay with Bob's niece Marcia and her husband, Fred Pope.

"Since you have never met Marcia Baker Pope, your cousin, I'd better fill you in. Your dad's big sister Carolyn, your 'Aunt Sis,' and her husband, Jim Baker, have a daughter, Marcia, and three sons. Marcia married Fred Pope, rector of the parish here in Ferguson. [Image 7.4]

"And about the Popes' children, more cousins ... their daughter, another Carolyn, is married and living in Chicago. Chris and Molly still live at home, and Fred Jr. and his new wife are up from Rolla visiting their parents."

Fred welcomed us in the driveway. When we told him of our ongoing car problem, he reassured us, "I can help you with your car, but not until Monday, so let's enjoy the weekend together."

What a fun family Marcia and Fred possessed. They were warm and welcoming. We stayed up late telling stories. Interested particularly in getting to know Mary, Fred suggested that she tell about her adventures in college and what she was up to now. Mary began by relating an experience she had on a visit to England with a stranger she met on a bus.

"I was eighteen and had just finished my freshman year at Cornell. A group of friends had planned a trip to England, where we would stay at the home of an American Field Service hostess in Deal, Kent, a not-too-long bus ride from London. Mother had warned me to be careful of familiarity with strangers, particularly with men whom I knew nothing about.

"Dad was even more cautious about a young girl traveling overseas. 'Sure, I want you to go ahead with the girls, but not if you take a charter plane as you have planned. I will gladly pay the extra if you take a regularly scheduled flight. It's safer.'

"I arrived on my first trip abroad carrying a heavy suitcase. As I walked the streets of London to get to the bus station to Deal, I had offers from guys to carry my suitcase. I smiled but refused.

"I found a place on the bus next to a window. The seat beside me was soon taken by a person who appeared to be a commuter. He nodded politely and I returned his greeting, noticing his well-groomed mustache and tailored clothing.

"After a few miles and several stops, I felt a sudden insecurity ... a fear that I might miss the station where I would be met by my hostess. So I asked the stranger next to me, who was obviously British, if he would warn me when my station drew close. He said, 'It would be a pleasure.'

"Then he tried to engage me in conversation. I felt uncomfortable, but I turned to him and answered him politely and quickly, then resumed watching the passing countryside through the window. He did not give up and inquired where I came from in America. Sometime later, my intuition told me that this was a kind and harmless man and that I was not only being over-conscientious, but rude.

"For the rest of the trip, we exchanged information about our homelands, and he gave me his thoughts about what I should see in England. When we approached the Deal station, he picked up my luggage, lowered the suitcase onto the pavement, clung to the railing by the open door, and with a teasing grin on his face, said loudly for me and for all the passengers to hear, 'Isn't it amazing that two people who have never seen each other before and who will never see each other again can fall so madly in love?'"

When the laughter died down at the end of Mary's story, Fred said, "Marcia, can you share some of your youthful recollections of your Uncle Bob and Aunt Ginny?"

She launched into a story about playing the game "Murder" with a bunch of young married couples when she was a teenager.

"I think I was about fifteen. Uncle Bob and Aunt Ginny had been married for about a year and I loved being invited to visit them. We were still feeling the effects of the Depression and often created our own entertainment. A popular pastime was acting out the game of Murder, trying to solve a mystery with a bunch of people and few clues.

"I'm not sure that the game is still popular, but this had been a special version of Murder, written by Aunt Ginny's brother-in-law, Harry, and I was included. I was very intimidated to be playing the game with these married people who seemed so old.

"The game was like a drama and the stage was all over a very big three-story Victorian house on the side of a hill. A murder was always the focus of the game. Each player was a character in the drama and had his own personal script and stage name that interacted with those of all the other players. Each player would listen for a clue, indicating his next move. During the course of the play, a 'murder' was committed. Eventually all the players were directed downstairs to the kitchen, where we heard the rattle of the dumbwaiter descending. The door opened and out tumbled a corpse, actually a stuffed, full-sized doll clutching an unfinished message written in blood. Everyone was shocked. We could make out four letters ... MAFI.

"All the players had to figure out who among us was the murderer. As we questioned each other, everyone but the murderer had to answer truthfully. Only the murderer could lie.

"Who was the murderer? Was the corpse trying to tell us it was his daughter Ma Fille, or perhaps Mafitte, one of the player-characters?"

Marcia continued, "I became the hero. Because I knew French, I solved the mystery of the murder and figured out it had to be Mafitte, not the murdered man's son or daughter."

"That was a scary evening for all of us ... and I had not realized how threatening it was for you as a teenager, Marcia, but you met the challenge," I recollected.

The conversation had led into scary stories and I had a good one to share.

"I have a scary radio story. About the same time the game of Murder was popular, a big source of our entertainment and news was radio.

"Around 1938, the world was tense as we followed the increasingly threatening moves of Hitler. A charming musical program or play that engrossed us was frequently interrupted by the earnest voice of an announcer, 'We interrupt this program to bring you the latest news from Germany. Hitler has moved his troops ...' or 'The British prime minister has flown to Germany ...' In America, we were ill at ease but tried to go on with our peaceful lives.

"I actually was listening to a rare live broadcast on the radio, announcing the arrival of the lighter-than-air German passenger airship called Hindenburg, due to land near Lakehurst, New Jersey. I could hear unusual enthusiasm in the announcer's voice as he reported on the Hindenburg's historical arrival. Suddenly, he started screaming, 'It's on fire, the ship is on fire!' and 'Oh, this is horrible!' He started weeping into the microphone as he continued describing hysterically the people jumping out of the ship to try and save themselves. It was as though we were right there witnessing this disaster altogether.

"That was one of the scariest moments I experienced. But there was another I have to tell you about as well. Later in 1938, Bob and I were celebrating our second anniversary at dinner with my sister, Mary Lou, and our brother-in-law. After dinner, we enjoyed a game of bridge. The radio was quietly droning with a symphony in the next room when we heard the noisy interruption, 'A special news flash ...' We could hardly concentrate on the bidding. An increasingly excited announcer kept interrupting the broadcast, describing a strange object that had landed on a farm in Grover's Mill, New Jersey. Officers had assembled at the scene.

"When the announcer described with apprehension in his voice that the airship might be from outer space, Mary Lou and I dropped our cards and ran to the radio.

"The station announced that it had sent reporter Carl Phillips and a professor from Princeton University's astronomy department to the scene. The announcer went on to say, 'Well, I just got here. I haven't had a chance to look around yet. I guess that's it. Yes, I guess that's the thing, directly in front of me, half buried in a vast pit. It must have struck with terrific force. The ground is covered with the splinters of a tree it hit on its way down.'

"We were glued to the radio by now, but so were thousands of other Americans, who were tuned in that night, October 30, 1938. Not our husbands, though, who wanted more than anything else to play the hands they had been dealt.

"Harry said irritably, 'If a spaceship has landed, every station in America will have the story.'

"We turned the radio dial and heard an episode of some foolish series, maybe *Fibber McGee and Molly*. The men were right after all. We had been totally taken in by Orson Welles' radio play, *The War of the Worlds*, because of the remembrance of the Hindenburg just a year before.

"Director Welles closed this adaptation of H.G. Wells' classic novel *The War of the Worlds* [1898], with this statement: '*The War of the Worlds* tonight has no further significance than as the holiday offering it was intended to be: The Mercury Theatre's own radio version of dressing up in a sheet and jumping out of a bush and saying boo!' This apology must have been prompted by a great number of calls from panicked listeners."

"I've got a scary story, too," piped up nine-year-old Chris. "It was the game of Sardines. I was scared once playing Sardines in a big dark house. I was 'It' and was supposed to hide quietly in an open closet or cupboard or some dark place in the house. The rest of the group was to find me and take a place quietly beside me, until everyone was packed in one small space like sardines. I stood there for a very long time in the dark, but nobody came to find me."

"That was a dirty trick, wasn't it, Chris?" Mary piped in, putting her arm around him. *Poor frightened kid,* I thought. Usually the hide-and-seek-type game of Sardines ends up with a bunch of people so tightly packed that they give themselves away by their giggles.

"We had a game that was more fun, which we played on Easter Sunday instead of an Easter egg hunt. We called it 'Finding Things in Obvious Places,'" Mary continued.

Chris asked how you played that one and Mary explained, "Well, for example, I would hide ten small items, such as a penny, a bright bracelet, a bobby pin, et cetera, in a place that could be seen by everyone in the room but somehow camouflaged by familiar surroundings. Then, I would give each hunter a list of these things to look for and check off when they discovered them, each player being careful not to show any expression that might give away the hiding place. The first person who found the ten items won the game and got a prize."

We reminisced a while longer on games we played as children, until we were all bleary-eyed. That night with the Popes in Ferguson, we went off to bed, still in our childlike frame of mind.

7.1 Original painted floor cloth by Virginia Wade Ames in the
John Marshall House Museum entrance hall—view from above.
Historic gesso and pigment mix on 9'x12' unprimed canvas.

7.2 Virginia Ames steps out of Bob's '36 Rolls Royce as Chair of the Alexandria Christmas Walk.
That year's event theme was a celebration of the Scottish founders, with Scottish games,
and a parade of old cars, including our antique Rolls from Scotland.

7.3 *Double Arches*, original pastel by Virginia Ames,
painted at Arches National Park, Utah

7.4 Robert Ames' niece, Marcia Baker (Pope) as a teen

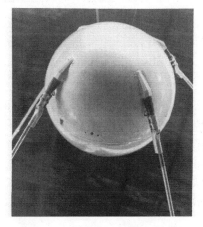

Diagrammatic drawing of Sputnik, source NASA

CHAPTER 8

Sunday, October 18, 1970
Odometer at St. Louis: 26,651

St. Louis, Missouri
Trip meter at St. Louis: 651

What Is the News of the Day? "They Say a Balloon Is Gone Up to the Moon"

The next day at church, we heard Fred Sr.'s sermon on "knowing which way the wind blows" and "by whose grace it blows at all."

Mary and I talked about the sermon later. "Mamsie, perhaps Fred was thinking of Bob Dylan's 'Blowin' in the Wind,' that Peter, Paul and Mary made famous in '63 when we were singing in hootenannies. Because it was considered a freedom song by the Civil Rights movement and a peace song by our anti-Vietnam War movement, Fred might have been thinking that the 'answer' was not going to be found blowin' in the wind, but somewhere beyond."

After the service, we joined the congregation for a church picnic. Sitting around the table together, when the locals heard we were from Washington, D.C., they bombarded us with questions about life there.

"It must be pretty interesting for you living in the nation's capital," one parishioner commented.

"Other than seeing lots of 'pomp and circumstance,' one of the most exciting events I remember was the day the *Washington Post* announced the Russians had put a satellite into orbit, a satellite that would pass over Washington, D.C., at a specific time that night." I turned toward Mary. "You were about nine years old. The neighborhood children, and some of the adults too, gathered in a circle in front of our house. Although it was cloudy, from time to time we could see bright stars in the dark sky between patches of white. We kept our eyes focused on the southeast as the newspaper suggested. Suddenly, we saw it ... a star moving from right to left in the dark sky between clouds while the other stars remained fixed in their places. The children whooped with excitement. I did too, but then my excitement was dulled by a feeling of growing anxiety." [Note 9 – Sputnik]

"For years after that first Sputnik sighting," Mary reported, "my teachers stressed how important it was for us students to learn mathematics plus all the sciences, as we were way behind Russia. It was up to America's young people ... they stressed the point ... to catch up with our enemy, Soviet Russia. I remember how they scared us into studying harder, because if we did not, the Russians might someday control outer space."

I added, "Some months after Sputnik, America launched Echo into orbit. When we got word that Echo might be visible, we ran through a pine woods until we could see open sky above. Echo rose like a giant silver planet. We watched its passage across the heavens, and I felt proud of the United States for our progress in space exploration but was aware of how far we had to go. A cold wind drove us to cover with an unearthly chill ...

"Mary, do you remember, years later, after we had put men in space and brought them safely back to earth, you had a Washington experience you might share with these Missourians?"

"You mean when the astronauts were given a parade in Washington and I had the nerve to run into the street to greet them?" Mary turned to the parishioner on her right. "When I broke out of the crowd and ran up to their limousine to congratulate them, Gus Grissom took my hand and said, 'Hello there, kid.' It was certainly exciting growing up in D.C. You never knew whom you would see. I always felt as though I was a part of history while it was being made."

"It has been a pleasure when members of our family come to visit us and we are able to share our Washington experience with them. We had a visit from Dad's brother, Uncle Mac, and his son, Johnny Ames, to see us and the nation's capital."

Mary grinned. "I remember that visit. Muffin admired her older cousin John, who in turn was intrigued by his older, more glamorous cousin Lucy, and Muff felt so invisible."

"Our Cincinnati relatives were eager to visit the newly installed national sculpture honoring the heroes of Iwo Jima. They also visited the museums on The Mall and, with Muff, climbed up and down the 999 steps of the Washington Monument." [Image 8.1] [Note 10 – John Ames]

Mary digressed. "Mams, whenever I think of these astronaut experiences while growing up in Washington, I recall this Mother Goose nursery rhyme:

What is the news of the day,
Good neighbor, I pray?
They say a balloon
Is gone up to the moon."

"And that rhyme reminds me of John Christian, who used to recite it. We had just moved into our little rambler under the oaks in Virginia Heights. You may not remember when Mr. Christian walked into our lives, Mary. You were so young, though you remember his poem. It was a very special day for me. The sun was sending rays through the leaves, making them sparkle like ornaments."

"Who was John Christian? It sounds like a story worth sharing with all of us," another parishioner interjected.

"Well, that morning, a young worker sauntered down our winding road into our Virginia Heights neighborhood, whistling a tune as sharp and clear as the morning air. With his tune, the words to it came back to me from my childhood. Mother used to play this Thomas Moore melody on the piano and we would sing:

> Believe me, if all those endearing young charms,
> That I gaze on so fondly today,
> Were to fade by tomorrow,
> And flee from my arms,
> Just like fairy gifts fading away ...

"The sentimental song he was whistling wafted me back to the South. That moment made me thrilled that Dad and I had chosen to remain in Virginia to rear our girls.

"That same morning, Mr. Christian came to us looking for work for the first time. His slow gait revealed that he was aging, but I could see that he was strong and steady as he approached our house carrying a large saw in one hand and a brown bag in the other. He greeted me politely and introduced himself as John Christian, with the mellow voice shared by Black people of his generation, and it reminded me of my father softly talking to me. He offered to saw firewood from the young oaks that were felled to make room for our new home. I worried that this might be too strenuous for the old man. But he looked prepared for the job, so I said yes and went to find the two sawhorses he requested.

"He came every morning for three days and set to work with slow deliberation. He never seemed pressed and worked steadily for long periods. Fireplace logs began to pile up. When he needed a break, he sat and rested, and if I was nearby, he would tell me stories. Maybe eighty, he couldn't remember the Civil War, but he did remember Freedman's Village, founded in 1863, the year of the Emancipation Proclamation. Many former slaves made their way north believing that Father Abraham would help them make a new life. The federal government sponsored the building of homes to house these refugees, trained them in new skills, and educated their children. Freedman's Village was located on the land where the Pentagon now stands. After a brief period of employment in the village, residents had to leave in order to seek jobs elsewhere and to make room for new arrivals.

"John Christian lived in Arlington County, between our house and the low land along the Potomac. When he came to work for me, he said, 'My father and I were not educated men, but we could count. When we drove our wagon to the town of Alexandria, there was a policeman directing traffic, standing on a platform in the middle of the street where Washington and King Street cross. The policeman held a pole with two signs on it, which he could turn. When we counted two letters on the sign, we knew we could go, but if we counted one-two-three-four, our wagon had to wait.'

"I asked him what he had in his brown bag, and it was no surprise to learn it was his lunch. He added that he always brought an extra helping of meat or a good bone. 'On my way to work I pass a lot of folks who have dogs. Most dogs are friendly and only bark to protect their homes. But now and then there'll be a mean dog that follows me up the street, growling and threatening to bite. I toss it some meat and it becomes my friend.'

"He also told me about the nonsense stories he shared with his Great-Half-Aunt Lucy that always began with Mr. Christian asking,

115

'What is the news of the day?' and Great-Half-Aunt Lucy would re-late an unlikely story that was always amusing.

"I chide myself because I did not write down these stories, but I shall never forget John Christian's pleasure in the telling of them."

One of Fred's parishioners was not smiling, and the mood be-came serious and changed.

"It must have been rough living in Washington during the up-heaval around the country over civil rights and the protests over the Vietnam War."

Mary picked up on this. "By the time I entered Cornell in 1965, civil rights and the Vietnam War divided almost everybody into two camps. One of our students had gone down to Alabama to support those protesting for civil rights, and he had been murdered while there. By the time I arrived at Cornell, the student body was galva-nized into positions for and against both the Civil Rights Movement and the Vietnam War.

"Mom, when I called to say I wanted to come home for the Peace March there and to bring a group of my friends with me to Washing-ton, you were hesitant."

"Yes, and I told you that of course you could come home, but I was not ready to sponsor a protest group. 'Bring your friends here for dinner the night before the march,' I instructed, 'but ask them to stay elsewhere.'"

I reflected on my thoughts and feelings at that time. Mary had called me "hesitant." Ambivalent might have been a better word. Basically, I am a pacifist. I object to war as a means of resolving a conflict because, when peace at last is declared, conflict has seldom been resolved. This was not the case during WWII. Hitler had to be stopped. He was a murderer and would stop at nothing to take over Europe, countries Germany had never owned but he claimed they had. When Mary asked about bringing protesters down, I was still remembering the unprovoked attack on Pearl Harbor by the Japanese and Hitler's evils. Patriotism had a strong significance for my generation. Protest made me uncomfortable.

I resumed, "Bob and I *did* want to hear what the young people had to say, so we arranged a discussion after dinner with knowledgeable friends to present pro-war points of view ... a theologian and an army officer. Our Army colonel friend and spokesperson held that the military should finish the job it started, and our theologian stood for ridding North Vietnam of Godless communism. The Cornell students arrived at our home twenty-five-strong.

"It was a great night. The college students were so much more eloquent in presenting their reasons why they did not believe we should have gotten into the Vietnam War in the first place that, by the end of the evening, Bob's and my points of view were in sympathy with them. These young people taught me that the Vietnam War was entirely different from the principles and actions we believed so deeply in during World War II.

"As they got up to leave, I asked the girl-protesters, 'Where are you going to sleep?' They responded, 'If we are lucky, on a church pew, and, if not, on a park bench.' I looked at these starry-eyed idealists and said, 'Oh, no, you can sleep right here.'

"The next day, I asked Mary to stay home when her determined friends joined thousands reported to be amassing around The Mall. It was a good thing she stayed home, because it was reported that over 200,000 protesters were there and the police were nervous, spraying mace on the 'rowdy troublemakers.' The mace spread and fell on innocent people, including the sister of one of our Cornell friends who ran in terror to escape. This massive protest doubtless was a great influence on President Johnson's decision to get out of Vietnam.

"The threat to our freedom also came from within our own White House when Nixon became president and tried to cut off funding for National Public Television because he said it was 'too liberal.' Fortunately, he and his henchman, Clay T. Whitehead, White House Staff Assistant, did not succeed in killing educational TV in its infancy."

"Mom, tell them about Dad's role in bringing educational television to D.C. in the first place."

"My husband, Bob, your rector's uncle-in-law, worked with Mr. Willard Kiplinger and members of a committee, that I believe included newscaster David Brinkley and the presidents of Howard University and Catholic University of America, to found a public TV station for the Washington area. Kip's friend, Pat Oliver, was the volunteer secretary.

"They were successful in getting a license to launch the first educational television station in D.C., with call letters GWETA, renamed WETA in 1961. Shortly after that, after investing large sums to support this effort, Kip said to Bob, 'Go over there and show them how to raise money to finance the station.' And he did just that. Mr. Kiplinger extended Bob a letter of credit of several thousand dollars to finance Bob's first direct mail appeal. The first letter brought such an enthusiastic response that they did not have to use any of the credit. He spent two days every week for the next few years working at WETA. During this time, he wrote a pamphlet outlining how public television could solicit membership to support itself by direct mail. When he needed an assistant to share the increasing workload, they found Susan Richmond, a young, capable, and creative worker who has continued to rise in the ranks to this day.

"One of WETA's first programs was *Washington Week in Review*, broadcast from Yorktown High School in the metro area. In 1964, the station moved to Howard University.

"Soon WETA added on-the-air funds solicitation to the direct mail campaign. Celebrities came to Washington to speak in support of WETA during membership campaigns, many from Britain. Following the airing of his show, Sir Kenneth Clark, British broadcaster and art historian, visited. Jean Marsh, writer/producer of *Upstairs, Downstairs*, made a big impression when she confessed during a luncheon speech, 'Just imagine, I am a successful writer and producer and my mother was in domestic service in England.' When my husband, Bob, picked her up at the airport in his antique Rolls Royce, she exclaimed, 'This is really *going upstairs!*' Actress Lynne Redgrave also came to speak on behalf of membership.

"Bob heard Julia Child's unmistakable voice at the studio when she came to promote her cooking show. I had just read an article in the *Washington Post*, revealing what a character she was. In part, the story described a woman in D.C. who asked her husband what he wanted for Christmas. His answer, 'I want Julia Child to cook Christmas dinner for me.' Julia agreed immediately to make his wish come true, and on Christmas she went to their home, carrying supplies from wine to chocolate soufflé, and prepared the meal of his life."

"Were you jealous of Dad working with all of those exciting people in a new industry?" Mary asked.

"I can honestly say I got a vicarious thrill from his experiences. Mr. Kiplinger was interested in a lot more than public television. He formed a school of journalism and had a dinner to celebrate its inauguration. I sat next to James M. Nabrit Jr., the president of Howard University, and asked him to tell me how Booker T. Washington managed to create Tuskegee University.

"He told me that Booker T. Washington's mother was very influential in his success. She told her son, 'Never say you cannot do something because you are Negro.' And this was why he had the courage to do the impossible ... to create such a successful educational institution for Black students ... Tuskegee.

"There are always exciting figures to meet in Washington. We were fortunate that our dear friend, Herbert Sanborn, Exhibits Director at the Library of Congress, invited us to many presentations at the Library. He introduced us to luminaries there, like American Poet Laureate Robert Penn Warren at a reading of his poetry."

Fred and Marcia and their parishioners continued to ask us about our lives in Washington. One of them told us of a young friend she knew who was studying at the Virginia Theological Seminary near our home in Alexandria.

"Our church, Immanuel-on-the-Hill parish, has always been af-filiated with the Seminary, but the congregation grew so rapidly that we built our own chapel, parish hall, and offices near the Seminary."

At the mention of the Seminary, Mary brightened and told about how some of the young Seminary students became beloved Sunday school teachers during her grammar school days. In her teens, many of them became special role models as sponsors of the Young People's Group.

I too was thinking about my participation in the Immanuel com-munity and wanted to tell them about my experiences as the Su-perintendent of the Children's Sunday School. "Since I was the first woman to hold such a position, I asked our minister, Reverend Tom Heath, for permission to speak to the youth from the new Zabriski Chapel pulpit. I had never seen anyone but a man speak from the pulpit before. Disregarding all norms of the time, he told me, 'Of course you can!' I had taught the children how to use the Book of Common Prayer and wanted to help them understand and practice the prayers and ways of the service before going with their parents to the big church.

"Please forgive me, but I can't help myself. I have to tell you folks another story about what happened once when the Ladies of the Church held their monthly meeting in that parish hall.

"It has been said in jest that when three or four Episcopalians are gathered together, you will always find a 'fifth.' This may be hy-perbole, but that meeting lends credence to this assertion.

"For purposes of my tale you need to know that some distance west of Alexandria, in an oak forest, a fine local family owned a small business known as the Smith Bowman Distillery, where they pro-duced excellent sour-mash bourbon. One brand was named 'Old Tub' ... but the smoothest, finest was aged 'Virginia Gentleman.'

"At the Women-of-the-Church's monthly meeting, heads of vari-ous committees were called upon to make reports on their activities during the preceding month. Time came for Billie Miller to report her progress in selling subscriptions to the diocesan newsletter, *The Virginia Churchman*. She told the group that she had secured only three new subscribers since last meeting, bringing the total number of subscribing families to a mere nineteen. She mentioned to the group how important the information in each issue was to all parishioners and ended her pitch with these words, '*Every* Episcopalian should get *Virginia Gentleman!*'

"A polite hush fell on the gathering, followed by an explosion of laughter that filled the hall. When Billie realized that the slip of her tongue had created such hilarity, she found it as funny, and as truthful, as everyone else."

When the Ferguson parishioners finished laughing, I followed with what happened next. "Downstairs in the church office, the minister, no doubt, raised his eyes toward Heaven, shook his head, and smiled at the levity. But he might not have smiled had he known that the next order of business upstairs was to be a discussion of his arbitrary plan to share with the bishop *half* of all funds received in our church for the bishop to spend as he saw fit, including the significant funds the *women* had worked so hard to amass.

"Every year in the fall the ladies held a bazaar where they sold items they'd spent all year assembling and fabricating by sewing, knitting, painting, and cooking. It had been their pleasure for years to meet and decide which charity was most in need of the profits from their labor. But not this year apparently. With the minister's un-consulted decision, the women would have only half of their hard-earned funds to dispose of as their own principles guided. The meeting mood shifted as dramatically as the change of wind direction in a sheer. Currents of resentment swelled.

"With their charitable funds halved, there was deep concern that many homeless might suffer, battered women and children would not find shelter, and migrant workers would be left neglected. Feelings ran high and the righteous arguments grew strident.

"One confident member, Eilene Eddy, stood up, and in her strong calm voice said, 'Madame President, I suggest we have *one minute of silent prayer*.' Calm descended. Order was thankfully restored. It was I who was assigned the chore of informing the minister that the women's group opposed his decision. The letter I crafted to send to the minister was sincere and honest, couched in conciliatory language. In the end, the Women-of-the-Church did not win, but at least a breach in the church was avoided."

"Mom, tell them about your flag project. It is such an important Washington story."

"Well, I don't yet know if I will get this commission, but it looks likely, and I really hope I do. For the Library of Congress Bicentennial Exhibition, ten of the flags known to have flown during the American Revolution will be replicated in giant size to hang in the Great Hall of the Library during the celebration. I've been researching and find that all thirteen colonies had militias for their own protection and each militia had its own banner. These were the banners that the colonists rallied around when the fight with Britain erupted around them. Before we left on this trip, I met with Elizabeth Hamer, Assistant Librarian of Congress. She is in charge of shepherding the Library's American Revolution Bicentennial Program. She employed two historians to verify the accuracy of everything the Library would do for the Bicentennial, including the making of these flags. I am optimistic about the outcome because Herb Sanborn said my skills qualify me to apply for this project." [Note 11 – Flags]

Fred's parishioners were enjoying our anecdotes about Washington. "It is seldom dull in the D.C. area. I recall another occasion when the press was full of the news of an imminent total eclipse of the sun, which would be best viewed at Wallops Island. The island is NASA's center for the study of weather and atmospheric conditions and is only a short drive from our home. On the appointed day, Bob and I, along with our friends the Sanborns, decided to watch the eclipse from the NASA Wallops Flight Facility. When we arrived, we found a small stadium-like bleacher on a vast grassy lawn for observing the island's regular weather-rocket launches, and we made ourselves comfortable. Others followed until the mini-stadium was filled with visitors. Soon the lawn was obscured by hundreds of people with telescopes and binoculars. When the time came close for losing the sun behind the moon, a group of officials ordered all of us to vacate our viewing stand and join the crowd on the lawn. We were replaced immediately by a group of officials led by Senator Barry Goldwater. We recognized Werner Von Braun among them, the eminent German rocket scientist who came to America when Hitler took power in Germany. He's the one who became a U.S. citizen and helped us develop the atomic bomb. Such is life in the D.C. area. We all have to make way for dignitaries."

That night, after our long day with Fred and his congregation, as we crawled into our guest-room beds, Mary and I reflected back about our own congregation in Alexandria at Immanuel-on-the-Hill, acknowledging how similar yet different they were from our new acquaintances out here in the American heartland. [Note 12 – Immanuel]

Recollections of our unique Washington experiences kept us chatting in the dark.

"I am intrigued, Mary, with meeting Robert Penn Warren, hearing his poetry, and wondering about the creativity that is engendered when writers get together. During Warren's student days at Vanderbilt University, he was a member of a seven-man poetry group who named themselves 'The Fugitives.'

"They were amazing characters ... that Fugitives group. One of them was Ridley Wills, who became a newspaperman. He wrote *The Golden Mean and Other Poems* with Allen Tate in 1923 and whimsical verses for his children. He has an interesting link with our family.

"In the mid-1930s, Mary, your dad worked for an advertising agency that served the *Cincinnati Times-Star*. At one point in his tenure, the newspaper had a special edition to celebrate a significant point in its long history going back to 1893. The project was too big for the regular staff, so it hired Ridley Wills, the newspaperman and Fugitive member from Tennessee, to edit this special issue.

"When Wills came to Cincinnati, he and Bob hit it off immediately. After that, he became a frequent visitor to our home, where he entertained us with some of his witty poems. When you girls were old enough to enjoy it, we would recite Ridley Wills' humorous poetry aloud to you. Remember the one Muffin liked in particular, about the "hippopotamusketeers"?

> Where hippopotamuskadines
> Grow gracefully on trailing vines,
> There live (and have lived many years)
> Three hippopotamusketeers.
> Whenever there's the slightest fuss
> Among the hippopotamus,
> These hippopotamusketeers
> Rush forth to war with three loud cheers.
> When warfare comes and folks are flustered
> These three are hippopotamustered
> Before the strife has fairly started,
> For they are bold and valiant hearted.
> On hippopotamustanges fleet,
> They ride like mad down every street,
> Their hippopotamuskets ready,
> Their eyes all set for aiming steady.
> At twilight where the grass is lush,
> They dine on hippopotamush
> And hippopotamuscatel
> Which liquor store inspectors sell.
> Once as they sat in hostile grass
> Some hippopotamustard gas
> Rose from a place they'd dropped a bomb at,

And rendered all three hors d'combat.
But they are gallant soldiers three
(And, for a fact, they ought to be)
They ought to win in any tussle,
With so much hippopotamuscle.

We rolled around in bed in bemusement. My thoughts flowed on, like water down a stream bumping into new pebbles. "There was another Vanderbilt student, not a member of The Fugitives, who followed the class of Ridley Wills, by the name of Ralph Emerson McGill. McGill did not graduate because he was suspended his senior year for writing an article in the student newspaper criticizing the school's administration.

"Later, as an editor of *The Atlanta Constitution*, McGill spoke out against racism. In response, many angry readers sent threatening letters to him. Some acted on the threats and burned crosses at night on his front lawn in Atlanta, fired bullets into the windows of his home, and left crude bombs in his mailbox. The articles he wrote earned him a voice as executive editor of the newspaper, which he used to highlight the evils of racism.

"It's not surprising that he became a hero during the period of social upheaval in the '60s. He is mentioned by name in Martin Luther King Jr.'s *Letter from Birmingham Jail* as one of the few enlightened white persons to understand and sympathize with the Civil Rights Movement. At the time of that letter, spring of 1963, Mary, Mr. McGill was a real hero.

"I have another interest in *The Atlanta Constitution*. In my high school days in Mobile in the late '20s, three of us were great pals: Helen Head, Isabelle Willey, and me. We dressed alike and called ourselves 'The Three Coconuts,' inspired by the Marx Brothers' recent movie with the same name. We even had a '3C' logo embroidered on our dresses. Among our classmates at Mobile High School was a newcomer from the Gulf Coast area, Celestine Sibley, a quiet

125

and thoughtful person. Years passed and we Coconuts went separate ways, yet Helen and I kept in touch. In one news-filled letter to me, Helen said that Celestine had written for *The Atlanta Constitution* for many years. She had also published half a dozen of her novels set in the South, including one called *Jincey*. Helen sent me one of the weekly columns that Celestine had written for the newspaper where she reminisced about her high school years, describing 'The Three Coconuts' and saying she had often wished she had been one of them. As an adult, I felt sad and wished she had told us back in high school that she felt that way, because having her friendship over the years would have been a wonderful thing for me." [Note 13 – Celestine Sibley]

Mary and I returned to contemplating the Washington scene that our Missouri hosts here in the Midwest did not have to contend with, for better or worse. "I never told you, Mare, about a little technique your dad and I have tried for dealing with those big Washington social gatherings. Because of his business connections, he and I are obliged to attend some big to-dos, perhaps a cocktail party at the Willard or the Roger Smith Hotel, a party where we seldom know anyone, you know, where people shallowly promise each other 'we'll meet again.'

"On one such occasion it was to be at the former home of Felix Frankfurter, the renowned former Supreme Court Justice, where, it was said, the sculptor Gutzon Borglum had drawn a sketch on the tablecloth depicting his proposed sculpture of four presidents' heads for the face of Mt. Rushmore. This smaller party promised to be more interesting than other big affairs. Your dad suggested that when he and I arrived, we should look around until we saw the most fascinating strangers there, aggressively introduce ourselves, and hope to talk meaningfully with only that couple before departing early.

"Our new acquaintances were warm and outgoing, and I found myself giving an interested man details of how I processed raw clay for making puppet heads with my children. At his request, I promised to send him the directions. Bob found the wife highly intelligent too and really enjoyed his conversation with her. When Bob and I reluctantly left our new friends and headed for home, I told him about my delightful conversation.

"'Do you know who he *was*?' your dad asked me. 'The gentleman you were talking with about processing clay was the nephew of Gutzon Borglum.'

"I hid my face to hide my embarrassment."

"'Don't worry about it, Gin,' he consoled me, 'I was talking to his wife about how to write and she's probably a descendent of Shakespeare.'"

Mary and I rested well that night at the Popes', knowing we would be seeing their mechanic in the morning and hopefully getting back on the road with Betsy once more.

8.1 Lucy Dunbar Ames at new Iwo Jima statue, 1957,
taken by her Uncle Mac, Malcolm McEwen Ames

CHAPTER 9

Monday, October 19, 1970
Odometer at St. Louis: 27,001

St. Louis, Missouri, to
Waynesville, Missouri
Trip meter at St. Louis: 1,001

Image of the bulb-style ah-OOO-gah
horn from early autos
(original sketch by MABurgess)

Heart of Tex's

The following morning, Fred Pope's mechanic declared we would have no more trouble with the fuel line—he pronounced it "taken care of."

We were traveling southwest through sparsely-settled farmland with little sign of life, where we had the unpleasant experience of Betsy's engine missing yet again and the incident at the small station where the greasy young attendant had scared us. We were thankful to have left that place with Betsy under her own power, especially thankful to be rolling on without trouble—and without having to buy a new carburetor.

"The fact that we successfully avoided being conned into buying anything at that station reminds me of one of Mother's stories about a garage in the early days of the automobile. Maybe I better put it in context for you, Mary. The First World War proved that the automobile was here to stay. No longer would people shout in derision, 'Get a horse!' By 1919, laws were in place providing for the construction of a system of national highways, and this vastly increased the demand for cars. Up until then, few cars could be seen on the streets of flourishing towns. Things have sure changed a lot since chickens and dogs fled and nursemaids gathered up their charges in a flurry when one of those noisy vehicles came careening down the unpaved streets at twelve miles an hour. But some things have not changed all that much.

"This is Gran-gran's tale, and I will retell it in her own words as well as I can recall how she told it to me:

*It was soon after **1900** in Alabama when my sister and brother-in-law, Hattie and Brooks Forbes, purchased a Franklin automobile. They were given license number 148, as I recall. That license reflected the entire number of cars in the State of Alabama at the time.*

There was a loosely organized fraternity of men who owned cars in Birmingham, and they would plan family outings on weekends for mutual pleasure and assistance, should there be a flat tire among them ... which there usually was.

One Sunday morning, as often happened, my brother-in-law heard the telephone ring in the box on the wall. He put the receiver to his ear and recognized the voice of his friend Mr. Yates, who asked him where he was taking his family for an outing that day. He stepped closer to the mouthpiece and told his friend that he thought he would take them across country to Roebuck Springs, about five miles out of town.

A motorcade was organized and several families, with picnic baskets strapped to their automobiles, headed to Roebuck Springs. Alas, when only halfway there, Mr. Yates' car came to such a sudden stop that only the picnic basket remained in place. The passengers were shaken up but unhurt. No matter what the men did, the car would not move forward. So Mr. Yates sent the family home on a streetcar with instructions for Mrs. Yates to call Drennen's, the only garage in town, and ask that they send a tow truck to bring his car in.

When Mr. Yates arrived in town with the Franklin in tow, Mr. Drennen examined it closely. With furrowed brow and lips pursed, Mr. Drennen declared that it would take at least a week to repair and the bill would be $75.00.

"That was a lot of money in those days, Mary, maybe a thousand dollars in today's currency. But that was not the end of the story. You would have to understand the gregarious nature of Southerners and their love of anecdotes to believe the outcome. So this is how Grangran's account continued:

Years later Mr. Yates was walking along the streets of downtown Birmingham, when he was approached by a stranger who said to him, 'Mr. Yates, you don't know me, but I used to work in Drennen's garage. Do you remember years ago when you brought your crippled Franklin in for repairs and Mr. Drennen took a long time finishing the job and charged you a fortune?'

The stranger went on to say, 'Did Mr. Drennen ever tell you what ailed your car?' When Yates shook his head the stranger said, 'Well, Mr. Drennen is dead now so I can get this off my chest. He looked under your Franklin, saw that you had hit a chicken and its head was lodged in the chain drive. He just pulled the head out, kept your car for a few days, and hit you up for $75.00.'"

"Mom, that story has a familiar ring. You're right, some things don't change."

"There's another anecdote that your dad tells from the early days of motorcars. By 1919, a family car in the garage was a status symbol and few people owned one. Your dad's oldest brother, Bill, twenty years his senior, bought himself a billed cap and a duster, a long raincoat-like garment intended to keep you dust-free as you sped down unpaved roads while leaving a small cloud in your wake. Bill had no car of his own, but he arrogantly and hopefully dressed for a ride. Bill would sit swinging on the porch, hoping that his affluent neighbor would notice he was ready and invite him to jump in.

"My father, as a young man, had no automobile but nonetheless had learned to drive. He took Mother, Mary Lou, and me on an extended vacation by train to California that I mentioned to you before. We explored by streetcars and cabs in the cities and went by limo to the beach, the missions, and the sequoia forest. But at that time in the late nineteen teens, there was no transportation available for us to see the Lick Observatory on Mt. Hamilton. My father seriously wanted us to visit this observatory, so he rented a car to drive us up himself.

"The road was a single lane, zigzagging all the way up the mountain to the summit. Our nervous father drove to the top, hugging the mountain to his right because there was no railing to protect us from the precipice on the left. To preclude our meeting another car coming down, a guard telephoned from a small gatehouse at the bottom of the mountain to the top to say that a car was on its way up. Regardless, my dad remained tense and asked us to talk in whispers to keep his nerves steady. Few of today's drivers could have faced that drive with equal courage."

Mary and I were elated to be on our way and out of that threatening situation, even though we knew the car problem was still a mystery. What a relief that the Wayfarer did not have any further trouble that day! However, the unpleasant encounter with the mechanic and an unresolved problem made the drive fatiguing. For diversion, I continued to muse about my own parents and the *changing times* they had lived through.

"Thinking about Dad and Mother in the 1920s, the rapid shifts in fashion and social mores must have seemed more dramatic to them *then* than even the 1960s have felt for me. It heralded in skirts above the knees, never before above ankle-length, short bobbed hair, and women's early sexual liberation described by the euphemism old folks called 'trial marriages,' sex outside of marriage like the 'free love' of the '60s. The women also freely drank, smoked, and danced the wild Charleston in public, instead of waltzing or doing the fox-trot. Although I was young, I remember clearly the times Mother and Dad talked of these changes. I recall Dad saying to her, 'Don't you ever cut that beautiful hair,' which she did anyway when Dad was on a business trip. She had her long chestnut hair cut in a popular short bob, outfitted herself with a gorgeous new dress and a panama hat. With me and my sister in tow, she met Dad at the train station. When he looked down at our family from the platform, he paused, smiled, and said, 'I like it,' much to Mother's relief."

Mary and I and Betsy arrived in the little town of Waynesville, Missouri, well before dinnertime. In the heart of the town was a small motel, not sleek and new, but there were flowers blooming around the office door showing that someone cared. In the office was a big man with thinning blond hair who, we later learned, had been a Marine in the U.S. peacetime army in Japan following World War ll. Tex Keels was expansive and friendly, a blessing after what we had been through. There was a room for us, and we signed in, washed our hands and faces, brushed our hair, and went into the dining room. Tex, apparently also chief chef and first waiter, served us a delicious meal. Mary told him his Texas-style dinner was "fantastic."

Tex declared, "The most expensive steaks I ever saw were in Guam, and I've seen 'em all." And he kept talking.

"I would never run away from the law, but one time I passed a police car going the other way and when I saw his taillights in my rearview mirror, I did step on the gas."

Tex was so friendly we told him all about the trouble with our car and asked if he knew of a good garage where we could have it checked out.

"I know it is the carburetor without even looking. First thing tomorrow morning, I will take you to one of the best garages in Missouri. I have friends there who will treat you right."

He introduced us to his wife, who sat down at our table. She was Japanese, beautiful, and affable. And she appeared eager to talk with us. She pointed out her ten-year-old son, who looked remarkably like Tex.

"Oh, Tex is such a nice man. He is so kind. He sent for me to come from Japan with our baby." So we guessed the baby, conceived during service in Japan, was the lad helping behind the counter and also clearing the tables. This motel was a family affair.

We enjoyed our dinner very much and when we asked for the check Tex said, "There will be no charge." Surprised, I thought, *He has seen our car, knows that it is twenty years old, and knows that it has a problem.* This well-traveled man could not have missed that we were educated and well-dressed. And though he could not figure us out, he asked no questions. He was ready to help two women in need.

We said, "Oh, thank you very much, but we cannot let you do that for us. We insist upon paying for that excellent meal."

He acknowledged our appreciation, shaking his head.

It was still early when we retired to our room, relieved that Tex's mechanic might really be able to fix Betsy this time.

The bedspread was nicer than the usual motel's linens. Mary turned it down, stacked the pillows under her head, and plopped down. I sat in the one big easy chair, delighted to have some quiet time for talking. Here were some uninterrupted hours to spend just with Mary.

"So tell me more about your first year as a reporter for the *Alexandria Journal*," I requested.

"It is a really emotional time to be a reporter and very interesting because of the issues of integration, particularly in Alexandria. My friend John says he no longer likes being the Assistant Superintendent of Schools here because there is so much tension surrounding the integration of the new T.C. Williams High School. The whole community is tense. I'm glad you started Muff and me out at Burgundy Farm Country Day School, because it was integrated before integration was law and we didn't have to carry the racist baggage that you, Mom, had to get rid of."

"Well, fortunately my parents were intelligent, gentle people filled with compassion and a sense of justice, so I had little baggage in regards to racism to deal with ... at least within my own family. But being in the Deep South did present me with major confusion and challenges growing up."

Mary continued about her work as a news reporter. "I learned that the judge who presides at the Federal Courthouse in Alexandria owns low-income housing that was maintained so badly it broke all the rules. As a reporter, I questioned him about this, and, interestingly, conditions were soon improved on his properties. On a visit to his courtroom, I was amazed to see that he had a Confederate flag displayed. I asked him if he knew that the Confederate flag, in the minds of Black citizens, was a statement that a person was against integration. Subsequently, I was glad to see that the flag was removed. It was hard for me to believe that a judicial representative of the Federal Government could so blatantly thumb his nose at the spirit of the law." [Note 14 – Titans]

"So it took a young, white, female reporter to call his bluff and tacitly embarrass him into fairness!" I was feeling extremely proud of Mary and her work as a conscientious journalist.

"Mom, you said you really didn't have significant baggage to overcome thanks to the way your parents conducted themselves. Can you tell me more about your experiences growing up?" Mary asked.

"When I was young, Mary, my parents never spoke ill of Black people. Before I entered the first grade, my best friend and playmate was the son of the cook at my grandmother's house. Several of my cousins lived nearby, and I liked them a lot, but nobody was quite as important to me as Jim. After decades, I still remember how black his pupils appeared against the white of his eyes.

"When I was preparing to begin first grade, Mother told me, 'You won't be able to play with Jim anymore.'

"I was devastated and asked why. Mother said, 'Because he has to go to a different school than yours.'

"That was my introduction to segregation.

"In spite of being without my best friend, entering first grade was an exciting and happy time for me because I had a warmhearted and sensitive teacher, Lockie Wingo. She taught us the beginnings of drawing and introduced us to 'stick men'; little figures of boys and girls, heads, arms, legs, and triangle skirts for girls. When we came in from the playground one day, Lockie Wingo said, 'Children, you have fifteen to twenty minutes to draw whatever you like.' I drew the playground and all of its equipment with little stick people see-sawing, swinging, and riding the merry-go-round. The teacher came around pointing out the good things each child had done and when she got to my desk, she said not a word but gave me a hug that pulled me out of my seat. I'll never forget the total acceptance I felt in that moment. It spurred me on to later explore my love of art.

"Towards the end of first grade, over the dinner table at the home of my mother's older sister, Harriet, I was listening quietly to the adult conversation one evening. Aunt Hattie, as we called her, spoke about the time when she and Uncle Brooks were planning to build a home on Highland Avenue, in a rapidly growing part of Birmingham. They had just employed Sylvia, a Tuskegee University graduate, as their primary servant. Aunt Hattie told Sylvia they intended to build a small home for her on the back of their ample lot, and they inquired whether she would prefer an entrance from Highland Avenue or from the alley, which would be more accessible to her neighbors.

"Sylvia replied, 'I prefer an entrance from the front because "familiarity breeds contempt." So says Emerson.'

"At this point in her story, Aunt Hattie made a self-deprecating smile at her own ignorance and said, 'I conferred with the judge's wife across the street and we found that indeed Emerson *had* made this statement.'"

"Do you think your parents' attitude influenced your feelings that night?"

"Quite possibly, but I think that children have a great sense of fairness, and I remember feeling very sad that Sylvia had to be the maid while her less-informed employers joked about their own ignorance."

"Mom, later on, didn't your family have a Black servant who became your mammy? Did she have a big influence in your life?"

"She surely did! Aunt Ida was like a member of our family ... an affectionate disciplinarian who took it upon herself to teach me and my sister good manners. In the afternoon when we had bathed away the soil from a morning of outdoor play, we could select dresses to wear from those Mother had fashioned for us, and the three of us would go out for a walk.

"One day, when a new lady in the neighborhood approached us, Aunt Ida said quietly but firmly, 'Show your *'telligence*, Chillin!' Since I did not know where my intelligence was, I substituted a wan smile.

"Once, when a stranger was close enough to observe Mother's handiwork, the embroidery on our dresses, she asked Aunt Ida, 'Whose children are these?' I do remember how our nurse raised her ample breasts, gave her head a haughty tilt, and pronounced, 'These is *Albert Wade*'s chillin,' as though he were the mayor of the town.

137

"Though Aunt Ida took seriously her self-imposed task of improving us, she let down her hair during her rest period. When Mother was away from the house, it was then that she opened her little tin of snuff, chewed a matchstick until it became a brush, pulled out her lower lip, and whisked the snuff between her lower lip and teeth, gently curling her lower lip to hold the snuff in place. She would sit quietly and happily absorb the nicotine. One day, she washed out two empty tins, so that there was not even a smell of tobacco in them, and filled them both with sugar and cinnamon, one for my sister and one for me. She showed us how to make a brush with our matchsticks and took us to sit on the stairs outside the kitchen, she on the top step, my sister below, and I next. We mimicked her as best we could by brushing this snuff substitute between our lips and teeth, and the three of us sat quietly for many minutes enjoying our stimulants of choice.

We had had so much fun with Aunt Ida pretending to be dipping snuff that the next day an idea occurred to me. I loved to see my dad light his pipe in the evening, hold it in his hand, and blow smoke rings into the air. He looked so relaxed and handsome that I knew we must make pipes for ourselves. A giant oak tree next door dropped acorns the size of a pipe bowl. We reamed out the acorns to make the bowls and used weeds with hollow stems for pipe stems. For tobacco, we 'borrowed' some coffee from mother's kitchen and set it afire. We felt grownup for a moment, until we inhaled the first smoke.

"Aside from watching over us, Aunt Ida had simple chores for dinner ... to set the table and prepare the vegetables for cooking. Mother enjoyed preparing dishes for our family. One evening before Aunt Ida left for the day her intention was to place Mother's casserole in the oven to warm it for supper. There was a small explosion in the kitchen. Aunt Ida came running out shouting, 'What has Ida *did?*'

"Mother hurried to her to assure her no harm was done, that she was sorry that Ida had been frightened. It dawned on Mother that Ida probably had a big iron cookstove in her own kitchen and that she had failed to tell Ida about their new gas stove with its pilot light. Aunt Ida was only badly startled, not injured. Mary Lou and I adopted her 'What has Ida *did*?' line whenever we made a mistake. Most of the time this made Mother smile and she seldom mentioned our error.

"Aunt Ida belonged to the United Daughters of Africa, a company of women dedicated to attending the funeral of any member of the society, whether a friend or acquaintance. She was very conscientious about attendance and always told Mother what day she would not be coming to work in order to attend a funeral. Mother respected her feelings and always gave her time away from work so Aunt Ida never had to pay the fifty cents penalty for non-attendance of the funeral."

I mused on, "Today it seems to me that too many of our fellow Americans have little regard for what I consider good manners. It is as though they have never learned that these small courtesies smooth out the inevitable rough spots that occur when people get together. They buy you time; they clear the air and help you to decide what to do next. I find myself wishing many others could have had an Aunt Ida in their lives.

"I sure missed Aunt Ida when we left Alabama. I am grateful, Mary, to both Aunt Ida and also to my father's mother, who remained my constant role model thereafter. I'm sorry she didn't live long enough for you kids to know my grandmother, whom we all called Bigmother. She was strong and wise, and a handsome woman."

"I wish I'd been able to meet Bigmother too. From everything you've ever told us, she seems to have been a wonderful woman." Mary paused and then continued, "Mams, you said you and your family moved to Florida when you were young. That must have been a big change for everyone in many ways. I've never heard very much about what took place."

"Well, now's as good a time as any to tell you more about the moves our family made, and what I faced. When I was going into second grade, my father was transferred by his railroad company to Florida. We spent our summers in Jacksonville and winters in Miami. Mother would take us exploring when we were out of school. But on school days, if Mother would not be at home, she hired Irene, a young woman of mixed heritage from Bimini in the Bahamas, to be at our apartment.

"I look back on Irene with great curiosity. She might have been a mixture of everyone who had ruled that island at different times … the indigenous Taino and the Europeans from France, England, and Spain.

"Irene spoke English with an exotic French accent. We liked to hear her talk but, better still, we loved to hear her play the piano. Jazz rolled from each finger with a Latin rhythm. Though Irene often stayed after Mother got home, she never played the piano when Mother was there. Mother would have loved that music. I wish I had had the sense to ask Irene to play jazz for her.

"One of my father's relatives was a great fan of Ragtime music also. She taught music at the Birmingham Conservatory of Music around the turn of the century and was captivated by the music of Scott Joplin that had become so popular in some circles. Enamored of Ragtime, she wanted her students to learn some of his music. However, the racist faculty refused to allow her to teach anything that Scott Joplin had written. I heard my mother, on the other hand, play one of his popular Ragtime jazz numbers, 'Maple Leaf Rag,' with gusto.

"Mary, I just thought of another fascinating character from my years in Florida, a man who worked for Mrs. Oliphant, a friend of Mother's. This gray-haired Black man helped her tend her lush tropical garden. Once, when she went outdoors to pass the time of day with the old man, he stopped working, leaned on his shovel to be cordial, and asked, 'Mrs. Oliphant, does you tell your husband everything you know?'

"She paused, 'Yes, Uncle, I think I do.' That was a term of respect in those days.

"'Tain't right! Tain't right! You should *tell* some, and *left* some.'

"He was silent for a moment and then said, 'I knew a perfectly nice woman once who told her husband everything she knew and ... and he *quit* her!'

"I had a watercolor teacher who shared some of that old man's wisdom. She told us art students, 'Even when painting realism, you should leave a part unfinished. The viewer then can fill in the blanks in his own fashion.' Yes, 'Tell some, and left some ...'

"Miami, Florida, was a lively place in the early '20s when we spent two winters there. Real estate was booming. Agents worked the crowds even after dark.

"Our family of four went fishing and swimming in the ocean at Miami Beach, which was not yet crowded with hotels and high-rise apartment buildings. I remember going out into Biscayne Bay in a glass-bottom boat to view a pristine coral reef alive with brilliant tropical fish and waving anemones.

"Mother and Dad took us to our first concert there, and the memory of it rings in my ears to this day. In 1924, we were thrilled to hear Paul Whiteman's band's introduction of Gershwin's 'Rhapsody in Blue.'

"Hard to believe, the Florida East Coast Highway was then a single lane paved with bricks, with wide shoulders of sand on each side. If you met a car coming at you, somebody had to decide who would hit the sand."

Mary grinned. "It reminds me of the game of 'chicken' that foolish teenagers played in my generation."

"And it worked fairly well because traffic wasn't heavy. The biggest things on the road were the buses bringing tourists by the hundreds to take part in the bourgeoning real estate frenzy. Everyone wanted a part of the action in Miami.

"The first winter there, my dad found an apartment for us in a beautiful suburb. The next winter, there was little room anywhere, and we had to move downtown.

"Everybody, it seemed, was heading for Miami, including several executives of the Louisville and Nashville Railroad who depended upon my father, a youthful member of the L&N, to provide them with proper entertainment. Despite the Volstead Act, or maybe because of it, one could buy Bacardi rum on the sly from illegal rum runners from Cuba. The men from the main office of the railroad seemed delighted to be a part of this intrigue. Once when they made their purchases, much to my father's surprise and chagrin, one of them was naïve enough to present the bootlegger with his business card!

"In the second winter, Mary Lou and I had to go to school in the inner city of Miami with children who were different from us: Cubans, Mexicans, and poor Anglos. I felt lost and frightened in this unfamiliar community.

"At lunchtime, we were allowed to cross the street to a little grocery store to buy treats. On my way there, I carried an unopened box of cheese crackers from the lunch Mother had prepared for me. I walked back to school. When I arrived, I saw the grocer hurrying to the principal's office to report that I had stolen a box of crackers. Mother was called to the school, talked to the principal, and set things straight, but I had been traumatized. On another occasion, while we were walking home from school we were joined by a classmate. Her dress hung from emaciated shoulders, a dress that badly needed to be washed, a dress with tears that should have been patched. She tried to start an argument with me but I ignored her. Next day the principal wanted to know why I had hit the poor girl and torn her dress. Once again Mother cleared my name."

"Mams, you must have felt helpless in a threatening land of Oz."

"At the time, I thought that poor girl was evil and unkind without cause. Now I realize her lies were because she had been deprived her entire life of healthy food and enough of it to build a strong body;

she had no pretty clothes and no adult who could keep those clothes clean and repaired, no parents who could fill her imagination and give her hope. I had all these things, and she must have been consumed with jealousy.

"I believe that simple jobs should be created for families like hers who have fallen between the cracks. Our lakes, streams, beaches, hiking trails, and parks need custodians. With good food and adequate shelter, workers like these require little training. No American should go to bed hungry. That is not socialism. It does mean that I believe we should lend a hand to the desperate, which hardly makes me a socialist.

"If we are Christians, or simply goodhearted people, we are our brothers' keepers. We should feel the responsibility of making medical care, education, and hope for a decent life available to anyone willing to work for these things.

"Moreover, how about the worker in this changing world who finds his kind of work is not needed anymore? These differences are the stuff that revolutions are made of. I learned a lot from those early experiences in Florida."

When my soapbox cooled down, I continued with more thoughts of Florida in the '20s. "Miami in the real estate boom was flooded with thousands of newcomers anxious to buy land. Mother and Dad described storeowners in the heart of the city keeping lights shining in their entryways as late as midnight so that agents could set up temporary stalls and continue selling into the balmy night. One innovative dealer added music in order to lure eager buyers from competitors next door. There was never enough land, so developers drained rich swamplands and created two communities, Coral Gables and Hollywood-by-the-Sea. The joke circulating among tourists was, 'Why are you so happy?' The answer: 'They found *land* on my property.'

"Miami was unreal to me, and really more than I could handle as a child. I was overjoyed when my father was given a new assignment:

Orlando. Dad was enjoying driving the first automobile of his own, a Dodge touring car, which in those days was a convertible. It sported the recently developed balloon tires with inner tubes instead of the hard rubber tires used previously. We rolled off the highway taking us north at a sign that read 'Orlando this way' and were overjoyed that the air was filled with the scent of orange blossoms. Inside the city limits the road widened, paved smooth with bricks. We were on Orange Avenue, which took us through the heart of the town.

"Orlando was a little residential town in those days, beautiful and tranquil. Mother and Dad rented an apartment in a complex a few stories high, set back from Orange Avenue. The building had a lawn in front with several lawn chairs for residents. At the rear of each floor was an open veranda for residents to enjoy balmy weather and each other.

"Unlike Miami, Orlando was a safe place. While we were living there, Mother gave us a loose rein, and in that climate my confidence flourished. Wider horizons stimulated my imagination as we were given freedom to venture out on our own. Tropical plants flourished around the many lakes in the residential part of town. Mother allowed us to walk from the large apartment a block into the heart of the neat little city, cross the main street where few autos sped by, to the library where we secured our own library cards and selected our favorite books to bring home. We were soon inspired to write a play. With the help of a wispy little girl from the apartment down the hall, we rehearsed and produced our play a week later. We dropped notices at the doors of all the tenants, and opening night had a good-sized audience on the three open porches. After the performance, when the smattering of clapping ceased, my big sister suggested that those who enjoyed the performance might want to drop a coin or two in the basket on each level. They laughed a friendly laugh and some complied, but my mother groaned with embarrassment, leaving me with the feeling that it was bad for a girl to receive money for services. As a result, for years I was ashamed to ever ask for money in exchange for work that I did.

"Directly across Orange Avenue was a tidy store selling staples as well as vegetables, fruit, and flowers. But their biggest sellers were orange blossom honey and orange marmalade.

"One block into the city on our side of the avenue was a specialty shop selling merchandise made only in Japan ... little China baby dolls with arms and legs that moved. There were dolls of every age dressed in beautiful Japanese silks. They also had an intriguing oriental paper form that appeared to be pressed pulp, but when you put it in a saucer of water, you could watch it absorb the water and grow into a surprising bouquet of colored flowers. I could have lingered in that shop all morning.

"We certainly take small things for granted in this day. Back then, two new things changed our way of life. One was cellophane. Someone showed me a pack of cigarettes wrapped in cellophane. I had never seen it before. It was like magic. I had an idea of how to use it, so I put it in my dollhouse windows and they looked like they were made of real glass.

"The other was a machine to take the place of our hand printing. Our little playwright friend grew excited by the idea of publishing a newsletter with Mary Lou and me, for our apartment community. Hand printing stories for each copy would be difficult, but we were young and enthusiastic. A new tenant to our complex, working for a while in Orlando, learned of our plan and offered us the use of his typewriter, not the big machine we had seen in the movies but a small machine he called a 'portable.'

"He showed us how to hit each key with one finger until we finished each sentence, pointing out the comma, period, and question mark. He asked only that we use his portable carefully. We spent many hours typing out our stories one letter at a time, and when we were finished it looked like a real newsletter. Alas, Mary, our first issue was our last.

"Our family loved taking trips to the ocean. One weekend, after a long period without rain, a much needed storm wet the highway we were taking from Orlando to New Smyrna for a relaxing visit to the beach. The combination of oil and water on the road was so slick that our automobile slid into a deep ditch along the highway. Remarkably, it landed upright, and neither the car nor the passengers were hurt. My sister had the presence of mind to put her arm around me. With her other arm, she held tight to the accordion-like ribs that held the roof secure, and I was not thrown from the car. The unbattered car was towed back onto the road and we went on to enjoy our weekend.

"In order to reach New Smyrna, we turned on the eastern highway until we reached a wooden bridge across the sound that led to the one-street island town. There was a sign 'apartment for rent' at the biggest white frame house in town. We inquired about the rental from the matron, who told us one apartment on the second floor was available for $1.50 for the weekend. It had a kitchen, running water with a shower, and beds for four people. We took it.

"That was the beginning of our acquaintance with Ma Dewey. She told us she was the widow of a fisherman, and from her different accent I guessed they may have lived in New England. Perhaps he had brought her to Florida to fish in warmer waters. What a character she turned out to be! She became friend to the children renting her apartments and told us that one of those houses built out on the dunes was haunted.

"One night when the large moon rose, it appeared to be coming out of the Atlantic, and a warm breeze blew from the west over the land, bringing heat and mosquitoes. Ma Dewey had all of us kids from our big house pile into the car, and we drove northward over the hard sand until we saw a lonesome, dark house on a dune. Silently, we tiptoed from the car and up the stairs and gathered on the porch of this lonesome cottage. One of us must have snickered or made some sort of noise, when a roaring voice bellowed out of the second floor, 'Who is that?' We turned and ran so fast that we knocked poor Ma Dewey flat on the sand in our rush to get back to the car. As we were driving away, Ma Dewey said, 'That must have been the new minister I heard was going to move into the neighborhood.'

"Before we left Orlando, your grandmother had relaxed into the easy life of that pleasant city. Further down Orange Avenue was the movie theatre where during intermission there were prize drawings from the number found on your ticket stub. Mother was one of the lucky ones. She had to walk up on the stage to collect her prize ... a beautiful French automobile horn. Parading back to her seat and pointing the horn from one side of the aisle to the other, she squeezed the bulb, blasting everybody with loud '*ah-OOO-gahs*.' Mary Lou and I laughed heartily along with the rest of the audience. Mother always saw the humorous side of life and made fun for everyone.

"Although we didn't stay in the state for long, Florida remained a special place to us. Many years later, your dad and I made a trip by car to Florida. The East Coast by that time had a major highway all the way to Miami. Before we left, an avid gardener friend, Andy Gould, where I was working at *U.S. News and World Report*, told us to pause in the low country of Georgia when we crossed a beautiful little river named the Altamaha and to look for blossoms."

"What makes the Altamaha significant?" Mary inquired.

"In the early days of our country, John Bartram, a botanist and plant explorer who lived in Philadelphia, discovered a previously unknown tree that grew along the Altamaha River. It was a glossy-leafed, low-growing tree with unbelievably beautiful white blossoms. He was so excited to discover this new tree he harvested its seeds and took them to his garden in Philadelphia to propagate them. He named this tree *Franklinea* for his good friend, Benjamin Franklin. Years later, he went with his grown son back to the Altamaha, and the two of them were unable to locate a single *Franklinea* tree. His beautiful tree would have been extinct had he not propagated the seeds from his first visit. [Image 9.1]

147

"The next big move we had after Orlando, when I was about ten, was because Dad was offered a more responsible position in a larger city. When our family packed up to move back to Alabama, this time to Mobile, I knew I had grown older and more self-assured because of our time in the beautiful little town where the air smelled so sweet. Mother had enjoyed Orlando too.

"Mr. Alec Payne had been head agent in the freight office of the L&N Railroad in the port city of Mobile for a long period, and soon he would be taking over business in the larger port of New Orleans. While he was preparing Dad for his new responsibilities, Mrs. Payne became Mother's dear friend, and their daughter Catherine, ours. Our families visited each other many times over the years. Once when we were visiting in New Orleans with the Paynes, they had a visit from a relative they called Cousin Kate. A young man arrived for a date with Cousin Kate dressed in a uniform and we ignorant kids thought he was a policeman.

"In my maturity, we were delighted when we received a letter from Catherine Payne saying she was bringing her mother to Washington. They were to go to dinner at the home of her Cousin Kate, who was now married and living there, and invited us to come along. We arrived at the Anacostia Naval Station where Kate lived in Quarters One, the Senior Officers' quarters. We were surprised to find that Catherine Payne's Cousin Kate's 'policeman' was now an admiral in the Navy! [Note 15 – Connections]

"The time in Mobile was the happiest of my youth. I entered grammar school in a suburb of Mobile, and it was the first time I became aware that there were boys in the world. One day, one of them brought me a bouquet of white dogwood blossoms. I was so appreciative that the next day he brought me a whole branch off the dogwood tree. The third day, to please me even more, he showed up at my house and presented me with a three-foot limb off that same dogwood. Yes, Mobile sure was a great town in which to grow up. [Image 9.2]

148

"When I was in fourth grade, my teacher wrote a play, *Titania, Queen of the Fairies*. Her plan was to have everybody in the class produce this play for our parents. The story unfolded with conversations between Titania and the King of the Fairies. The rest of the boys were elves and the girls, fairies with wings but no crown. Titania was the star, and she spoke most of the lines. Every little girl in the class wanted to be Queen.

"The teacher chose Minette for the part, a small girl with curly blonde hair. The rest of us were the members of her court. The Saturday of the performance, Minette, Titania's real name, fell from a swing early in the morning and fractured her arm. The doctor told her mother that it was not a bad break but the fracture needed to be protected in a cast until it healed. Minette insisted on being on stage because her role was so important.

"When the curtain went up that night the King began the dialogue with the Queen. They were well into their conversation when he asked her a question. There was no answer. He gave the cue again. No answer. He spoke again. Silence. Frantic, the King spoke into thin air. I had been hesitant, but I knew the lines. Although I wasn't the Queen, I was compelled to answer the King. Poor Minette had suddenly felt so ill she slipped backstage for help, where she had fainted.

"The King of the Fairies, relieved, turned toward me standing tall among the fairies, and thus we completed the play and the curtain came down. If the audience noticed the change in the cast they accepted it quietly. Our teacher was ecstatic.

"When she learned that Minette was better and in the care of her parents, the teacher rushed forward to thank all the elves and fairies. Then she covered me with hugs and kisses and did the same to the uncomfortable King of the Fairies. This 'positive reinforcement' influenced my future of public speaking and my love of attending plays.

"Mobile continued to be a wonderful place, opening me to the world. I went from grammar school to what was our junior high, seventh grade. Three unmarried sisters of Portuguese origin, the D'Ornellas, lived in Mobile. Two of them had a significant impact on me during that time ... one, a principal of Old Barton Academy Junior High and a second who taught math at Mobile High School. In junior high, the principal came to our class one day, paused at my desk, pushed my bangs from my forehead, and said loud enough for all my friends to hear, 'My, what an intelligent forehead!' These things one never forgets. I was so embarrassed.

"The next year, when I entered Mobile High School, my friends told me to avoid taking math from the second Miss D'Ornellas because she was so strict they were afraid of her. I was assigned to be in her class that had three-too-many students, so when the principal came around, I readily volunteered to be switched to another class. Later, I learned that I had made a big mistake. In my senior year, I was made president of the National Honor Society with Miss D'Ornellas as the faculty adviser. After she and I finished a society business meeting, she rose from her seat behind the desk, smiled, and said, 'May I kiss you?', and she did ... on my forehead. She stood back and said, 'Virginia, if I had ever had a daughter, I would have wanted her to be exactly like you.' I was deeply touched. I was old enough to realize how significant a statement this was. I left, ashamed that if I had not been a foolish teenager, I would have realized what a wonderful math teacher she could have been for me.

"I joined with enthusiasm a world of friends. On Friday evenings, our dads would drive us to the parish hall of the Episcopal Church, where we taught each other how to dance to the popular songs of the day played on a large Victrola.

"At the start of my high school years, when the doors of Mobile High School opened, so did whole new vistas for me; I became an avid student of literature, history, and the arts. I was unaware at the time of the bias that required females to take such classes as home economics, to the exclusion of science, business, and math. Later in college, I realized that I ... and all girls ... should have been far better trained in mathematics.

"There was another incident in Mobile that makes me look back and smile. One night when we were in high school, Helen Head and I, along with our dates, drove to an orchard to pick up satsumas ... those large, sweet tangerines that had dropped onto the ground. How naïve we were! For a time, nocturnal nabbing of satsumas was an exciting adventure, popular with lots of our friends. Helen and I waited in the parked car as the boys hopped the fence and disappeared. After what seemed like ages, the boys returned, closely followed by two men holding rifles at their backs. The orchard owner had employed guards to protect his property. The guards took me and Helen home and the boys to the orchard owner's house. The boys protested that they had only picked up the fallen tangerines, but the owner was so enraged by the vandalism his orchard had suffered at the hands of other kids that our dates bore the brunt of his anger. He wanted someone to learn that you do not have the right to destroy others' property. So, he said that they would each need to work to make money and pay him five dollars, at that time a week's pay for a teenager.

"Helen was the head of an in-school committee that resolved minor infractions by their peers. Always honest, Helen felt that she could no longer judge her fellow students and exclaimed, 'Now that I am an accomplice to a misdeed, I must resign that committee.'

"My mother's reaction was quite surprising. When I told her that the boys were escorted from the orchard with rifles at their backs by the men who had brought me home, she began to giggle at the image of her straight-laced daughter being brought home by armed guards.

"It was our custom every day after school to stop at Helen's house for a snack. Her mother often had johnnycake ... a thin cornbread cooked with bacon ... on the bottom of the iron skillet for us, a typical Southern dish we delighted in eating. Afterwards, Helen played the piano and we sang the songs of the day. Next, we would go to my house and have fruit, cookies, candy, or ham sandwiches. How remarkable that we stayed so thin!

"At fifteen, Helen and I continued to be part of our group of friends. Our crowd swam together in the freshwater Dog River or the saltwater of Mobile Bay, or sailed there. On summer nights, we would drink a coke at the corner drive-in drug store or just cruise Government Street to see who else was there.

"At sixteen, we began to pair off. One day we were swimming where the bay meets the saltwater of the Gulf. When Jimmy McLemore and I did a porpoise dive, we discovered how clear the water had become. I saw him alright, gliding toward me, short black hair waving like an anemone. Just before we surfaced, his lips brushed mine.

"The same old friends were splashing and laughing, but Jimmy and I emerged different people. Afterwards, he asked me to wear his class ring to show we were special friends. Jimmy's grandmother had purchased it for him. He was very fond of his grandmother, so the ring was precious.

"The stock market had crashed while I was in high school, but my father protected his girls from the worry of it. He announced on graduation night that the railroad had offered him a position in Cincinnati and he had accepted the offer because the university was available to us there. We were shocked to learn that otherwise he could not afford to send us to college. He chose Cincinnati because it had a 'streetcar college' where many students were able to live with their parents while attending.

"Time came for me to board a train for the north. Jimmy put his strong young arm around me and with knitted brow told me, 'If you ever need me, no matter where or when, I'll be there for you.'

"When I got to Cincinnati, I missed the teens that had been a close circle of friends in Mobile and didn't know anybody. Everyone in Cincinnati spoke with an accent, at first strange and offensive to me. I missed Jimmy most, as he was such a good friend.

"At last, in October of 1931, now moved to Ohio, Mary Lou and I became acquainted with a young immigrant Cincinnatian whose last name was Cocanougher, an interesting name in a town in which eighty-five percent of the people were of German descent. In the course of our friendship, he said he'd like to introduce us to a visitor from Germany, a gentleman who wanted to meet some young Americans. Mary Lou and I agreed to a double date. The four of us went out dancing to the sounds of a live Big Band. Returning home reasonably early, we asked the men if they would care to come inside, where we continued dancing to records on our Victrola. The courtly Oswald Hartmeyer volunteered to teach us how to tango. During one deep dip, he brushed an ashtray, which fell to the floor and broke. He was very apologetic ... although Mary Lou and I assured him it was not an important thing.

"We talked awhile before they left, of his father sending him to study American journalism at *The Cincinnati Inquirer*. I regret that at seventeen I was not interested in politics and asked him very little about his life in Germany. But Mary Lou and I were absolutely intrigued to be taught the tango. It was great fun, and before he departed Oswald said, 'You know, in Germany, *proper* young women would not have invited two men into their homes.' To which I replied, 'And in America, *respectable* young men would not have accepted!'

"That evening is very clear in my mind, although I cannot remember Cocanougher's first name. A few months later, on Mary Lou's birthday, a package arrived. Inside was a handsome ashtray. After that night, and thereafter through the difficulties of World War II, I often wondered what happened to the young Oswald Hermann Hartmeyer. [Note 16 – Hartmeyer]

"Later, as a college student in Cincinnati, I was working on a social service committee at the YMCA and attended a luncheon meeting of members from all across the city. A young African American woman about my age sat next to me. Because of social mores that I had unconsciously grown up with in the South, I had never actually sat at a meal with a Black person. No matter how close, our servants would never have sat at dinner with us. I was so uncomfortable I could hardly swallow my food, but when I faced her for the first time, I saw that she was painfully timid and much more uncomfortable than I was. Then I remembered how I truly felt about Sylvia and Aunt Ida. Fortunately, my upbringing demanded that I at least introduce myself and learn her name.

"Thankfully, politeness led to empathy and made me a child again, unencumbered by social rules that had governed me unwittingly. We talked for a while and were soon exchanging stories, laughing and enjoying ourselves as young people do. I bring this up because I think my life, my awareness of racial relationships, and my behavior changed in that moment ... and from then on."

Our conversation paused with the significance of my self-realization, and we listened to the crickets outside the motel window. At length, Mary changed the subject and pressed me to reveal more about my old flame, Jimmy McLemore.

"Toward the end of World War II ... when our family moved to the Washington, D.C. area ... my life was full, and youthful memories were buried along with a variety of trinkets and souvenirs, Jimmy's ring among them. Mary, when I turned forty I began dreaming of the South again and yearned to show you girls places where I'd been extremely happy. In the summer of Lucy's sixteenth year, we were ready to make a vacation trip by car to see old friends and remembered places: Birmingham, New Orleans, Mobile, and the Florida East Coast. I so enjoyed introducing you to relatives and friends in Birmingham ... and hearing music blaring out of open night club doors as we walked down Bourbon Street in New Orleans."

"Yes, I remember thinking, 'If my friends could see me now.'"

"After calling on my parents' former neighbors in Mobile, we spent time returning to my two still-beautiful schools among the live-oak trees. Mobile stirred up recollections ... the ring ... Jimmy. I had told you girls about our parting when my family first moved north, and I thought maybe I could return his grandmother's ring while we were there. Helen had written to me that she thought Jimmy might still be living in Mobile, so I had brought it along. Next morning, before we left Mobile to head for Florida, I told your father that I wanted to go by Jimmy's house. At breakfast I found the address for James Tilford McLemore in the phone book. It had to be Jimmy for sure. When I asked your father if he would stop by the McLemore house on the way out of town, hesitation was written all over his face. 'If you don't telephone him in advance you probably will miss him.' I had to smile to myself over this. Since your father had such strong feelings about the situation, I decided not to call in advance ... just to go and get it over with.

"And you, pixie Mary, under your breath, whispered, 'No matter where or when, I will be there for you.'

"Dad parked the car way up the street from the house. His head sank deep into his shoulders as he watched me approaching Jimmy's house followed by three pre-teen to teenage girls, duckling fashion. As I rang the bell, I noticed an old sports car and a motorcycle in the side yard. Through the open windows I heard jazz music playing, so I rang again, but nobody answered.

"Disappointed, I led the group back to the car, painfully aware of your mirth and the repeated line I fervently wished I'd never shared with you. Your dad had that *I told you so* look on his face, but he gave me a hug and grinned before he started the engine .... Gads, that's enough of *my* memories." [Note 17 – Jimmy's Ring]

"You haven't really told me much of your impressions about when I was a little girl growing up in Alexandria or some of our early family vacations. Maybe just one more story?"

"Oh, that was a delightful period in our lives. You loved going to the beach and swimming in the Atlantic. I recall stopping at farmers' markets along the highway en route to Nags Head. Each farmer would offer his summer bounty, and we would fill our car with trea-

155

sures of produce along the way to the shore. We were always raven-
ous at the beach.

"One July, my friend Ruth Poggenpohl told us about her favorite
farmer's stand along the way, and we found it, a well-built structure painted dark green. The neatly arranged produce caught our
eyes from the road. We pulled over and were charmed by the colorful array of this farmer's harvest: rectangular bins of red tomatoes,
yellow summer squash, green beans, orange carrots, collard greens,
and white turnips with leafy tops, not a blemish on the bunch. This
farmer manned his own market and was well worth knowing. His
white curly hair was a stark contrast to his dark skin, and his eyes
sparkled. We had difficulty saying 'enough' when making our selec-
tions, but when I spied the shiny dark-purple of a large eggplant I
had to add that too. I suggested he put several vegetables together,
and he said to me, 'No, each vegetable gets its own sack. When I was
a kid in the Depression and the grocer sent me home with all my
vegetables tossed into one sack, I hated it. So now I use an *excessive*
number of bags for each customer.' I kept thinking of his use of the
word 'excessive,' and was so moved by his skill, knowledge, and pride
in his work. We carried away a wealth of produce as well as memories of that impressive Black man." [Image 9.3]

"When we rented that cabaña on Hatteras Island, it was great
fun to explore other islands on the Outer Banks," Mary piped in.
"The best part was seeing the Chincoteague ponies in the wild on
their island after we read the book, *Misty of Chincoteague* by Marguerite Henry. The characters Paul and Maureen became our imaginary best friends. You and Dad told us that we could visit their cottage on one of our trips and we might even see Misty, the wild pony
that belonged to Paul and Maureen. But when we went down the
road to their real-life home, they were now teenagers and did not
want to talk to outsiders curious about them. We saw them riding
up the dusty road from their house on horseback and thought, *How
could our 'old friends' ignore us?* [Image 9.4]

"Mams, with our fun beach memories why did you call the Outer Banks the Graveyard of the Atlantic?"

"Well, when swimming on Cape Hatteras, do you remember how cold the ocean water was, coming down from the north? This is where the Arctic current flowing south meets the Gulf Stream flowing north. The two collide near the Hatteras lighthouse and form a current that carries sand out into the Atlantic. The moving sand continues to build under the water's surface. Many early ships were wrecked on the shallow sandbar. It is said that some sailors saved their lives by swimming to this remote shore. Some who couldn't swim were saved by floating to shore clinging to molasses barrels.

"Pirates profited enormously from these tragedies. They'd hang a lantern on a donkey's neck and walk it along the high sand dunes to give the captains the illusion of ships in a harbor, making them think they were further out to sea. That's how Nag's Head got its name. When the boats foundered on the bar, the pirates would steal the contents.

"This isn't the only strange tale about the history of the Outer Banks. England's first settlement in America was here on Croatoan Island, now Roanoke Island, North Carolina."

"Near Cape Hatteras."

"Yes. Mare, you might have been too young to remember the 'Lost Colony' play we saw on Roanoke while on vacation. It was a re-enactment of what happened there. In 1585, Queen Elizabeth I gave Sir Walter Raleigh permission to form a colony in America. Under his direction, 100 Englishmen attempted to found a colony on Roanoke Island. Although they succeeded in building a town with a fort, they could not survive. They were short on food and other necessities, so artist and poet John White returned to England with a few of the settlers to get necessary provisions. When he got back home, he found that all vessels had been commandeered for the Queen's Navy in its fight against the Spanish Armada, leaving no available funds for him to return to Roanoke Island.

157

"When White left Roanoke, he instructed the colonists to let him know if they moved to another location. When he was finally able to come back, in 1590, the colony had been deserted. The only clue to their whereabouts was the word *Croatoan* carved into a tree where the village had stood. Chief Manteo was the leader of the Croatoan Indians, a tribe that had befriended the early colonists.

"This story is one of the great mysteries of the colonization of America, for none of the settlers were ever seen again. There are competing theories as to what might have happened. In later years, the explorer John Lawson proposed that they might have gone to live on the nearby island of Manteo's people. His evidence was based on the belief that some of the Croatoans possessed European features and spoke English words. Another theory maintains that the colonists moved to the Pembroke region of North Carolina, because the Pembroke Indians could also speak English and many had the same last names as English colonists.

"When you girls had outgrown vacations with the family, your dad and I continued to visit the Outer Banks. One wonderful day, Mary, I took a book, blanket, and umbrella to a deserted beach and was quietly reading. Looking up, I saw the eyes of a hundred land crabs that had emerged from their dry, sandy homes, just high enough to be silently staring at me. I was aware of their presence in a way that almost made me self-conscious, as if everyone had turned around to look at me in a theater because I was snoring or something. I flipped the butt of a dead cigarette in the air near me, and instantly and simultaneously they disappeared into the holes I hadn't seen until that moment.

"Here's another crab story. This one took place when my family moved to Mobile. Soon after we got there, Dad and Mother built a beautiful little white cottage with columns on the tiny veranda and a kitchen I shall never forget. A house painter did the kitchen. His praises should be sung, because he was an artist who cared about his work. The chair rail built into the kitchen was worthy of a formal dining room, and our unsung painter made the area above it, ceiling and walls, a warm off-white. Below the chair rail, he employed his creativity by painting the wall as *faux* marble.

"After we moved in, an event occurred so out of keeping with our formal kitchen, I laugh today when recalling it. One morning our family of four, carrying the makings of breakfast ... a crab net, a burlap bag, and old scraps of beef for bait ... had waded out into Mobile Bay. Our destination was an old sunken barge in the shallow water near the shore, and from it we scooped up many crabs. Dad dropped each crab into the burlap bag, secured it, and took the catch home to our pristine kitchen. Friends had told Mother to put a large pot on the stove with plenty of water, and when it boiled, to drop the crabs in. Dad opened the burlap bag and held it over the boiling water. A few crabs fell into the pot. The rest clutched to the heavy burlap fabric with their claws. Dad shook the bag furiously. A few more dropped into the pot but most escaped the stove top and scurried across the kitchen floor. 'Close the door to the dining room! Grab them from the rear, so they won't pinch you with their claws!' Dad shouted, laughing. From his cage in the kitchen, our parrot began to squawk and swear ... as he had been taught during his earlier life as a seaman's pet. It was a raucous madhouse for a while, until things quieted down as the last crab succumbed to its fate. We became old salts after a few more crabbing and fishing trips were behind us. But remembrance of this hilarity bemused us for years." [Image 9.5]

After our long conversation covering the miles of time and memory, Mary and I had a comfortable night's sleep in Tex's lodging. Next morning, refreshed and checked out of his motel, we followed Tex to his favorite garage, where his mechanic did a thorough job replacing Betsy's carburetor as well as her fuel pump.

9.1 *Altamaha River, Georgia*–sketch by Virginia Ames. A botanist discovered an unknown flowering tree here and lived to see its disappearance in nature.

9.2 Virginia, sister Mary Lou and friend–our first musical instruments in Mobile, Alabama, 1924

9.3 Produce stand near Nag's Head, North Carolina

9.4 Lucy, Muffin, and Mary at the Atlantic, summer of 1960

9.5 *Blue Crabs*, original watercolor by Virginia Ames. These crabs modeled for Virginia years later on the Outer Banks during another quieter family crabbing experience.

Sally Louise Powers-Wade, 1930s

CHAPTER 10

Bigmother

(Letter to Muffin, from Waynesville, MO)

October 20, 1970
Dear Muff,

Mary and I are really having an "abventure," as little Clo would say. We left home Thursday afternoon for Cincinnati, having had the car thoroughly checked out by your dad's favorite mechanic. The mechanic said, "She is solid. She is safer than one from the showroom floor. I have fixed the miss you heard at 60 mph, Mrs. Ames, by replacing points and plugs!"

163

But he was wrong. Since then, the car has caused us much anguish. It has misfired repeatedly. The first time was when we climbed the long hill up to the Pennsylvania Turnpike. It felt as though Betsy had developed the symptoms of angina pectoris of the fuel valve. Remarkably, we arrived in Cincinnati with no more trouble.

Mary and I enjoyed the warm hospitality of the Kassons in Cincinnati and the kind service of their favorite mechanic. We bought a rebuilt fuel pump to carry, just in case. The mechanic replaced the fuel filter and said, "Now it's repaired. Have a good trip."

Harry and Mary Lou sent us forth joyously.

Fifty miles east of St. Louis, the car missed again—almost stopped. Another pit stop at an East St. Louis garage enabled us to move again but we felt the basic problem still needed to be solved. No doubt you can imagine the relief we felt when we arrived in Ferguson, just northeast of St. Louis, and rolled into the driveway of the home of relatives, Marcia and Fred Pope. You may remember that she is your dad's niece and her husband is an Episcopal minister. Two of their children are still at home; their elder daughter is married, living in Chicago. Their son Fred Jr. and his young wife were visiting from their home in Rolla, Missouri. All of them greeted us warmly.

When our host learned about our car problem he said he knew just the man who could resolve it. Everybody has referred us to their favorite mechanic, but maybe this one can really fix it, I thought. Fred invited us to spend the weekend with them because his friend would not be working until Monday.

All weekend we swapped anecdotes about our lives since we last met, when Marcia was a teenager. We enjoyed their church service, their church picnic, their beds, their food, and their love. Early Monday morning, Fred took us to his favorite mechanic, who checked out the car and said everything looked fine to him.

Alas, fifty miles out of St. Louis trouble hit again. It was nip and tuck whether we could cross the double highway to a little garage that suddenly caught our eyes on the opposite side of the road—an ancient Shell station with a lecherous country boy in charge. I couldn't decide if he would help us because of Mary's blonde hair or capture us permanently for the same reason. He took the carburetor out and we made him put it back so that we could high tail it out of there.

The next morning, for reasons known only to Betsy, we traveled eighty smooth miles to Waynesville, Missouri. The owner and manager of our motel is a big, slightly balding man, aptly called Tex. We decided to stay here overnight and hope to find a good garage with a civilized mechanic in the morning. We want to get to Seattle with time to spare for Mary to get back to her job. And we hope we might even be able to see the Grand Canyon and to stop and see you in Tucson.

If we have solved Betsy's problem (and there are few areas left where the fuel line can be improved), we will have the neatest, smoothest little car in the country. And because Mary and I are in this together, it's just a great challenge—not a threat! If you want to contact us, we will check in at the Museum of Northern Arizona in Flagstaff, hopefully on Thursday.

Wish you were here,
Mamsie
Wish we were there,
Mary

We posted the letter to Martha and left with a warm feeling for Tex, a big man ready to help anyone in need, and gratitude for a mechanic's "job well done."

Railroad tracks ran parallel with our highway and vast farms filled the lonely land. Ahead a group of grain elevators, seemingly tall as skyscrapers, pierced the blue sky. Mary read aloud some of the signboards:

Welcome to Greenfield, Missouri
International Home of the Assemblies of God
and
End Republican Recession

Driving on through Missouri, Mary noticed that Senator William Stuart Symington's face appeared on most of the campaign signs. Some even read that there was little doubt he would be elected to another term.

In this big sky country there were few trees. Where grasses once grew there were now endless cultivated fields. Rows of corn were like thin legs that raced in the opposite direction at the speed our car was moving forward. Soon a huge farm separated us from the railroad track, but a freight train pulling perhaps a hundred cars was visible. We could see it from engine to caboose. Mary remarked that it looked like a child's toy from our vantage point.

"Mary, your granddad worked for the Louisville & Nashville Railroad all of his life, and like a kid he never lost his enthusiasm for running that railroad. I wish you could have known him. He would tell me stories of the early days of railroading, about a steam engine named The General that was a prize during the Civil War, commandeered by Union troops and then recaptured by the Confederates. He was so enthralled by railroad history.

"Your grandfather told me that the first time troops were ever transported by rail in our country was to the battlefield at Manas-

166

sas. On another occasion when Confederate forces were desperate for reinforcements in Kentucky and Tennessee, General Braxton Bragg was ordered to bring the troops under his command in Louisiana to reinforce the beleaguered Confederate Army in the East. On this long march, they found relief by boarding the short-line railroads they found along their way. The many troops boarded the trains of six small railroad lines, some of which were only ten or fifteen miles long. They would board one line until it came to its end and then march until they arrived at another rail line, which they boarded.

"Your grandfather liked to recall a railroad story that he said would not be in history books. Railroading in the South was young. Most lines, built in the decade prior to the Civil War, covered short distances. One line was centered in Louisville and another originated in Nashville, Tennessee. They merged to become the L&N. The merger proved a good one, until Tennessee belatedly joined the Confederacy while Kentucky remained neutral, so war actually broke out within the company over who owned the valuable rolling stock, that is, the engines, cars, and rails. Peace in the company was finally restored even though Kentucky never went with the Confederacy.

"When my father was a child in Montgomery, Alabama, he said that he remembered giving food to the troops riding the train on their way to fight in the Spanish-American War. This was his first memory of his relationship with trains. When he was made general freight agent of the L&N, he and Gran-gran moved to Louisville, headquarters of the line. He was being groomed for an important role in running that railroad.

"My dad was conscientious like his mother, Bigmother, but unlike her his personality was tempered by a wonderful sense of humor. Bigmother had such an enormous influence on me. She was born Sally Louise Powers in the 1860s in Florence, a small town in northern Alabama. Like most people in the agrarian South, her father must have farmed, but never on a large scale. I do not know if he was a slave holder.

"Men in Bigmother's generation were professional people. There was a doctor, perhaps her brother, and a cousin, James Powers, a professor who became president of the State of Alabama Normal School for training teachers and later president of the University of Alabama. Though healthy as a child, Bigmother contracted what I believe was typhoid fever and took months to recover. During her enforced rest she taught herself Latin, read Shakespeare, and doubtless studied the Bible. The members of her family were devout Methodists and never failed to attend camp meetings.

"One day, when Bigmother was five years old, just old enough to remember the War Between the States, while playing outside in the yard between her home and the servants' quarters, she was terrified by Union troops from Ohio scaling the fence, dropping down near her, and running unbidden inside to ransack the house for food. She remembered the terror of the women left unprotected. One soldier opened her big sister Pony's hope chest, spilling intimate apparel all over the floor. Pony slammed the trunk lid down in a fit of anger and embarrassment, cutting the soldier's finger. Both girls were paralyzed with fear, but the soldier did not harm them.

"Bigmother also remembered vividly a scene in the kitchen where a young Negro servant girl was working. Another soldier believed there had to be hams hanging somewhere but found none. This servant, who was small enough to crawl through the hole into the attic, had hung the family larder from the rafters for safekeeping.

"The young man in a blue uniform pointed his gun at the little servant's heart, threatening to kill her if she did not tell him where to find the hams. Bigmother said this heroic girl threw her two arms behind her back, faced him bravely, and shouted, 'Shoot!' His arm dropped slowly, and he turned away to join his departing comrades.

"The soldiers did not leave without loot, however. They drove the family livestock, horses and cattle, ahead of them as they departed. The women and children watched helplessly from the veranda. One of the horses was lame and had been put out to pasture because it could no longer work. The Yankees led him back down the lane to the house and shot him in front of the stunned group huddled there.

"My grandmother remained a person of her time and place. She held steadfastly to her prejudices, refusing to visit us for years after our family moved to Ohio, remembering those Ohioan invaders, even though my father was her favorite son. Family tradition finally triumphed over her war memories, and she came to my sister's wedding in Cincinnati after she was eighty.

"It was a few years later when I visited her with my Ohio-born husband. She was bedridden in her Alabama homeland and held court from her pillowed throne. When the family rose to go, she asked the two of us to tarry, telling us solemnly, 'Even though Bob was born in Ohio, he is an *aristocrat.*' In the devastation after the Civil War, when most in the South were reduced to poverty, all that was left to the citizens was pride in a good family and in having refined manners. Both virtues elevated one to the aristocracy in Bigmother's opinion. Your dad qualified.

"Though she was proud, she was never arrogant. She was the quintessential grandmother and mother, compassionate and capable. She told me of the romantic man whom she married, Alexander Corson Wade, a handsome young Virginian who had come down with a fellow worker vending their products in the Deep South. When they saw Sally, Bigmother, crossing a street in Florence, Alec said to his friend, 'That is the girl I am going to marry.'

"'What is her name?' Alec's friend asked.

"'I don't know. I haven't *met* her yet,' he replied.

"My grandfather Alec Wade had been orphaned young and had gone to live with John Hancock, a relative in Lynchburg, Virginia. When I heard this from Bigmother, I thought at first I was related to one of the signers of the Declaration of Independence, but this John Hancock, she told me, was a wealthy merchant and owner of tobacco fields.

"Life must have made my grandfather Wade serious. He was probably not an easy man to live with ... somber and righteous with a short temper. Bigmother, who admired the writings of St. Paul, often said, '... let not the sun go down upon your wrath,' [*Ephesians 4:26*], and with this precept she maintained a happy marriage and family.

"Your great-grandparents Alec and Sally Louise Wade had ten children, eight of whom lived to maturity. Sally cared for them herself, nursing them through illnesses, as she had also cared for the Negro servants employed by her family. She helped her husband with his businesses ... a small hotel in Calera, Alabama, and the telegraph office. He also owned the local feed and grain store. As was the custom, he extended credit to the small farmers annually, providing seeds, fertilizer, and feed for their stock, and securing his loan with a lien on their farming teams ... their horses and plows. He deplored the fact that in good times many farmers squandered their harvest money on liquor while their families suffered, and some ended up without enough to pay their feed bills. He worked hard to drive all the saloons out of town.

"After two drought years, when he received no payment because of a scant harvest, he told his wife, 'We have two choices. We can foreclose on all these teams and many families will suffer, or we can forgive their debts and we will ourselves suffer bankruptcy.' Bigmother supported him in his choice: bankruptcy. They lost everything and moved to Montgomery to start over.

"About sixty years later, while driving through Alabama, your dad took me on a side trip to Calera to see my grandparents' early home. The town's chance for glory had been aborted when the builders of the Louisville & Nashville Railroad decided to bypass Calera in favor of Montgomery. The town we now saw was unchanged from the time it had been a thriving agricultural center. It remained a small country town dying on the vine.

"The brick hotel that might have been the heart of the county seat when it was new was now a building strangely out of sync with the world we knew, like a skirt that covered a woman's ankles. A recent addition to the hotel was a building that housed a drugstore with a soda fountain. Thirst and curiosity pulled us into a dimly lit room where turn-of-the-century soda tables fought for space with a wall lined with apothecary supplies. A white-haired pharmacist shuffled toward us holding a shaking tray of sodas.

"'Do you remember who built this hotel?' I asked him.

"'A man named A.C. Wade, an ill-tempered man who folks didn't like.'

"He had to mean A.C. Wade, the grandfather I never met. Apparently, my grandfather was remembered for driving the saloons out of town and *not* for sacrificing himself to save many farmers from ruin. Shakespeare said it best in *Julius Caesar*, 'The evil men do lives after them; the good is oft interred with their bones.'

"In Montgomery, Bigmother told me that his good reputation had preceded him and the bankers extended him a loan of $25,000 with no collateral. He was so anxious to build up his business and retire his debt that he insisted upon attending a meeting with a client when not totally recovered from influenza. Soon after this meeting, the influenza was complicated by pneumonia from which he did not recover.

"Resourceful Bigmother moved her fatherless family to Birmingham and established a boarding house, a genteel profession for a woman who had no other means of support. Her great skill was homemaking and managing a large household. Her 'guests' were carefully selected and included schoolteachers and musicians, some of whom she bartered board for lessons for her children.

"Bigmother saw to it that the boys in the family went to work to help send the girls to teachers' college. No daughter of *hers* would face an uncertain future like hers without training for a career.

"She was deeply religious, refused to play cards on Sunday, never drank alcohol, and thought that lying was the worst of sins. She refused to tell her age to avoid that sin, but when she turned eighty,

171

she relaxed a little, began boasting about her age, and even drank a little wine before going to bed.

"I never saw Bigmother when she was not beautifully groomed and appropriately dressed. She had a lovely gown set aside, should she 'have to go to the hospital,' and she kept a complete outfit ready for her own funeral. Having prepared for the worst, she faced life with optimism.

"Bigmother was not pretty ... she was what I call handsome. She held herself erect and carried her chin high. I have a lingering picture of her in my mind in a black-and-white outfit, her thick white hair dressed in the latest fashion and a string of beads around her neck. It consisted of a set of three beads repeated around the strand. The first was of sand cast glass, frosty white; the second a faceted jet-shining black; and the third a clear crystal that sometimes made its own little rainbow.

"Her strength made us all secure, and her sense of joy filled us with happiness. She continued to love me even though I teased her about her belief that Jonah lived inside a whale. She was from Scotch-Irish stock, though I have no genealogical charts to substantiate this fact. Her father was a Powers, and she made it clear that his was an Irish name and anyone who was Irish could not take one drink of alcohol without subjecting himself to alcoholism. My sister and I had been warned that we had 'Powers-blood.' Because of this conviction and because she was a Methodist, she was a teetotaler. What forces combined to make this strong, responsible, and loving woman? She told one story about a female ancestor, which became oral tradition in the family. She was quite certain it was very real and not mythology.

"In the early days of Virginia colonization, the king granted a Scotsman, the Earl of Dunbar, a parcel of land in Northern Ireland where he made his home. He had two small children, a son and a daughter. Their nurse had strict orders that they never be taken down by the docks. When the nurse disregarded this rule and took the children to the docks, a rough sailor grabbed the daughter and disappeared with her. According to Bigmother's story, his ship must have sailed immediately, for she was never heard from in Ireland again. According to the family legend, when the ship landed in Virginia, the sailor was accosted by a Virginia gentleman who must have noticed the child's beautiful but bedraggled clothing and blonde hair. He ransomed the child with no questions asked and reared her as his own daughter. Bigmother told us, 'Years later, Lord Dunbar was able to make contact with the man who had reared his daughter and sent his now-grown son to America to bring her home. The story has it that the boy was lost at sea in a shipwreck on his way west. His sister would never leave the only home she ever really knew.'

"Over the years, this girl's descendants might have followed the Scottish migration pattern, south through the Appalachian valleys and into Alabama. Bigmother's people had made their home in northern Alabama for a few generations before her birth in Florence. She told me that her own mother knew an ancestor who remembered an earlier kinswoman who had personally seen this Colonial matron, the little girl from Ireland and first progenitor of the family that produced Bigmother. That knowledgeable forebear described the little kidnapped girl as a regal matron, elegant and wise.

"I would love to think I might research the genealogy that would bring the little kidnapped child a sort of second life, but if I am not able to do this, perhaps someone in our family will do it in my stead."

Still rolling down the highway with great confidence, Mary said, "You told me that at the time your parents moved to Louisville, they were barely settled when most of Louisville went under water because of the great flood of 1937."

"That's true. Ohio River waters were so deep in the downtown area it flooded the first floor of the L&N Railroad headquarters building. The officials located a boat and rowed in through the big front door to get to the upstairs offices and bring order out of the chaos created by the flood.

"Meanwhile, my dad told me that Gran-gran, who prided herself in being a good cook, was in their apartment on higher ground, preparing greens and cornbread for dozens of refugees whose homes had been washed away. Flood victims were being housed in the garage on the first level of the building where my parents were living. Soup kitchens had not been set up yet, and Mother could not stand seeing the dispossessed hungry. She used fresh vegetables that Dad grew in his garden near our home. Later, after World War II broke out, when they had a bigger yard, he was able to keep the whole neighborhood in fresh food. [Image 10.1]

"Whenever Mother had 'help,' she insisted on doing most of the cooking herself, because she liked her own cooking better than anyone else's and demonstrated her love for everyone through her cooking. Want to hear a funny story about my mother's particular choices about food?"

"Sure."

"Food displayed in open containers at the local stores was forbidden to us. She would not buy it nor allow us to do so. It had to be packaged. But while traveling on the train through El Paso, for some reason in this new territory the old rules didn't hold, and she did not hesitate to buy tamales from local vendors handing them through the open windows of the train. When we returned home from that railroad trip, Mother was inspired to teach herself how to make fresh tamales, a brave undertaking for someone who didn't have a Mexican cook for miles around to show her how.

"My parents had a wonderful life in Louisville after the flood. They built the home in which they hoped to spend the rest of their years and enjoyed the many new friends they made there. Most often they saw the Terrys, because there was so much to share from their mutual days back in Birmingham when both couples were young. Mother said Charlie Terry was so well liked in their crowd that he was best man in at least a dozen weddings.

"Mother loves to tell of the time Charlie Terry was entertaining a business acquaintance from the North. Charlie told Mother, 'You know, that fella started talking *business* before we finished our first martini!'

"Fate had smiled on the Terry family, but Montez, Charlie's wife, harbored one worry. Charlie was a social drinker. He was so gregarious, Montez worried that drinking might get out of hand, threatening his health and maybe their future. So she put her foot down. Charlie, with disarming charm, slipped out from under that pressure from time to time. One such episode is worth sharing."

"Please do. Sounds entertaining."

"There was a big affair at the Paducah Country Club. It might have been a wedding the Terrys attended with another couple ... I don't remember those particular details. While the ladies were powdering their noses, Charlie and his companion slipped away to the cocktail bar. Imbibing a second drink there, Charlie discovered he was next to an old acquaintance, the writer and great Southern humorist, Irvin S. Cobb. As he greeted Cobb, he saw Montez approaching the bar from the other side of the room. Her head was held high and her gait determined. He knew he was in trouble. He set down his glass, gently touched Cobb's elbow, and guided him firmly toward Montez. Using verbal deflection tactics, Charlie said, 'Mr. Cobb, I would like you to know my wife, Montez. *You* have always been a particular favorite of hers.' Bowing slightly, Cobb replied, 'Mrs. Terry, I share your weakness.' Being thrust into being a fan, what could she say after that to either of those conversation-stoppers?"

"A good lesson in how to divert oncoming criticism with a good offense," quipped Mary.

I continued elucidating more family history for her. "When Mother lost her own mother, she was a teenager, only fourteen years old. Her older sister, Harriet, and her husband, Brooks Forbes, opened their home and their hearts to my mother. Their own two children

175

received gifts on Christmas; their adopted daughter was treated with equal love. [Image 10.2]

"Mother always took great pride in Uncle Forbes, the man who treated her like a daughter. She was especially intrigued with one of the stories of Brooks Forbes' Virginia ancestors listed on the chart he displayed proudly in their home ... one of the Knights of the Golden Horseshoe."

"Mams, how does it happen that I've never heard of these Knights before?"

"It's a little known episode in the history of early colonial expansion. Listed among the members on the chart was Governor Robert Brooke, one of fifty members of a special expedition led by Colonial Governor Spotswood ... I think of the Colony of Virginia ... to explore the unknown land of the Appalachian Mountains in order to claim new lands in the name of King George I. It is said that after crossing the Blue Ridge Mountains into the Valley of Virginia, they buried a bottle on the banks of a river, inside which they had put a paper whereby Spotswood claimed the place in the name of George I. Upon returning home, each member of the expedition was given a golden horseshoe pin by the governor, studded with jewels in honor of their successful journey. It's funny that none of the original gold pins have been found to date."

Mary grinned, teasing me. "Those *were* the good old days."

My mood became serious and I said to Mary, "You know, those good old days lasted through World War II. History books record the grim details of battles but seldom mention that a warm spirit filled our land even through wartime. People were kind and helped one another ... not only family and friends but also total strangers. This made life tolerable in those difficult years of depression and war.

"When your father was beginning his naval communications training as a Lieutenant Junior Grade at Harvard, I left Lucy with Gran-gran and traveled from Ohio to meet him in Manhattan, as his next assignment was to be shipped out to the Pacific. The taxi driver who took us to dinner refused to accept the fare. Your dad insisted. But glancing at Bob's uniform, he replied, 'There will be no charge. I have a son in the Pacific.'"

"Sure doesn't sound like Vietnam, does it?" Mary exclaimed.

"Another form of wartime good sportsmanship comes to mind. The gasoline coupons that were issued were inadequate, so neighbors carpooled to work, to the grocery store, and wherever necessary, with no questions asked."

I was on a roll thinking about the many small "heroisms" at home during wartime.

"Your grandfather was fifty when Japanese planes destroyed our Navy in Pearl Harbor, along with our irresolution about getting involved in that war. Of course, because of age, he would not be drafted. His railroad work, however, made him essential to our effort here at home. Most Americans were unaware that German U-boats lurked in the Gulf of Mexico off the port of New Orleans, making shipping of arms erratic. Much-needed supplies for our troops and our allies piled up in the rail yards and on the docks in New Orleans. A gridlock brought shipping to a virtual halt. My father was the person from among all the rail executives chosen to undo this gridlock. With his penchant for memorizing long rail car serial numbers and his sense of the larger system, he succeeded, and shipping resumed.

"Toward the end of the war, one of the L&N freight agents presented him with another problem. The U.S. Army wanted to make shipments to Huntsville, Alabama, but had failed to note on the bills of lading what the contents of the shipments were. Dad made a call to the Pentagon, saying it was illegal for the railroad to accept a shipment without knowing what was being shipped. The next day two strangers appeared in my father's office and flashed their identification cards. They were FBI agents. Their message to him was, 'Mr. Wade, don't ask!' But he remained curious down to his final illness. Dad repeatedly said, 'I wonder what they are *doing* in Huntsville.'

He didn't live long enough to learn that components of the first atomic bomb were being assembled there."

When Mary and I arrived in Waynesville, we had been so confident that replacing both the carburetor and the fuel pump had solved everything that when the engine became rough yet again, as we drew near Tulsa, our spirits took a nosedive. By 3:15 p.m. the engine faltered once more, and we limped into Tulsa just before it cut out completely at about 27,400 miles.

Mary and I hobbled into Bob and Larry's Skelly Station to fill the gas tank and ask for a recommendation for a close-by motel where we might spend the night. We crept into the nearest one and, outside the office, we sat limp in Betsy—waiting for our emotional fog to lift. They had a room for us and we registered. This was the first time we truly doubted the wisdom of continuing our journey.

We reviewed Bob's parting words when Mary turned on the ignition, "Dump the car and come home if you do not like what you are doing."

The night before in Waynesville, when we checked in with Bob by phone, he'd told me that he could be reached the following night at the vacation home of a very nice person with whom he worked in Washington. Bob said to write down her telephone number because her house was on the eastern shore of Maryland, some distance from D.C.

I knew she was a recent widow who had lost a husband quite young and Bob was a compassionate person for anyone in need of support. It was good of him to send her telephone number. Once we got into our room, I decided I would call him. I had to contact him. Although he was dining with *another* woman who needed sympathy, I knew she was not the *only* one needing sympathy. *I am his wife and need moral support and guidance*, I thought. Knowing it was little of me to be jealous I still couldn't help feeling low.

And when I spoke to him, he told me again, "Jettison the car and come on home if you want." Like Scarlett O'Hara, I decided to think about it tomorrow.

Mary and I purchased vodka and tomato juice, returned to the motel, and drowned our sorrow in not one but two Bloody Marys. When I was floating into blissful sleep, Mary aroused me.

"Mams, I have been lying here thinking about that character Dad knew in the hospital in Charlottesville who was more deeply involved in alcohol than we are tonight."

"Mary, you were only five years old then," I groaned.

"But Dad told me that moonshiner's story later when I was old enough to understand. Tonight we just put a toe in the water. That character had been a bootlegger in the mountains of West Virginia. He confided in Dad that on one occasion he had been transporting a cargo of moonshine so heavy that the rear of his car was riding real low. 'That caught the eye of a highway patrol officer who pulled me over,' he said. 'The officer leaned in with his elbow on my open window. I was caught red-handed and didn't know what I was in for, so I says to him, "I've got a mother in heaven, a father in hell, and a sweetheart in Bluefield. Which one am I going to see tonight?"'"

And how was it going to turn out for us and Betsy? We chuckled and sleep came easily for both of us that night.

10.1 Ginny's father, Albert Thompson Wade, August 24, 1890-November 21, 1944

10.2 Ginny's mother (Grangran), Pearl Mae Guscott (Wade) as a young woman, 1892-1981

CHAPTER 11

Wednesday, October 21, 1970
Odometer at Tulsa: 27,456

Tulsa, Oklahoma, to San Jon,
New Mexico
Trip meter at Tulsa: 1,456

A Day of Decision – Heroic Hearts

Iron Star support ornament from Birmingham railroad
station, silkscreen on fabric by Virginia Ames

The next morning we drove into a Gulf station on Yale Street in Tulsa, where a perceptive mechanic named Daniel Vann replaced the vacuum tube. Then he suggested a radical idea. "Let's use the air pressure hose to blow the fuel line *backwards.*" He said that he didn't know why, but this had been known to work for up to 500 miles. This clever man's idea filled us with hope once again. We also knew we still had three or four days' margin of error before Mary had to return to her job.

"Let's go for it," Mary decided.

Though much is taken, much abides; and though
We are not now that strength which in the old days
Moved earth and heaven; that which we are, we are,
One equal-temper of heroic hearts,
Made weak by time and fate, but strong in will
To strive, to seek, to find and not to yield.

(*Ulysses*, Alfred Lord Tennyson)

Heading southwest on Route 44 toward Oklahoma City, we passed myriad campaign signs dotting the roadside. *Dewey Bartlett is Governor of Oklahoma and Colonel Sanders is even better known.* Other signs boasted *Democrat David Hall, Tulsa County District Attorney and former law professor.*

"Mary, how difficult it must be to win an election. Mother told me that when he was quite young, Hugo Black, later a Supreme Court Justice, had to accept the support of the Ku Klux Klan in order to be elected to his first public job in Birmingham, Alabama. Years later, when he was nominated for Justice on the Supreme Court, he made this statement, 'I was a member of the Klan. I am no longer a member of the Klan. I do not agree with their ideology and, furthermore, this is the last statement I will make on this subject.'"

"Mom, didn't you know him?"

"Only for one delightful evening. The Honorable Hugo Black sat next to me at a dinner at the Army Navy Country Club, which is across the Potomac from Washington in Virginia. Our hosts were a Navy couple with no legal interests in common with Judge Black. The wife had become his friend while they were enjoying games of tennis together.

"Early on I had wondered why our hostess had selected your dad and me for this intimate gathering. Your dad had little connection with the legal or political community. He was in publishing and advertising, and few of his clients were in law or government.

"My friend told me she wanted us there because she thought Justice Black and I might have mutual interests. He and I had Alabama in common. Birmingham was hometown for both of us.

"Prior to the dinner, Dad and I familiarized ourselves with Justice Black's decisions during his tenure on the court. Almost all of the Warren Court's civil rights decisions during Black's tenure unanimously favored civil rights. Therefore, anti-integration groups in Birmingham and elsewhere may have considered Justice Black a traitor to the Southern cause.

"We found that Black's important dissenting opinion in the 1949 decision, *Adamson v. California,* was his most unique contribution to the court. Prior to this decision it was clearly understood that the Bill of Rights restricted only the federal government's legislation, leaving the states to pass whatever laws they pleased. In his opinion, Justice Black said that the Bill of Rights was 'incorporated' into the Fourteenth Amendment that guaranteed rights, privileges, and immunities of citizenship, due process and equal protection, specifically limiting state governments in certain ways. This interpretation, the Incorporation Doctrine, is now standard. A precedent was set by his dissenting opinion and affected all subsequent Supreme Court decisions.

"Justice Black arrived at the dinner party with his new and relatively young wife and they seemed very compatible. She laughingly said that their marriage had set off a series of May-to-December unions in Washington, including that of Justice William O. Douglas to a very young bride. The Blacks were an attractive couple and spoke of their recently purchased home in Old Town Alexandria.

"Black was concerned that nearby neighbors believed having a Supreme Court Justice who owned a home in the area would increase the value of all property and raise taxes for everybody. Why, he wondered, would ownership of land by a Justice of the Supreme Court have any effect on real estate values? His sincerity and lack of arrogance was charming, and I felt comfortable in his company, but when our mutual background was mentioned, instead of inspiring sparkling conversation, he became withdrawn and silent, and the festive mood faded as quickly as brightness does when a cloud rolls in front of the sun.

"We had been naïve not to be sensitive to the effect Justice Black's liberal civil rights decisions had had on his private life. By some, he was considered a hero, by many others, too liberal, even radical. When he returned home to Birmingham, it is said that he was reviled by the racist element in town and snubbed even by conservative friends who had put him into his first political office. I knew immediately that my challenge was to put him at ease as soon as possible ... to let him know as subtly as I could that I was not one of his detractors. At that moment, I was grateful for my Alabama parents who taught me tact and for the Black nurse who taught me good manners.

"I talked to him about my mother's older sister, Harriet Forbes. Did he remember her? She was a good friend of his first wife, Josephine Foster Black. He did. We talked of Vulcan, the giant sculpture that stands atop Red Mountain, symbol of the steel industry that made Birmingham wealthy, beautiful, and sometimes brutally tough. He knew the sculpture was created to represent Birmingham at the World's Fair in Chicago in the 1890s. I told him that when city water came to Birmingham, my grandmother suggested they put the old mold from Vulcan in her well, as she no longer needed her well. He was interested to learn how they disposed of the mold in which Vulcan had been cast, and the more we talked of 'old times,' the more relaxed he became.

"The band was playing a waltz and he asked me to dance. This interesting man, who served both his country and a tennis ball with equal skill at eighty years of age, whisked me around the dance floor with the grace of a young athlete.

"As Dad and I learned more and more about Hugo Black's career as a jurist, we felt fortunate to have shared one brief evening with this very humane man."

Outside Oklahoma City, Betsy took us past the Western Electric Plant that looked big enough to be one giant high school for the whole of Oklahoma. We were still in Oklahoma at 27,583 miles as we passed through Watonga, whose annual cheese festival we'd missed by a week. At the first opportunity, we pulled off the road at a Standard station by a Cherokee trading post, where a turquoise-bejeweled attendant adjusted the carburetor to the tune of $2.00.

Low blue hills loomed for the last forty miles of Oklahoma as we headed toward Amarillo and the Texas Panhandle. At 27,666 miles, everything remained okay and Betsy hummed on. We talked of spending the night somewhere in New Mexico on the way to visit Muffin in Tucson, Arizona. We knew we were in Texas when congressional campaign signs appeared on the horizon saying *Bush Can Do More*. Near them was a sign for Democrat Lloyd Bentsen, who was vying for a seat in the Senate.

"Hurray, we made it over the New Mexico border!" It was 8:00 p.m. Central Time. An hour later, we pulled into the M Motel in San Jon and discovered it was still only 8:00 p.m.—Mountain Time. We played the jukebox over dinner at the San Jon Café. *Everything is beau ... tiful ... in its own waaay ...* We tried calling Muffin to talk about whether we might have time to make the detour to Tucson and then called Bob. Neither was in and we collapsed into bed.

CHAPTER 12

Thursday, October 22, 1970
Odometer at San Jon: 27,956

San Jon, New Mexico,
to Grants, New Mexico
Trip meter at San Jon: 1,956

As Others See Us

Mary in a tree, seeing through the camera lens

We returned to the San Jon Café for breakfast where everyone was either Spanish-American, Native American, or both. While we were eating, a big old touring car, crammed with what appeared to be household possessions, pulled into a space. Out spilled five bedraggled, unkempt people—a mother, father, baby, and two other adults. They sat down at a table next to us. The baby's dirty face was covered with emerging sores, and the whole group reminded us of Okies, the name given to desperate migrants heading to the "promised land" of California from Oklahoma and the plains in the 1930s, when drought and dust storms ruined their farms and livelihood. The sight of them brought a discouraging pall over us that we struggled to overcome.

Then, as if that were not enough, at 27,984 miles the odometer cable broke. We stopped at a Chevrolet repair garage, where the mechanic sounded just like Tonto, the Lone Ranger's sidekick. "Tonto" greeted us and said he thought our car was worth $1,500. We agreed and said we had the *bills* to prove it! While he was solving the cable problem, we asked him also to blow the fuel line backwards with a pressure hose—just in case. It had been close to 500 miles since Daniel Vann first exercised this solution. Tonto scratched his head, looked up at us, and asked, "Are you sure?" But he did it.

Soon after, we were back on the road again, Betsy sailing smoothly. I saw a sign indicating a right-hand turn north to Santa Fe.

"I would really like you to see Santa Fe, Mary. It is as fascinating a town as it must have been when it was the important outpost of New Spain, the name the Spanish gave Colonial Mexico. Shall we take a detour to the north and eat lunch there?"

With a wry grin, knowing this spontaneity might change our path significantly, as in Frost's poem "The Road Not Taken," Mary responded, "Maybe we can eat at the old La Fonda Hotel you've been talking about all my life."

At the Vaughn exit, we turned north onto Route 285. I was driving now on a rounded gravel road at 55 mph when we heard a loud explosion, a blowout on the right front tire. The car lurched to the right. Our Wayfarer predated power steering, so I had to use all my strength to keep it from veering into the ditch to our right. After what seemed an eternity, we came to a stop, still on the road. Odometer reading 28,079. Still some miles from Santa Fe, we sat quite still for several moments. For the first time, Mary and I were faced with the challenge of changing a tire on this heavy car. But before we could get the tools out, a sleek new Buick drove up behind us and stopped. Out stepped a military officer in a neatly pressed uniform, smiling and ready to help change the tire. He introduced himself, a colonel stationed at Cannon Air Force Base near Clovis.

His wife and two teenaged boys, who surely were his sons, remained in the car while he quietly went to work. In no time at all,
the stranger was done. He wiped his hands on a clean white hand-
kerchief. With curiosity he did not try to hide, he asked our destination. He could not place us. Why would a pretty young girl with an
educated voice and a middle-aged mother wearing a tailored suit be
driving this old automobile to Seattle? And by way of *here*?

Sincerely grateful, I offered him a jar of our homemade chutney
I'd intended as a gift for the Copasses in Seattle. He hesitated too
long and then thanked me profusely. Maybe he wondered in what
kind of kitchen our gift had been made. He obviously could not figure
us out, and I somehow felt sorry for him. He hopped into his car,
stepped on the gas, and waved goodbye while his wife and sons continued to ignore us.

I sighed, "You know his wife will *never* open my precious homemade chutney." We burst out laughing. I thought of a passage from
Robert Burns, my favorite poet in high school days, and quoted him
for Mary.

> O, wad some Power the giftie gie us
> To see oursels as others see us!
> (Robert Burns, "To a Louse")

A few billowy white clouds hung in the blue sky above the mountains ahead. Each cloud dropped its shadow, like a purple silk scarf
that drapes itself over the folds of the mountains below. We were
transfixed by the clouds and their shadows, by their color and shapes.
Mary asked to stop in order to capture on film this moment we might
never experience again.

Pulling back onto the highway, I told Mary of a similar experience Muffin and I had had while driving across Monument Valley in
northern Arizona. There were pullouts along the way for visitors to
contemplate the towering monoliths scattered throughout Monument

Valley. Muffin, knowledgeable about geology, explained how eons ago this area, now a vast valley, had been as high as the tallest rock formation. Erosion over the millennia had carried this overburden away, but some of the harder rocks resisted erosion and still stand today, towers of varied shapes but all sharing the same rock strata.

"The colors of the distinct layers were a variety of rose and yellow hues, beautiful in the bright light of the lowering sun. Noticeable was a very thick streak ... vertical, flat, and smooth ... stained with desert varnish, a thin coating created over time by the chemicals in the rock and rainwaters. We were enjoying the scene when I was startled to realize that the slick streaks that appeared down every rock formation in the valley had suddenly turned blue, a rich reflective blue. Muffin saw this phenomenon also. Surprised, we tried to figure how and why. While we were speculating on its probable cause the blue disappeared as quickly as it had appeared. Had the setting sun cast a desert shadow? 'Muffin, since we are watercolorists we have learned much about color, but what we have just seen makes me want to know more about the nature of color and the effect of light hitting something or passing through it.' She commented that many people do not see ... really *see* ... color. It is a trick of physics and light waves.

"Mary, you have been very quiet for a while ... a penny for your thoughts."

"I was just thinking about art and color, inspired by the marketing of the Coca Cola Company. A friend of Dad's who handles the Coca Cola advertising account once told him that wherever the name Coca Cola appears ... and it is everywhere ... always red. Someone in the advertising agency thought this logo would have a greater impact if Coke's reds were as similar as science could make them. They must have spent a fortune developing red paint for metal surfaces and printing inks to be used on paper."

"That's fascinating in itself. But how does that square with Muff's thought that some among us can't really see color very well?"

"Some clever art teacher used Coca Cola's red to test each student's skill in color perception. The assignment was for all students in the class to spend one week locating and studying as many of the company's logos as they could. The following week when they entered the classroom, they saw on the board a dozen identical squares, each painted with a different red. Only one card was painted with the Coke red. When the tally was made, only three or four students recognized the Coke logo red accurately."

"Maybe that art teacher learned as much about her students' ability to remember a color *later* as it did about color recognition. Something your dad and I experienced while visiting old friends on the eastern shore of Virginia best illustrates Muff's idea that some 'people often don't see, really *see*, color.' We were visiting old friends Charlie and Essie Wessels in the little town of Oyster. They took us sightseeing in the lowland near the Chesapeake Bay shore. I saw a spot that might turn out to be a quaint subject for a painting, and I asked them to stop the car to capture it on film. A fishing boat was abandoned upside down among the weeds next to a deserted wooden building that Essie told me had been once used for processing seafood. At one time the building must have had many coats of white paint. Now the old structure was stained with drips of color like a contemporary painting. There was soft red oxide from rusting nails, black streaks from molding leaves and other debris caught in the sagging V in the metal roof, and soft greens, perhaps from the old copper flashing around the chimney. When I shared these musings with Essie she said, 'Funny, I always thought this old building was white.' Almost everyone might have said the same, but I could see multiple colors vividly.

"Mary, I had another color experience when I went to visit Lucy and Michael in Seattle. It was a crystal clear day as I flew across the United States. Somewhere in the Midwest I could see the farms below with their different colored fields and shapes. What I really saw was the possibility of an abstract painting. I had my forehead pressed against the window while I made colored sketches of green and yellow fields below, with big circles and rectangles and squiggly irrigation patterns that zigzagged across multiple crops. In my artsy fog, I became conscious of a couple in the seats behind me who were having a gay ol' time with cocktails. At one point, the gentleman tapped me on the head and said, 'I think you're seeing something we're not seeing.' I laughed and replied, 'I think that is quite possible.'"

Fresh dry air of New Mexico blew through our hair, further crisping our sense of sight, and our spirits. We were approaching Santa Fe. When we arrived in that charming old town, we found a tight parking space for tank-sized Betsy, chose a Mexican restaurant, The Shed, and had a delicious lunch. Over our green chili burritos, I reminisced about my first visit to New Mexico as a member of the debate team from the University of Cincinnati.

"I was reared, like many Southern girls, Mary, by a mother who believed that it was prudent to defer to a male, particularly to his intellect. 'Men are very sensitive if a female appears smarter than they are.' I just couldn't buy that. When I got to college and an English professor said, 'I want you on the debate team and I want you on the Speaker's Bureau of the University,' I knew I wanted to do those two things even if I never had another date and no man ever married me! I sincerely considered that could be the likely outcome. The debate team turned out to be one of the most transforming experiences of my life.

"Let me put this experience in perspective for you, Mary. It was 1935. Professor Postle proposed an ambitious plan for the women's debate team: to challenge other teams on a grand tour of the West. The effects of the Great Depression, which began with the stock market crash in 1929, lingered for a decade. Budgets were tight, and the University was no exception. We, the two women who were selected for this tour, had access to railroad passes, as did my mother, who was to be our chaperone. We traveled by train to Denver, then Salt

Lake City, Los Angeles, and finally Albuquerque, New Mexico. We debated in the daytime at the convocations of various schools. In the evenings, the universities provided us with dates. In Salt Lake, a young man tried to convert me. Although he was charming, I remained true to my own church. In Los Angeles, I was amazed when a tall, handsome, brawny football player appeared at my door. After an evening of dancing, he promised to see us off the next day. When he arrived, he confessed that his mother had said, 'You have a second date with a *debater*? I can't believe it.'

"In New Mexico, we were met at the railroad station by a professor who pointed out a striking middle-aged Indian. He was finely dressed with stylish slacks and a Pendleton blanket around his shoulders. The professor said, 'Remember that man. He is Tony Luhan, married to Mabel Dodge, the woman who dictates the social life of Santa Fe and Taos.' When I returned to Cincinnati, I looked up the Luhans and I learned that she had enough wealth to be the social arbiter in that growing community of fine artists. Not surprising, there was gossip that Dodge locked horns with another strong woman who came to live and paint in that area, Georgia O'Keeffe.

"Your dad tells me he fell in love with me in 1934 because of the *very* thing that I feared would prevent such a relationship. He had been deeply impressed by my debating. One of the first gifts he ever gave me was a fine fountain pen that he mailed to me in Albuquerque during that debate tour.

"Right after we returned from this debate tour, I was surprised to learn that my father had been transferred from Cincinnati to the main L&N office in Louisville because he had been made an executive, which left me, in my senior year, without a home and family in Cincinnati. Luckily, my sister invited me to live with her and her new husband in their generous-sized apartment, which allowed me to have my own room, until I graduated and married your dad in 1936. When we decided to be married where all our friends were ... in

Cincinnati ... Mother agreed, even though she and Dad would have to travel back there to attend the wedding.

"A funny story about our wedding day happened when all of the bridesmaids, my mother, and I had gathered at my sister's apartment for the final primping before the ceremony. There was a knock on the door. The woman who was doing our hair answered the door and exclaimed, 'The groom can't come in here! You can't see the bride until she walks down the aisle!' Somebody said, 'That's not the groom, that's the bride's *father*!' The hairdresser then responded with, 'My God, I'd marry *that* man myself!'

"Later, in the candlelight of the church, turning onto the aisle on my father's arm, I was rigid with tension. Dad leaned over and whispered, 'How am *I* doing?' which kindly diverted and helped me to relax and regain my composure."

After lunch, sniffing cedar wood smoke in the air, Mary and I took a whirlwind walking tour through the adobe pueblo of Santa Fe, visiting several art galleries, artists' studios on Canyon Road, the La Fonda Hotel, and the Cathedral of St. Francis of Assisi, founded in 1610 and made famous by Willa Cather's book *Death Comes for the Archbishop*. On leaving town, we stopped to talk with an Indian girl displaying her crafts. "I go to school with mostly Spanish, Anglos, Negroes, and hippies, but very few Indians," she confided. "But I go there because it is close. Everybody loves my leather headbands. All the teenagers in the village buy my headbands."

We asked her how long it would take us to drive to Grants.

"Well, that depends. Indians estimate it takes an hour to go the 108 miles; three hours to Gallup, which is 172 miles; and three days to Flagstaff, 350 miles." She added, "Truth is, Indians start off at 100 miles an hour and actually end up going 100 miles a day." We thanked this friendly girl and headed southwest to join Route 66 at Grants, elevation 6,466 feet, not knowing how long it might take Betsy.

It was cold and raining, so we stopped and bedded down early at the San Franciscan Motel in Grants, a typical southwestern adobe building. The manager told us it was snowing in Gallup, sixty-five miles ahead.

"We've had good luck with the car, but I am afraid we're running out of time."

"I was thinking the same thing. Let's call Muff first thing in the morning to tell her the bad news and how disappointed we are to not see her on this trip."

Ginny at the wheel of Betsy–off across the desert!

CHAPTER 13

Friday, October 23, 1970
Odometer at Grants: 28,381

Grants, New Mexico, to Grand
Canyon (south rim, Bright
Angel Overlook), Arizona
Trip meter at Grants: 2,381

The Harvey Girls and the Santa Fe Railroad

Still no answer when we called Muff's apartment in Tucson. We knew we'd have to let her know our change of plans soon.

We selected the Carpenters' "We've Only Just Begun" on the jukebox while eating breakfast at the motel's restaurant, thinking it fitting. As we waited in line to pay our bill, we noticed a sign by the register. It read, "Now, at reduced prices, large selection of deer horns." Mary remembered the disappointment she felt when she was fifteen and we discouraged her from buying deer antlers on a family tour of the West. There was no room in the car, and we would have had to tie them on the roof, an option her father would not consider.

197

"I have managed very nicely without any deer antlers," she concluded.

Whenever the opportunity presented itself, we traveled on the outdated, poorly maintained vestiges of U.S. Highway 66, the original East-West national highway from Chicago to Los Angeles. Since its completion in the 1930s, Route 66 had been the *road to opportunity* for truckers, escapees from the Dust Bowl, and many others. By now, almost the entire original road that connected the main streets of rural and urban communities along its course had been replaced by the modern four-lane Interstate 40.

Soon after crossing the border into Arizona we found ourselves in a kind of "Never-Never Land." Sandstone mesas and rills stretched out on all sides. Mary held an open map of Arizona in her hands as I drove and was scanning the barren land to the horizon in every direction.

"I see the map says those spires to the northwest are the Hopi Buttes. I wonder how they came to be. I wish Muff were here to tell us what they represent. With her geology studies at Brown and her penchant for interpreting the landscape, she could make the history of these landforms come alive. See those tiny blue bumps on the horizon way ahead on this flat plateau? Those are the volcanic San Francisco Peaks at Flagstaff, where Muff first plunged into exploring the Southwest. It was her enthusiasm for this Colorado Plateau Country that whetted our appetites for driving this route."

I was surprised to find that the path of the Little Colorado River we were crossing on its way to join the Big Colorado beyond Cameron began as snowmelt in the White Mountains of Arizona to the south of us. As we continued west, the sandstone landscape became flat and treeless. We were delighted to see a gateway into the Petrified Forest National Park. We looked at each other and knew without a word that we had to explore it by taking the time for a short hike within the park, as we had heard that it features one of the world's largest and most colorful concentrations of petrified wood.

Interpretive signs in the Visitor Center gave us a rich view of the past in this very place. The park had not always been here. Prior to the late Triassic period, when all the continents were one and had not yet drifted apart, this section of Arizona was located in the area of the equator. A dense forest grew here and rivers flowed everywhere. Then, ashes from distant volcanoes were carried by prevailing winds and deposited in river sediment. Fallen trees were submerged in the rivers. Before they could decompose, the groundwater-dissolved silica from the ash replaced every cell and cell wall in these logs, one by one. Once the dissolved silica finally crystallized, it reproduced the log in stone. Now oxidized minerals stained the glassy silica in brilliant oxide colors. Buried by time, this land—called the Chinle Formation—was covered and later exposed. And now, the logs we were looking at sparkled with color like a stained-glass church window.

At the trailhead, a park service map greeted us, showing all hiking options, plus suggestions to wear sunscreen and carry drinking water. At the bottom, the sign read, "If you should be so fortunate as to see a rattlesnake, please report it to the ranger."

"Are they kidding?" Mary said. "If I see a rattlesnake, I'm headed straight back to the car! No hunting around out here for a park ranger."

She wasn't scared—not the easily frightened type—but she was only half joking. Neither of us was familiar with western wildlife. We knew that harmless garter snakes might skitter across our path on our hikes back East, and we knew not to turn over logs or old tires without first checking for poisonous copperheads. But a deadly snake right in the path?

"They say a rattlesnake will warn you before it strikes," I offered.

"Yeah. They also say snakes travel in twos. I'm not skirting around one rattler just to bump into its mate."

An hour later we finished our short hike, feeling fortunate not to have encountered any snakes. Before we got into the car we noticed another instructive sign—this one directing us to look northwest toward the distant Hopi Buttes, which at that hour stood silhouetted purple in the afternoon sun. Mary draped herself across the hood of the old Wayfarer, breasts facing toward the heavens, and said, "Mom, take a picture of the Hopi Buttes." [Images 13.1, 13.2]

On we drove, westward into the vastness of the Painted Desert that covers much of northeastern Arizona. The flatland of the Chinle Formation was now covered by endless mounds, each revealing the layers of pastel sands and silts. This triggered a memory in Mary from a natural history class, and she volunteered, "This landscape has got to be two hundred million years old! Just to put time in perspective, over the next hundred and forty-five million years, different dinosaurs evolved and then disappeared forever. That was some sixty-five million years before today."

Mary continued her lecture, "If dinosaurs hadn't perished, humans might never have evolved. When dinosaurs no longer tromped over the earth, little insect-eating mammals came out of their hiding places, fed freely, and had a chance to flourish. From those little bright-eyed creatures, scientists believe that primates evolved over eons, including us. Ta-dah! Homo sapiens!"

By late afternoon, Mary and I arrived in Winslow, Arizona, where we peeled off the freeway onto a stretch of old Route 66. We found a pay phone in the middle of town and were able to reach Muff at last and let her know that time constraints and car uncertainty were dictating that we head north soon, instead of south to visit her.

With that done, we stopped to look at La Posada Hotel, a masterpiece of architecture by designer Mary Elizabeth Jane Colter, built in 1929 by the Santa Fe Railroad to serve its passengers, and now in a state of neglect. The Santa Fe also built most of the significant structures on the South Rim of the Grand Canyon and had hired Mary Colter to design most of them.

The Fred Harvey Company managed many of the Santa Fe Railroad's restaurants before dining cars were available on trains. His company was famous for the consistency and quality of both food and service. Harvey began using waitresses—the famous "Harvey Girls"—in 1883. These young women were well trained, smartly dressed, and very strictly chaperoned.

"I should tell you, Mary, about how, prior to the construction of La Posada, our family experienced the good food at a Harvey House, probably here in Winslow, when we went west by rail in 1919. I was almost five at the time. Before the train would arrive at a restaurant stop, a conductor walked through the cars counting the passengers who wished to eat at the next Harvey House. He'd telegraph ahead, and the food would be ready when we got there. When I ate those meals, little me was always terrified that the train would leave without us. Of course, it never did."

After we looked at the interesting old hotel architecture of La Posada, Mary and I cruised slowly through Winslow, the town the Santa Fe Railroad built in the 1880s. Until the 1920s, it was the largest town in northern Arizona. Somehow Betsy seemed right at home on this old stretch of Route 66. "We really know we are in the West now ... there are Indians on the city streets," Mary said. [Note 18 – La Posada]

Continuing west toward the blue peaks in the distance, up from the Painted Desert and Little Colorado River Valley and anticipating being next in Flagstaff, we were reminded of what Muff had told us about her experiences there.

I reminisced, "When Mother and I came out to see Muff in Flagstaff after her graduation in the summer of '67, while she was working at the Museum of Northern Arizona, I remember she took the wheel of our low-slung Ford Galaxy and drove us right off the highway and across the sandy desert to see an archaeological site where she had been digging with the research team. We just don't do things like that back East."

Mary was pensive about how Muff came to the Southwest. "I think the people she has met out here, the natural history, the research digs she's been on, and the Native culture she's absorbed here have surely changed her life. She is so excited about this tree-ring dating ... this dendrochronology thing."

"Mary, she told me that's the science of determining the age of ancient ruins by comparing the width of the growth rings in a building's wooden beams against an established chronological pattern ... and to push that established chronology ever farther back in time with the discovery of older logs and trees." I continued, "Did you know the science of dendrochronology actually started in Flagstaff by an astronomer at Lowell Observatory? Later, the study expanded to the Laboratory of Tree-ring Research at University of Arizona, where Muff is now deeply into her master's program in geochronology. Lord knows, she has met some amazing profs there in Tucson."

I continued on that theme, "Did you hear her tell of one of her heroes, Dr. Lawrence McKinley Gould, who taught her glacial geology? He had been second in command of the Byrd Expedition to the South Pole by dogsled in 1929 and was still teaching in 1969! As a weather-beaten old explorer, he had some vivid experiences to relate to his students. Two of Gould's friends ... Peter Kresan, another geologist/photographer, and Tad Nichols, also a professional photographer ... are friends of Muffin's too. Muff said she sure wishes you and I can meet some of these special mentors of hers someday.

"Muff has told me of two other of her heroes at U of A: Paul Martin and Ray Turner, with whom she rafted the Grand Canyon this year. It was Dr. Martin who introduced her to Arizona's amazing plants and who sponsored her on the recent *National Geographic* expedition to study ancient deposits in Stanton's Cave in Marble Gorge of Grand Canyon. That's where she excavated a condor bone in a packrat midden way back in the cave."

Mary contemplated, "Wouldn't it be neat if condors could return to Grand Canyon someday? Muff is always digging into something. This summer on a dig with her other hero, Dr. Haynes, in the San Pedro Valley of southeast Arizona, she described to me finding at that mammoth-kill site a Clovis point imbedded in the ribs of a huge extinct elephant. She uncovered a baby mammoth tooth at the bottom of an Ice Age spring where the animal had been caught in quicksand some 16,000 years ago. That was the dig where she met the character Barney Burns she talks a lot about, who is studying tree-rings and ancestral Pueblo bean crops."

Mary continued her musings about Muff. "Does she ever attend classes or is she always out in the field? Her latest letter reported another tree-ring dating field trip to the cliff dwellings of Canyon De Chelly where she met this intriguing field biologist, Tony Burgess, who was assembling a vertebrate reference collection for the archaeology team. What is this big draw of interesting scientists to Arizona? The diversity of researchers seems as varied and exciting as the landscape! Next trip we will definitely have to meet some of these scientist-personalities she's been telling us about." [Note 19 – Professors, Mentors, and Scientists]

As we climbed up the grade toward Flagstaff and San Francisco Peaks, we were relieved not to feel any complaints from Betsy. Whew! The air grew cool and we caught the sweet scent of Ponderosa pines that surround Flagstaff at 7,000 feet.

We had another decision to make. To approach Grand Canyon from Flagstaff, we had two options: go to Williams and north overland on high ground directly to the South Rim of Grand Canyon at Bright Angel Overlook or, the more interesting option, the longer route that I really wanted Mary to experience, foolhardy though it may be, to go north on Route 89 out of Flagstaff way down to Cameron (at 4,200 feet elevation), where the Little Colorado flows by on its way to join the Colorado River proper. Either route would lead us to the South Rim where we hoped to stay the night. We chose scenic Route 89 and stopped to read a sign explaining Wupatki Ruin to the east. We were lured in to see what Wupatki was all about.

Driving the loop road, we learned that the red-rock pueblos preserved at Wupatki National Monument were constructed in the years following the eruption of nearby Sunset Crater, sometime in the eleventh century. The eruption deposited volcanic ash that fertilized the soil, making it possible for Native people to build a community and thrive there. The ash, deposited in thin layers, retained moisture and improved the soil for farming by the growing population at Wupatki. Interestingly, Frank Lloyd Wright was inspired by the Wupatki dwellings and how the pink stone buildings seamlessly blended into the land—the original "organic" architecture. The Natives had included the giant boulders in the construction of their homes and used the smaller stones for the rest of the masonry on their big house, ball court, and amphitheater.

Light was fading, and we quickly got back on US 89 North. Betsy easily glided down the long slope of the road, once again into the Painted Desert. As we looked behind us, the eerie glow of the sky silhouetted the San Francisco Peaks, now a deep blue. Ahead, pink sky turned to dark violet over the Painted Desert.

I had to hold Betsy back as we continued our descent toward Cameron. Mary thought this feeling of going downhill was an illusion, brought on by darkness and rain, but she didn't realize that Flagstaff was 3,000 feet higher than Cameron.

By the time we reached Cameron, it was totally dark. I was feeling anxious about my decision to choose this lonely road. If dark had not fallen some time ago, we might have seen the Little Colorado again. I held my breath as we climbed the narrow, deserted, and torturous route up along a seeming canyon wall toward what said "Desert View" on the map. If we had car problems now, we would be in real trouble. And there would be no view for us.

We realized how tense we were when Mary gasped, "Mother, that sign says we are crossing over *Dead Indian Canyon*."

"Mary," I said. "If we are not gaining altitude now, Tuba City is sinking." She laughed as we looked down on the lights of that tiny Indian village in the distance.

Betsy still purred. We went very slowly, and she thankfully did not labor on the upgrade climb. Her tires were steady, engine cool and capable on that winding road-of-no-return-and-no-houses. As we neared the top of the Kaibab Plateau and headed into Kaibab National Forest, the largest junipers we'd ever seen loomed even larger than reality in our headlights. We sighed with relief when we spotted the tower at Desert View overlook in the darkness. A familiar landmark at last—another imposing piece of architecture designed by Mary Colter, inspired by prehistoric Puebloan towers in the Four Corners region.

Twenty-five miles later, along the South Rim, we reached Grand Canyon Village, where we hoped to find a bed for the night. Not knowing our plans in advance, and running on chance in Betsy, we had made no reservations.

El Tovar Hotel was full. As we awaited our turn at the Visitor's Center, a group of college coeds ahead of us were negotiating accommodations. The ranger took it upon himself to ask if they had a chaperone in their group. He was definitely not a man of the '60s. Their spokesperson was about to reply, "No, we do not," when a young lady piped up, "This is my brother. *He* is our chaperone." Grumbling and shaking his head, the ranger finally registered them.

"Doesn't that guy realize the world is not the way it used to be?" Mary whispered to me. Fortunate to get the last beds available in the park, we braved the cold and walked to our cabin. [Image 13.3]

13.1 View north to Hopi Buttes from Petrified
Forest National Park, Mary and Betsy

13.2 Mary on petrified log and Betsy, Petrified Forest National Park

13.3 We made it! Ginny in the Wayfarer at South Rim, Grand Canyon

Looking into giant sequoia treetops
(original sketch by MABurgess)

CHAPTER 14

October 24, 1970
Odometer at Grand Canyon: 28,981

Grand Canyon (South Rim,
Bright Angel Trail),
Arizona, to Kingman, Arizona
Trip meter at Grand Canyon:
2,981

California Dreamin'

I awoke Mary before sunrise, and we hastened to the South Rim near El Tovar. It was ridiculously early. I didn't have to dress. The temperature in the cabin was so cold that I had slept in my clothes for the first time in my life. Bundled in our jackets at the Canyon rim at Bright Angel Overlook and gripping the freezing cold guardrail, we looked into the dark abyss before the sun touched it. I was at last realizing my wish that Mary's first view of the Grand Canyon be as the rays of the rising sun torched the first peak below us, then another, and yet another.

As the sun overtook the darkness, more and more of the canyon's peaks came into view, among them Vishnu Temple and Buddha Temple, until finally the sun made a tiny mirror of the Colorado River below. As the cold wind blew up from the abyss, Mary and I found ourselves shouting with excitement. We had the world to ourselves as we shared this exceptional dawning.

The sun rose high as we explored along the rim. We were surprised to see a peace symbol painted on the brink of the precipice where only the foolhardy would dare venture. Clinging to the rock ledge nearby was a gnarled tree trimmed like a bonsai, perhaps by the stiff winds out of the canyon.

Hardy backpackers passed us on our way to visit El Tovar, the big hotel built in 1918 on the Rim for railroad tourists. We paused, meditating at the overlook to take in again the immensity of the natural wonder that a river had carved for our pleasure.

Mary broke the silence. "It's amazing that the Spanish explorers on first seeing the Canyon felt no wonder in it, only anger that it slowed their forward march." We turned toward El Tovar and passed the Hopi House, a stone structure replicating an Indian pueblo, also designed by Mary Colter as an early tourist attraction.

When Mary and I entered El Tovar, the aroma of the logs in the lobby brought back with a rush the same experience I had had in my childhood. It's amazing how your olfactory system can evoke and sharpen memory. I recalled my first view of the Canyon in 1919, when Mother had said, "Remember this, Virginia. Remember this canyon. You will probably *never* have a chance to come this far to see it again."

I reminisced aloud. "At that time, the Hopi House was an almost empty shell of a building. As a five-year-old, I had a most frightening experience there. A performance was scheduled for hotel guests that evening. Benches lined the walls, and Mother had us arrive early to get good seats. Tourists drifted in ... singles, couples, and families ... and just as Aunt Ida had taught us, Mary Lou and I politely slid down the benches to make room for them, as a result, separating us from our parents. Suddenly, loud chanting by strange male voices and drumming struck terror in my heart. A group of Indians bounded into the room, with faces painted, feathered headdresses flying as they danced. They were painfully close to us. Later, Mother said that she saw big 'crocodile tears' rolling down my cheeks.

"In 1935, when I did return to the Canyon on the University of Cincinnati debate trip, nothing much had changed ... except my perceptions. Even now in 1970, the old Kolb Brothers' photography studio still hangs on the Canyon's edge. Those brothers were really good entrepreneurs. They found a spot at the top of the trail that leads to the canyon bottom, where they set up cameras and photographed tourists on their way down. They would then hurry back to their studio, develop the pictures, and have them for sale the next day when the tourists emerged back up to the rim. Standing near El Tovar, the Hopi House still served as an example of native architecture, but now it houses a gift shop of Indian arts and crafts."

With reluctance, Mary and I bade *adieu* to Grand Canyon and headed for Seligman on the plateau to the west. On the way across flat high desert, Betsy's engine became rough for the first time since Tulsa, so we stopped in Seligman to test it and drain the oil. There, Danny wanted to sell us another fuel pump. We resisted, so, wanting to try anything, he replaced the clogged filter instead. When faced with going across yet more deserts, and remembering tire trouble on the road to Santa Fe, we also thought it provident to buy four new tires.

At a place called Grand Canyon Caverns with a Fred Harvey Restaurant, we were "served up" a big steak breakfast that Mary and I shared. Full and content, we walked to the parking lot, got back inside the car, and Mary turned the key in the ignition. The engine faltered once, then again. We tried adjusting the carburetor to make the mixture leaner. At last it turned over, warmed up, and we took off for Kingman, gliding again onto the irresistibly historic Route 66 and feeling a little aged ourselves.

"We'd better listen to the news soon. Washington could be bombed and we would not know it."

"Mams, *we* could be bombed and *Washington* wouldn't know ... That sign says land here is $100 an acre. Do you think we should go for it?"

"It may be a good deal. You never know. But it wouldn't be the first good deal that we've passed up. Did I ever tell you about your dad's wonderful idea that *The New Yorker* didn't buy?"

"No, but we do have lots of time."

"In 1935, the year the 'Lullaby of Broadway' was being played on every radio station, your dad and Uncle Harry concocted what they thought was a wonderful original idea they wanted to sell to *The New Yorker* magazine. And the four of us, Mary Lou, Harry, Bob, and I, got on the train for Broadway and the Big Apple. Harold Ross founded *The New Yorker* and was still editor when we made this trip. The magazine had a wide audience across the country but did not sell as well anywhere else as in New York. During the Great Depression, your dad had worked for a failing little magazine, *Inland Topics*, which purported to be '*The New Yorker* of Chicago.'"

"When did he ever work in Chicago?" [Images 14.1, 14.2]

"In 1934, when he graduated college in Cincinnati, the Depression was still going strong. Jobs were impossible to find, so at the beginning of 1935 your dad went to Chicago to 'seek his fortune.' He got a job working for *Inland Topics* as the sole writer. In lieu of cash, because very little real cash was circulating then, he was paid in 'due bills,' which were all that even the top companies could pay in exchange for advertising in the magazine. Without a salary, without any pocket money, the 'due bills' enabled Bob, essentially by barter, to stay at the Stevens Hotel and eat in the best restaurants. However, he often did not have the wherewithal for cigarettes to smoke after his delicious meals, and he often could not afford the dimes to take his shirts around the corner to the cheapest Chinese laundry.

"Dad stayed in Chicago for a year ... twelve issues. Each month he and the one other employee, the editor and publisher, took the finished copy to a small printing company in Cicero, at that time a sleazy suburb of Chicago. This was at a time when gangsters were having their way in Chicago and the St. Valentine's Day massacre was fresh in everyone's mind. One night after putting the magazine 'to bed,' as they said, your dad and the editor stopped into a bar for a much-needed late supper and drink. While they were waiting for their food to come, the owner of the bar slipped into a seat beside them and whispered, 'I have to get you guys out of here. My customers don't know who you are and they don't like it. Follow me and I will let you out to the back alley.' Happy to have escaped what might have been somebody like Al Capone's gang, they ran down the alley to their car.

"So, because of his experience working for *Inland Topics* in Chicago, it had crossed your dad's mind that Ross' magazine might be simultaneously published in four or five large cities and include different articles specific to *each city* in which it was printed. This would increase circulation and speed distribution. Circulation directors called potential subscribers to their magazines their 'universe.' Your dad believed that such geographically-specific issues would certainly increase *The New Yorker*'s universe.

"In New York, Harold Ross received Bob and Harry, listened to their *radical* idea, but was not persuaded it was right for him."

Mary shook her head. "I believe that system of simultaneous publishing is widely used today."

"And quite successfully, too! His 'radical idea' was mentioned later when your father received the 'Man of the Year' award in Washington, D.C., for his work in direct mail promotion. The award luncheon emcee included the story of your dad's visit to *The New Yorker* a few decades earlier. The emcee built his story of your dad's career around the fact that he revolutionized publishing when he was only in his twenties and concluded by saying, 'Today we are acknowledging who should get the credit.'

"In anticipation of that award ceremony, I was interviewed by the circulation director of *National Geographic*, who chaired the

213

awards committee. He wanted 'inside' information about Bob that would be revealed at the luncheon. He gave me a rare invitation to have lunch at the restaurant on the top floor of the prestigious headquarters of the National Geographic Society. As we walked to our table, I felt that no one looked at me, but their studied indifference told me they knew a strange female was in their midst. I felt as though I were walking through a London men's club. In those days, apparently women were not participants in the inner circle at *National Geographic*.

"My host's interest heightened when I told him of *The New Yorker* visit and Bob's idea so far ahead of its time. Your dad was surprised too, not only by the award, but also by being recognized as 'the man whose idea made a major change in the publishing industry.'"

By now, Mary and I were on the outskirts of Kingman. The lava rock beside the road was light-colored, unlike the sharp black lava that had flowed from Sunset Crater. It was defaced with paintings. The 3,280-foot elevation town of Kingman seemed new and pleasantly clean. Although it was early we decided to spend the night, grateful to find a motel of any kind. After settling in for the night, the two of us continued talking in the comfort of our room, anticipating crossing the state line into California the following day.

"Tell me, Mom, more about the time when the family brought you as a little girl to California."

"It's a long tale. Our first trip to California was a gift to my father from his brother-in-law, Fred Nowell. It came about soon after my dad's sister Minna died early in her life. Bigmother had taken over the care of Minna and Fred's four young children. Out of gratitude to Bigmother, Fred arranged an extended vacation in California for Bigmother, her unmarried daughter, Nell, and Fred's four children. He asked my dad to accompany them and tend to the details. Mother said, 'Oh, no! Not without our girls and me!'

"So, in the summer of 1919, ten of us boarded the Santa Fe train in Birmingham and headed to San Diego. Mary, he really gave us the 'grand tour' of California. In San Diego we watched, from the heights of Point Loma, the Pacific fleet as it arrived home through the canal into the San Diego Bay, victorious from the First World War. Mother and Dad were filled with such strong emotion that they talked about it for years to come.

"My first memory of the vastness of the ocean was from the cliff at Torrey Pines, north of La Jolla. As we approached, we were stopped in our tracks at the view of the immense Pacific. I was totally unprepared and overwhelmed at age five by all that restless water. I was almost afraid that the hugeness of the ocean and its powerful waves would wash the land right out from under us. I could hardly breathe.

"We continued north to Los Angeles. Our party of ten rented a house for a month in Beverly Hills as a home base. From there we traveled via two hired limousines to explore the recently established National Forest where giant Sequoias grew. [Image 14.3]

"Although we remained in the Los Angeles area for a month, the only memories I have are visits to the studios where silent motion pictures were made and seeing the open tar pits in the heart of the city. Some of these adventures are vague in my mind, but the Beverly Hills ghost house remains vivid even today. My parents knew we were able to rent the house because the mother who had previously lived there had lost a little child and subsequently died of grief. Even though I was five, I slept in this child's crib in my parents' room. One night, a few weeks after arriving, Mother awoke, frightened by what appeared to be an apparition, a woman standing at the foot of my crib. Mother gently awakened my father who whispered, 'Hush, I see the same thing you do.'

"The next morning my grandmother poo-pooed my parents' active imaginations and warned them not to frighten the children. However, at breakfast the morning after that, Bigmother was upset and whispered to my parents, 'We must leave this place.' She had been awakened that night by the rustling of papers so loud that she could not sleep. 'What is it you want?' she had shouted into the night.

To see our stalwart Bigmother disturbed was so unusual that we decided we should move on as soon as it was convenient.

"Traveling up the coast we stopped at Father Junipero Serra's Spanish missions all the way to San Francisco. Each mission site seemed to me an isolated rural oasis. What a pity that they are now engulfed by cities and no longer have that feeling of salvation for the weary traveler on horseback. From San Francisco we made a side trip to Yosemite.

"Because my father felt much healthier in California, our family spent a few months on another trip there while my father scouted for a new career. For several years back in Alabama, Dad had felt that the air near the train station where his office was located was bad for his health. Then, when he, along with all the rest of the family had gotten sick during the 1918 flu epidemic, he decided it might be time for us to move to a healthier place. That flu epidemic had decimated the population of Europe and took a heavy toll in America.

"In the past, my father had done favors for his brother-in-law Fred. In return, Uncle Fred suggested that, after this first trip to California, my father turn right around and go back to California in search of a new career. 'I will set you up in a new business in that clean climate.' Fred was a soldier of fortune whose wanderings had taken him to Cincinnati, where he threw in his lot with a University of Cincinnati geology professor and his lawyer friend, who were contemplating prospecting for oil in Kentucky. The three of them secured land, struck oil, and made a fortune. He was now in a position to return my dad's kindnesses. Dad took a six-month leave of absence from his job at the railroad, and our little family headed west once again by train with high hopes of making a new home in California.

"Everyone in Birmingham had warned us that California was a haven for 'foreigners' whom everyone called the 'Yellow Peril,' and to beware of religious cults, such as the followers of Aimee Semple McPherson's International Church of Foursquare Gospel.

"The custodian for our apartment building in Santa Monica was Japanese and must have admired my mother, because he gave her a toothy smile whenever he saw her. He never spoke to her, which frightened her even more.

"There were many firsts for us on that trip … coming from the provincial South. When Dad tasted his first avocado in a fancy hotel restaurant, he was sure he was being poisoned. This strange green fruit had been cut with a melon ball cutter and dressed with olive oil, and he refused to eat it.

"The days on the boardwalk and shady beach of Santa Monica are my brightest recollections. It was the era of silent movies, and the *Keystone Cops* was a popular series. While playing in the sand, Mary Lou and I watched the filming of a few episodes. For one of the filmings, the actresses were eight beautiful, long-haired women dressed in bloomer bathing suits with stockings. They sat in the sand, and all that was visible were eight umbrellas and sixteen legs. One of the cops appeared on the scene holding a false leg from which he was drinking whiskey. He hid his mannequin leg among the legs of the bathing beauties. So, whenever he reached for another drink, there was great confusion. The girls were aghast when he grabbed their legs, and he was horrified when he did not get his liquor.

"Another time, the cameramen brought their equipment onto the beach. When one of the Keystone Cops grabbed a baby out of its mother's arms, the cameraman began shooting while the child screamed. Whether these were actors or whether it was spontaneous, I have no idea, but I do remember that the mother was as upset as the baby.

"On another occasion, I remember going to a movie theater in L.A. and hearing songwriter Ernest Ball give the premier performance of his song 'Let the Rest of the World Go By,' a theme that was our family 'dream,' and we sang it thereafter whenever we gathered together around the piano."

With someone like you, a pal so good and true,
I'd like to leave it all behind and go and find
Some place that's known to God alone
Just a spot to call our own
We'll find perfect peace, where joys will never cease
Out there beneath a kindly sky,
We'll build a sweet little nest somewhere out in the West
And let the rest of the world go by.

"Mams, you were lucky to have experienced Santa Monica in those early days!"

"I guess I was fortunate. It was a special time for me. But, before my dad had a chance to establish himself in a new career in California, Fred Nowell died unexpectedly of a heart attack, *leaving no will*, and ending our dreams just like that."

Mary groaned. "Gads, that's tragic. Granddad didn't have any way of getting the money Mr. Nowell had promised him?"

"None. It was only a promise. Nothing on paper. No one imagined that a young man of Mr. Nowell's forty years would die without warning."

"I've heard Gran-gran play that song on the piano so many times that I know it by heart, but I never realized how much it meant to her and Granddaddy. She never told me about their dream of moving out west."

In truth, the incident wasn't as tragic as it sounded, and I didn't want Mary to think it was. "It's just as well that we didn't settle in California," I said. "Your granddad went on to have a fine career with the L&N Raiload. And, judging from what I've seen in recent decades, I don't think I'd want to be a Californian anyway."

Mary wrinkled her nose. "I don't think I would have liked that, either. I can't imagine having grown up anywhere other than the Washington area. So many things happen there!"

"It's certainly the place to be if you're a news reporter!"

"One thing I will say for Californians, though," Mary added. "They're often on the leading edge of political and social issues. Take the student antiwar movement. That really started at Berkeley in '65. It took us more than a year at eastern universities to catch on. And Californians are way ahead of the rest of us on environmental issues. Did you know they have a board that regulates air pollution? The federal government isn't doing anything, so California decided they'd better, before they suffocate."

"They surely do need to, if only in Los Angeles."

Mary laughed. "California is a crazy place. Half the people are rugged individualists with that old pioneer spirit. The rest are dreamers, like Gran-gran and Granddad. The first half has their foot on the accelerator and the other half is saying, 'Whoa, maybe there's a better way.' The funny thing is the rest of the country needs both types to keep it moving in the right direction."

"Mother and Dad had only one direction to go, once their California dream ended, and that was back to Alabama on the Southern Pacific. On that ride I remember a young Frenchman, a veteran of the World War, who attached himself to our family. He had been intrigued by the American boys he met in France during the war and shared many of the Europeans' curiosity about the American West. The train pulled into El Paso, where our Pullman coach was detached and we would sleep for the night. The Frenchman suggested we cross the Rio Grande into Mexico and dine in Juarez. Dad said, 'I will *not* subject my family to the uncertainties of Mexico.' He was doubtless remembering Pancho Villa's recent 1916 attack on the village of Columbus, New Mexico, and its proximity to this border town."

"I don't blame him. If I had known that, I would have stayed on the train too," Mary responded.

My eyelids were sagging after reliving those earlier trips to the Golden State and, slipping into my nightgown, I said, "I'm worn out and my bed looks mighty comfortable."

But in my weariness I continued to muse, "Had we become Californians we might have been there years later to greet your dad's older sister Carolyn, your 'Aunt Sis,' and her husband Jim when they moved recently from Ohio to a retirement community in Los Gatos. But this isn't the 1919 world of my childhood visit. It's the world of hippies and marijuana. The Bakers told me that one day some old ladies at their retirement home were all bemoaning social change and decided that the world had gone to pot, so to speak. One reported, 'Right in the middle of the city, my purse was snatched!' Another complained that her lovely grandson had been caught smoking marijuana. Before Aunt Sis could listen to a third tragic story, she sighed, 'I'm glad *I'm* not living in these times.'"

Before Mary fell asleep, she still managed to read a few pages from her copy of *The Body Has a Head*.

14.1 Bob Ames, college age, circa 1933   14.2 Virginia Wade, college age, circa 1933

14.3 Wade family photo with giant Sequoia tree "Wawona" on first family trip to California 1919. Virginia Wade, 5 years old, center bottom of photo. Back row left to right: Aunt Nell Wade, Bigmother (Sally Louise Powers Wade), Albert Thompson Wade, two chauffeurs. Middle row left to right: young Fred Nowell, Janice Nowell, Pearl Guscott Wade in horsehair hat. Front row left to right: the Nowell twins, Louise and Margaret, Mary Louise Wade in taffeta traveling coat matching Virginia's.

221

Vulcan, the symbol for the Birmingham steel business
displayed at the St. Louis World's Fair in 1904

CHAPTER 15

October 25, 1970
Odometer at Kingman: 29,311

Kingman, Arizona, to Mojave,
California
Trip meter at Kingman: 3,311

Best Laid Plans

Just southwest of Kingman at the city of Yucca, Mary and I noticed our first Joshua tree, a huge multi-branched member of the
yucca family, a visual surprise to us Easterners as it appeared so
surreal. Further along Interstate 40, we crossed the bridge over the
Colorado River into Needles, the gateway to California.

Among the presents that I had brought along for Lucy were several rare Glendale-hybrid azaleas that we had nursed across the
country. I had always known that California protects certain vegetable and fruit crops from unwanted invaders, but I never suspect-
ed that nursery-grown azaleas might be a problem. Alas, I had no
certificates from the nursery where I had purchased them, certifi-

cates that would have allowed their transport across California into Oregon and Washington. To my shock and dismay, at Needles, the Stateline border inspector cut off the plants above the soil line, dropping their root balls and pots into an incinerator. He handed me the cut stems in a plastic bag, reassuring me I could make cuttings. This led me to wonder ... if we had Virginia soil on our shoes would he have cut off our legs below the knees?

Crossing over the 2,700-foot-high pass twenty miles west of Needles, Betsy strained but never faltered. From this high point we could see the stark Mojave Desert basins and ranges stretching out below us. The mountains appeared like ships in a sea and seemed to go on and on as far as the eye could see. This range, called the Dead Mountains, borders the tri-state intersection of Nevada, Arizona, and California, and the Mohave Valley. Soon after we made it over South Pass, Route 66 split off from I-40 for a sixty-mile loop. Curious, we followed old Route 66, past a sign for Essex, California, population 100, elevation 100 feet, and another sign, "soda fountain 500 feet." It felt like the boondocks again. We stopped for lunch a few miles west in Danby, which boasted a population of 20.

Continuing along Route 66 for about thirty more miles, we arrived in Amboy, a desert town surrounded 360 degrees by volcanic mountains with absolutely no apparent vegetation on them. We passed a giant stone beside the highway carved with a peace symbol. Beyond the peace symbol was a trail of smaller stones brought there by human hands, and on each of them was carved the name of a different man. *A different boy*, I thought. Recent Vietnam losses. I was overwhelmed by a pang of those losses and with a desire to be home with my family around me. We barely heard the distant whistle of the thirty-three-car Santa Fe train looking so tiny from the road, too tiny to give to Lucy's Baby Mike.

At Ludlow we rejoined I-40. At last the air temperature began to drop. What a nice evening to be on the desert, driving at an easy 45 mph. Almost to Barstow, we saw a dust storm over dry Lake Bristol and the word "help" written on a stone, as if to remind us we were still far from "civilization."

Driving through this desolate land brought to mind a story that I had heard about soldiers who had been stationed in this desert with a certain amount of water in their canteens. They were so afraid to drink it—having been instructed to ration it—that they died of dehydration with water still left in their containers.

We continued west, past the Clipper Mountains and across the Mojave Desert to its western terminus at Barstow. Mary and I counted high-tension poles in the hope this foolish activity would hasten our arrival in the town of Mojave, where we stopped for an early dinner at Daggett-Kelly's Café. There we played "Cecelia" on the juke box and talked with the waitress. The waitress said she came here with a boyfriend who deserted her, and now she was working to make enough money to leave—to go "back to civilization."

"I remember how hot Barstow was when we crossed this same desert in 1919. The conductor walked through our railcar and said, 'I have a wet towel for each passenger. You can put it on your forehead to keep you cool as we cross the desert. We have water enough if all goes well, but you must be very careful to save a supply in case the train should have trouble and we are stalled in the desert. Don't waste the water!' We kids should have been spared. This was the second time that we feared for our lives on our train trip. When we were crossing the plains, the adults were thoughtless enough to tell us that the train was racing to keep ahead of a grass fire."

"What a lot of exciting travel experiences you had when you were little!"

"Yes, exciting and seldom dull. When my family's plan to move to California failed, Dad was disappointed, but the railroad had held Dad's position open, so we returned to Birmingham. There Dad purchased a charming home for the four of us, a bungalow in a new neighborhood in that rapidly growing city. The developer appropriately named his little community Mountain Terrace, because he

225

had chosen the level plane of a true geological terrace at the base of Red Mountain, which is the southwestern-most ridge of the Appalachians. It was a generous street with gutters, curbing, and sidewalks. He designed large lots for houses on both sides of the street and told prospective buyers that the bungalow would be perfect when the children were small and that the great area toward the front of each lot would be waiting 'when you are ready to build the home of your dreams. One day the bungalow in back can become a guest cottage or a home for your help.'

"Mary, you hiked part of the Appalachians in Virginia when you were little."

"Does the Appalachian Trail go all the way into Alabama?"

"No, it starts in Maine and ends in Georgia."

Mary added, "I do remember walking along the Appalachian Trail off Skyline Drive in the Blue Ridge. I always ate all of the chocolate you provided to keep up my energy ... before I barely got started hiking!"

"Our Mountain Terrace neighborhood butted up against Red Mountain at the end of our street. In the few months that we lived in the bungalow, I am reminded now of how much it seemed like the adventures of Tom Sawyer. Since we lived on a dead end with little traffic, the neighborhood kids played right in the street. I remember playing kick-the-can on most days. We had a mascot that played with us too, a short-haired Airedale. One time when a bum, with a stick over his shoulder and belongings tied to it like in the movies, came wandering down the mountain onto our street, the dog bared his teeth and growled. The bum pulled a knife out of his pocket and opened it up, ready to strike the dog down if he attacked, but all of us kids gathered around our dog and held him back so nobody would get hurt, and the bum finally folded up the knife and walked on, not saying a word or looking back. We never told our parents about that because we had handled it, sort of like Tom Sawyer who had to deal with dangers in his life.

"Another time danger brushed us kids was when there had been a big gully-washer storm with waters flowing down the mountain into the streets. After it abated, there was a huge rattlesnake left in the street, but we knew better than to get too close, so we stood at a distance and watched it. After a while it made its way back up the mountain, as if nothing had happened, which it hadn't. So we didn't tell our parents about that either. We had one adventure after the other in those Birmingham days, and it was a lot of fun having so many friends to play with."

"We said a while ago that we wondered how boys ever manage to make it through childhood, and here you are living a life like Tom Sawyer. What other crazy things did you do?"

"The streetcar that went to Lakeview Elementary where we attended ended its route just below our house. Since there wasn't a circle for the car to make a U-turn, the conductor would have to get off the car, pull down the line that had been under tension, connect the car to the power line overhead, and reconnect his streetcar to power at the rear. Then, he could go in the other direction. While the conductor was taking his end-of-the-line break, we kids would go to the track and put two straight pins crisscrossed one over the other on the track. When the heavy car rolled over the pins and flattened them, they became little dollhouse scissors."

After sunset, sitting outside our desert motel room in the warm dry air, we continued ruminating on old times and family history, in which my more mature Mary was beginning to take more interest.

"Years before I was born, my mother's father, Stephen Guscott, who had been brought to the United States as a child from England and lived in Chicago where he met my grandmother, was instructed by my great-grandfather, Stephen's new father-in-law, to 'move to a little place called Jones Valley in Alabama,' an agricultural area, 'because they have found in a mountain nearby the three components for making steel. That's where the *future* is.' Red Mountain, at the edge of Jones Valley, was once as tall as the Blue Ridge Mountains, but ages of erosion brought it down to about 1,000 feet. It was red because of the iron oxide ... iron ore. With its nearby sources of coal and limestone, it was a perfect industrial site for steel mills. When these elements were discovered, the quiet little town of Elyton that nestled in the valley below Red Mountain was infiltrated and later consumed by 'progress.'

"In 1877, Gran-gran's parents, my grandfather and grandmother, Mary Wheeler Guscott, moved to Jones Valley, where a boxcar served as a train station. They told me that on arrival, Polly, as Mary Guscott was called, was outraged and demanded, 'Oh Stephen, why did you bring me to a place like this?'

"But Polly's parents remained in Alabama and so did the young Guscotts. The little surrounding towns became rapidly growing mining towns and the family stayed. Stephen worked in the offices of the steel mill and Mother recalled that her father developed some metal parts in his home workshop that improved the steelmaking process.

"Old Elyton and Bessemer were small towns, with poor whites and uneducated Blacks, which grew in the rush of mining and steel milling, beginning in 1871 when Milner and Stanton collaborated on their big real estate deal. With an air of deceitful finagling, they brought their railroads together and established the plan for Birmingham, the Magic City."

Mary interjected, "Your people were there at a time of great change. How were the locals affected by the birth of this industrial center?"

"In that competitive mining era, Mary, hatreds were formed. Small wonder that Birmingham became so hostile, as it was based upon the entrepreneurs' manipulation of laws and their grab for wealth, an emphasis on social class and the division between the haves and have-nots, concentrated in a volatile time of rapid transformation.

"So, Mother ... your Gran-gran ... was born in a young Birmingham in 1892. The next year, in 1893, the huge statue of a steel worker, named 'Vulcan,' was fashioned out of cast iron, as tall as a two-story building. It was sent to represent the iron and steel industries of Birmingham at the St. Louis World's Fair in 1904. When the fair was over, Vulcan was returned to Birmingham and first placed at the state fairgrounds. Years later, when I was young and Mother took us to the state fair, I remember her telling us, 'If we get separated, go sit at the foot of Vulcan and I'll find you there.' In 1936, Vulcan found his final resting place on top of Red Mountain in the middle of the new park.

"By 1945, Birmingham had settled down into a relatively peaceful and wealthy community. By the '60s, however, fomenting social injustice issues peaked when the bombing of innocent children took place in the 16th Street Baptist Church, commanding everyone's attention around the country. Birmingham was the perfect hotbed for racism to be confronted, because the town was divided between poor, uneducated steel and mine workers, and wealthy, more educated people. Finally, Charles Morgan Jr., a prestigious lawyer of the time, could watch from the sidelines no more and spoke out against racism and against the people who had allowed it to continue. On September 16, 1963, Morgan addressed the Young Men's Business Club of Birmingham with a speech saying, 'And who is guilty? *Each of us!* Each citizen who has not consciously attempted to bring about peaceful compliance with the decisions of the Supreme Court of the United States ...'

"His book, *A Time to Speak*, so moved me, I actually keep and reference it, as it is one of those earthshaking documents like the Gettysburg Address that matter enough to memorize." My deeply mixed feelings about Birmingham, its joys and its frustrating prejudices, were boiling up and I continued quoting Morgan with fervor, "'Each of us! Each citizen who has ever said 'they ought to kill that nigger,' every citizen who votes for the candidate with the bloody flag; every citizen and every school board member and schoolteacher and principal and businessman and judge and lawyer who has corrupted the minds of our youth; every person in this community who has in any way contributed during the past several years to the popularity of hatred is at least as guilty, or more so, than the demented fool who threw that bomb.'"

With that, Mary and I retired early, drained and trying to cool the heat of my passions and recalled emotions, as well as the desert air—grateful for a good fan in our room.

CHAPTER 16

Monday, Oct 26, 1970
Odometer at Mojave: 29,536

Mojave Desert, California,
to Willows, California
Trip meter at Mojave: 3,536

A Man Ahead
of His Time

Photo of Dr. Gustav Eckstein and his pet macaw "Polly"
(original inspiration for caricature of Dr. Eckstein
with macaw and monkey by Miguel Covarrubias
published in *The New Yorker* in the 1930s)

We got up early, anxious to cover ground. Betsy climbed a long lava flow for seventeen miles, mounted the Tehachapi Pass, and rolled down to the town of Tehachapi onto the flatland around Bakersfield. "Reagan for Governor" posters dotted the landscape on the edge of orchards of fruit trees and fields of corn, avocados, potatoes, and other vegetables.

At 9:30 a.m. we were in the San Joaquin Valley, leaving Bakersfield and heading northwest on Route 99 to Route 5 and north.

"This desert is an unlikely place for such a great variety of fruits, nuts, vegetables, and cotton." Mary thought it strange to see rigs pumping oil in the middle of an orange orchard. "Speaking of oil, Betsy is getting a whopping 19.7 miles per gallon."

Route 5 between Bakersfield and Willows was monotonous, so Mary suggested that one of us read aloud from Eckstein's book, *The Body Has a Head*, which she was now drawn into.

"So, what is Dr. Eckstein really all about, Mams?"

"Mary, he is a complicated man … brilliant, impossible to categorize, and a century ahead of his time. My introduction to Eckstein was in an article published in *Harper's* magazine in 1931. This article told how he breezed through the halls of the University of Cincinnati Medical School, carrying a macaw named Polly on his shoulder.

"When I was working for him after 1936, Dr. Eckstein confessed to me that he surmised he was an achiever because he had not been pampered in childhood. He announced to me in hyperbole, *'Thank God my parents gave me the blessings of poverty.'* He was careful with his money. For instance, he is a vegetarian. Every day I shopped for his lunch, and when I presented him with a bill for his vegetables, he carefully went over each item. He appreciated those who assisted him, and in many ways, was generous with his funds. Years after I left his lab, I talked with a staff member of the medical school library who was delighted to speak with someone who knew him. 'Each Christmas holiday,' she told me, 'he gives presents to all the librarians, janitors, cafeteria employees … anyone who has served him in any way.'"

"How did you find out about this job you liked so much?"

"When I graduated during the Depression I was lucky to find any job, even a dull one. A friend, Sam Bell, alumni secretary of the university, needed help. I became his only assistant. My duties included keeping a roster of every student past or present, by year and by college. One day Sam put down the phone and told me that a fascinating professor of physiology at the College of Medicine, Doctor Gustav Eckstein, needed a part-time secretary to help him with his writing. Sam Bell was not only my boss … he was an old friend who knew I would enjoy working with Dr. Eckstein. He also knew he would personally profit by replacing me with a worker who might find it more fulfilling than I did to keep statistics on thousands of U.C. graduates, living and dead. I asked what qualifications an applicant must have. Sam smiled. 'Eckstein said that she must be a human being.' I qualified, and he hired me the morning we met.

"In the following two-and-a-half years, I gained insights and wisdom from this great man that have served me well ever since. Hardly a workday in his laboratory passed without an interesting event.

"Gustav Eckstein, the man, is about 5'4" with black wiry hair. He was in his fifties when I met him, quick in motion, and a tireless worker. He never walked. Rather, he scurried from one place to another. His evening secretary, Martha Keegan, said it all when she stated that, when the time comes, the marker on his grave should read, 'The only stone he left unturned.'

"His laboratory contained all of the facilities of a chemical lab, as well as an extensive library, one heating grill for preparing lunches, the usual tables, chairs, and typewriters, one wicker lounge, and a grand piano protected with a large cover.

"Dr. Eckstein has degrees in both dentistry and medicine from the University of Cincinnati College of Medicine. However, his interests range in many other directions. He loves music and plays the piano well. He was not only an innovative teacher ... he is also a successful writer and playwright.

"The book that brought him popular acclaim was *Canary*, published by Harper Brothers in 1936, a bestseller in America and England. By observing his canaries over many years he saw the unique characteristics of each bird, knew its habits, even saw relationships between them within the flock, and their different personalities and behaviors. On Saturday nights, when he left the birds and did not return until Monday morning, he wondered what they were thinking.

"When he was working on a play, he spent much of his time in New York at his younger sister's house. I think her name was Laura, but he called her Lots. Because he loved her dearly, he was overly concerned about her happiness, fearing, he said, that she did not have enough friends to stimulate her. When away, he always kept in touch with me through letters. In a September 6, 1939, letter he wrote to me, 'Remember me to all my 34. You have done very much for their lovely lives. How clearly one sees them in the brain, each with its separate beautiful shape and plan.' And on December 11 of that year he wrote me, 'Wonder what they think. They have the happy memory of lunch – Lai-lu particularly. What a swell being she is. How Lai-lu pleases, a bit like my mother. Makes me forever grateful of her.'

"In another he said,

> November 21, 1939
> Dear Virginia,
>
> I haven't got very much time to write, not yet. Thanks for all the hard work.
>
> We seem to have made it count at least to the point of getting a play to the announcements of a brief date for a rehearsal (announcing a rehearsal date on Broadway for the play).
>
> Can you hear Lots groan at the last? I can even hear you.
>
> Remember me to all the guys. Tell 'em the man busy with the drama, be back to ornithology (meaning wonderful, higher species, etc.) forthwith.
>
> Back in a few days. Keep me informed and I you.
> All the best,
> G

"Because he told stories of his birds and other animals in such a lively manner, he was in great demand as a luncheon speaker. His reputation after *Canary* was published brought him to the attention of the members of a group known as the Algonquin Round Table, a changing group of outstanding people in the fields of art, letters, and theater of New York City. They gathered regularly at their special luncheon table at the Algonquin Hotel in Manhattan. Harold Ross of *The New Yorker* is credited with getting this luncheon group together.

"In the 1930s, radio had become an important source of news and entertainment. Alexander Woollcott, 'The Town Crier' and member of the Algonquin group, had a popular weekly talk show featuring what was new in the arts. This series was sponsored by Liggett & Myers Tobacco Company. When Woollcott read *Canary* he was so taken by the book, he gave it a rave review on his show. He was so impressed with Eckstein when they met that he invited him to join the Round Table whenever he visited the city.

"Thereafter, many illustrious people in the theater and writing worlds, as well as world leaders and scholars in this country and abroad, wanted to see this vivacious man in his *canary*-filled laboratory.

"Eckstein's literary interests have been wide-ranging. His biography of Hideyo Noguchi in 1931 was his first important book. This Japanese bacteriologist did research on syphilis and its effects on the brain. Next, Noguchi studied yellow fever until he himself succumbed to that disease on a research trip to Africa.

"Eckstein has also been recognized for two more of his books, *Lives* in 1932, and now in 1970, *The Body Has a Head.*

"One of my jobs when I started with Dr. Eckstein was to type for him as he composed the play *Christmas Eve*, which he finally published in 1940, and to listen to him as he read aloud from his ever-changing manuscript. The theme of the play revealed how the birth of a baby changed the lives of everybody in one family. The action included a 'live' birth on stage ... not the sight of it, but the sounds.

"He became acquainted with the actress Katharine Cornell, who was married to producer Guthrie McClintic. McClintic decided to produce *Christmas Eve* on Broadway, so he and his wife were frequent visitors to the lab.

"On one visit when the two men were conferring about the production, Dr. Eckstein suggested that McClintic witness a live birth. After having this experience and upon returning to the lab, McClintic, white as a ghost, threw himself onto the lounge. Eckstein exclaimed, 'Quick, Mrs. Ames, find him a bottle of Vichy water!'

"When the play was to open on Broadway, Eckstein invited Martha Keegan and me to be his guests on opening night and to stay with Lots and her husband in their Manhattan apartment.

"We were tense in our seats waiting for the curtain to rise. The house was full. Unfortunately, many in the audience had brought young children, expecting to see the traditional Christmas story. When the birthing sounds began, many of them herded their children and left in the middle of the performance. They were 1930s people with lingering Victorian sensibilities and were shocked at the suggestion of a real live experience. The play failed miserably.

"The next morning, when we read the bad reviews, Dr. Eckstein said, 'When things go wrong, that's when you have to stop ... think ... then act.' He was not one to panic or accept failure. He rushed to Harper Brothers, publisher of all his books, and induced them to publish his failed play.

"Dr. Eckstein was obviously pleased by the enthusiasm so many felt for *Canary*. Illustrious people came from far and near to meet and to talk with him, and he was generous in sharing much of the excitement with me. One Friday, as I was about to go home, he said, 'Mrs. Ames, you might want to be in the lab around three o'clock on Sunday afternoon.' He told me that his visitor would be Sir Ronald Storrs, accompanied by his Cincinnati host and hostess. Sir Ronald had held important posts in the British Foreign and Colonial Office for thirty years, from 1904 to 1934. His area of expertise was the Middle East, and he served in a variety of capacities in Egypt. Storrs' friends brought him to the laboratory at his request. I made sure I was there.

"It was my duty to help all guests to the lab through the double doors, in order to prevent the canaries from escaping. When they arrived, Dr. Eckstein met and introduced the three people to me. The host and hostess swept by, the scent of the pre-luncheon cocktail drifting behind them, ignoring the introduction. But the courtly Sir Ronald Storrs said, 'It's a pleasure to meet you, Mrs. Ames.' He paused to look at the bookcases as he passed by and said, 'Lawrence of Arabia. I knew him, you know.'

"As he departed, Sir Ronald said quietly to me, 'All of London speaks of this man.' I think it was his book, *Canary*, that captivated the Brits.

"The next visitor to join us for lunch was Doctor Walter C. Alvarez, Professor of Medicine at the Mayo Foundation, a handsome man who talked medicine with Eckstein.

"Many of the visitors were in theater or were writers. Thornton Wilder came, and he thrilled me, an English major who had just finished reading two of his books, *Our Town* and *The Skin of Our Teeth*.

"Alfred Lunt and Lynn Fontanne were a couple, actors with an incredible number of smash hits on Broadway during the '20s and '30s. Their most recent success was *Amphitryon 38*, a comedy in three acts. The Lunts did not visit the lab during my time there, but Dr. Eckstein shared anecdotes about them with me and about many others from his travels. Miss Fontanne had told him that they'd decided to take *Amphitryon 38* off Broadway to New Orleans ... an unusual thing to do in those days. The box office reported that some in the audience had driven as far as 700 miles to see the show. The company arrived in New Orleans too close to curtain time to have supper but sent out for hard-boiled eggs to sustain them through the long comedy. Miss Fontanne said she had seldom played to such a responsive and enthusiastic audience.

"When Eckstein visited the Lunts' home in Genesee Depot, Wisconsin, probably at Christmastime, everyone dressed for dinner. Alfred Lunt's sister appeared at the table with a corsage in her hair. Fontanne, not to be upstaged, disappeared into the kitchen and returned wearing a corsage of fresh green parsley in hers.

"A most interesting day at the lab was the one that I spent doing my work at the far end of the room while Dr. Eckstein visited with Ethel Barrymore. Her companion was Alice Roosevelt Longworth, Theodore Roosevelt's daughter and wife of the Speaker of the House, Cincinnatian Nicholas Longworth.

"The only conversation I remember was when Ethel Barrymore, who obviously adored her younger brother John, excused his drinking habits by saying that his real ambition in life was to be a great artist. But when he stepped onto the stage and became such an immediate success, he had no choice but to follow the acting career. 'He was a victim of his own abilities,' she said.

"The following day, Dr. Eckstein told me of the discussion Ethel Barrymore had with him after my departure. She commented to him about his secretary's ... *my* ... Southern accent, and she said that try though she might, she would never be able to copy it. Her reasoning was that the consonants could easily be copied, but the vowels are the music of one's voice, which is determined early in a person's life.

"Alexander Woollcott came, of course. It was Woollcott who brought Eckstein to the attention of the committee responsible for awarding PhDs at Hamilton College, Woollcott's alma mater, and the result was that the college awarded Eckstein an honorary degree. At the same ceremony, Hamilton College also gave an honorary degree to Helen Hayes. In his acceptance speech, Dr. Eckstein told four animal stories in his own original way.

"One of those stories had been previously published in his book *Lives*. It concerned a cat's sense of time. His secretary Martha Keegan had told him that her cat usually was fed just before it went to bed, but on Mondays the cat demanded his food early. 'The cat knew Monday. The cat knew 8:00 in the evening. Each Monday, the cat left the house exactly at 8:00. It always returned two hours later. When the cat's knowledge of Monday became obvious to the secretary, she followed it one evening. The cat crossed the street on a green light, following the pedestrians, and wound its way along the street next to Good Samaritan Hospital. It then jumped up onto the ledge of a basement window through which it could see masses of people playing bingo. When the game was over, the cat jumped down and ran home.'

"Eckstein was an innovative teacher and his slant on almost everything was atypical. When he taught his students about stomach pumps, he made half of the class administer a stomach pump to the other half, until every student had experienced what he might do to his own patients in the future.

"Dr. Eckstein was ahead of his time. He fought for both women's rights and animal rights before either cause had become a popular movement. It was just in his nature.

"Margaret Snyder was an energetic young woman who ran the cafeteria in the medical school. Dr. Eckstein thought she would make a superb doctor and told her so. The thought had never crossed her mind. However, his insistence got her so excited about the idea that she applied for admission to the University of Cincinnati's College of Medicine. At that time, few women ever succeeded in being accepted into the medical profession, and every kind of roadblock was thrown up by the admissions office against this young woman. But Eckstein fought so effectively and doggedly for her that her application was at long last accepted. Years later I was glad to learn that she had become a well-respected doctor.

"Dr. Eckstein deplored the mutilation and suffering imposed on animals for medical research. He said that you could learn much more by observing the living animals instead of making them suffer unnecessarily.

"In 1938, Neville Chamberlain, Prime Minister of the United Kingdom, promised the Sudetenland part of Czechoslovakia to Hitler in exchange for his declaration not to take the remainder. Eckstein was hopeful. However, every subsequent move revealed Hitler's true ambition, to conquer Europe and England. A letter Eckstein wrote to me on September 6, 1939, five days after Hitler invaded Poland and war was declared, reflected the feelings of many:

> *The pain of all those people – it may be impossible to get one's mind from this for more than a few moments, and even when one does forget, there's the heaviness about the forgetting. I think I ought to pray for them.*

"Eckstein once told me that psychiatry would be unnecessary if a man were thoroughly trained in physiology. He did have an acute understanding of human nature. Often he and I would take a break from the lab and go to Mecklenburg Gardens, a German restaurant and beer garden near the medical school. This was a delightful place with meals served outdoors under an arbor heavy with grapes. Dr. Eckstein told me the story of one of the waiters he had known over the years. This man had held one goal in life. Though he was not wealthy, he wanted to buy the restaurant. Every penny he made in salary and tips that he did not need just to subsist, he stashed away in his goal fund. Year after year, he walked to work to save the bus fare and denied himself constantly in order to amass enough money to buy the place. After years of deprivation, the Mecklenburg Gardens was *his*. When Dr. Eckstein asked him how happy he was to be the new owner, he replied, 'It's not as great as I thought it would be. I have nothing to work toward now.'

"I was subsequently amused to hear that Eckstein had received a dual appointment at U.C. Department of Psychiatry and was the guest speaker when a psychiatric society met in Cincinnati.

"He probably prepared me more for bringing up children than I learned from anyone else or any book. He said, 'You can't *tell* a person anything—you have to *show* them.' I recalled this later when I read in an advice-to-parents column in the newspaper that children 'do what you *do*, not what you *say* to do.'

"He was a firm believer in facing reality and drove home this point with the advice, 'Lie if you must to the rest of the world, but never fool yourself.' His most memorable idiosyncrasy was his intolerance of lazy thinking and of those who assumed an air of authority they had not earned.

"I was absolutely fascinated with my job with him, could hardly wait to get there in the morning, and ran rather than walked up the steps to the laboratory each day. His a-polar view of traditional thought always resulted in new ideas to ponder, which I found thrilling." [Note 20 – Eckstein]

Since Betsy left Mojave, she had been running smoothly, but her engine began missing again at 29,330 miles. We stopped at James Reed Chevron in Pixley, where they put in yet another filter and we filled the tank. Although we felt confident we would get to Seattle, there was still one gnawing concern.

"We've fixed everything possible along the gas line, but no one has examined the tank. Let's stop at the Dodge dealer in Visalia and have them look at that."

Visalia was the next large city on our route. There we rolled into the repair shop of the Dodge dealership, a most immaculate reception area for ailing automobiles. We were greeted by a man in a white uniform holding a writing pad on which he recorded the symptoms of our car's trouble. Being careful to touch the Wayfarer as little as possible, he gave it a superficial examination, asked us a few questions, and made a few notes. We suggested he blow the line in reverse, as had proved favorable previously. He shook his head *no* and said that, without question, the trouble must be rust in the tank, and instead of blowing the line, he would clean the tank. That process would require three days, he told us—the first to exhaust the fumes, the second to remove the tank, and the last to replace and connect the new tank. We replied that while this might be a good idea, we did not have three days to spare.

He sniffed righteously. Mary got in behind the wheel while I hurried into the passenger seat. She stepped on the gas with such determination that the trunk of the car flew open and out fell two jars of my precious preserves onto his clean floor. We roared out, trunk ajar, stopping a block away to close the trunk. Pleased with ourselves for saving Betsy from yet another unnecessary probe, not to mention our pocketbooks and schedule, we followed the signs to Route 5.

The Wayfarer cruised north as though nothing had happened, passing grass fires on the plains for fifty miles before we approached the city of Willows, where we reserved a room for the night.

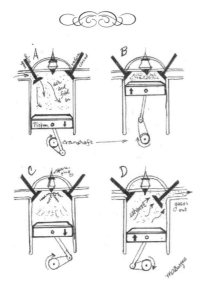

Gasoline engine 4-stroke diagram—A-suck,
B-squeeze, C-pop, D-phooey
(original sketch by MABurgess)

CHAPTER 17

Tuesday, October 27, 1970
Odometer at Willows: 29,961

Willows, California, to
Portland, Oregon
Trip meter at Willows: 3,961

Suck, Squeeze,
Pop, and Phooey

In the morning, we drove from Willows to Corning, where we stopped at the J & W Café and shared another steak-and-egg breakfast big enough for a small family, so big that we were sure we wouldn't need to stop for lunch. With our inquiry about the town name, our waitress told us that many artists in town used glass as their medium, but it was not inspired by either the well-known Corning Glass Works in New York State or by the International Glass Company in Corning, Ohio.

Sipping a second cup of coffee, I asked Mary if the hard beds in our motel the previous night had been a problem for her.

"At first, yes," she told me, "but once asleep I made it until after sunrise."

"Sleep did not come for me for a long time. Thoughts of another hard bed were stimulating me. I was remembering a letter written by your dad's Great-uncle John while he too was on an epic journey, his by canoe, with the Episcopal Bishop of Kansas. Uncle John Ames was a recent graduate from Johns Hopkins University when the older man asked him to accompany him exploring the Red River-of-the-North through little known and sparsely settled country. They were surprised to see a single teepee in a clearing in the forest beside the river. Living in this lonesome place was a grey-haired Indian couple who greeted them warmly and offered the canoeists shelter for the night in their woodland home.

"That night their bed was the hard earthen floor, and Uncle John reported hearing the bishop groaning, 'My bones ... my bones.' Next morning, after sharing breakfast with them, the old Indian man spoke, 'We have lived here for ten years contemplating what religion we should embrace. The coming of the Episcopal bishop is a sign.'

"They asked the bishop if he would baptize the two of them, and he said he would be most pleased to do so."

Mary reflected, "I'm glad to hear about Uncle John's letter and his adventure. It was like being on yet another journey, this time with two unlikely companions."

We paid the bill and returned to our car. "Mams, why don't I drive and you can tell me more about Dr. Eckstein and his laboratory?"

"In my maturity, Mary, someone told me that I had had an 'intellectual affair' with my mentor. And that is not totally untrue. Eckstein always saw the bigger picture ... beyond the here and now. His thinking was far ahead of the mainstream. I so respected how he deplored the injustices to women that he could see happening, and the cruelty to innocent animals. He remained a friend upon whom I could always depend, even long after I left his employment. When my dad was dying from leukemia, I turned to Dr. Eckstein for advice. He wrote me immediately with a letter that gave me courage through our rough time.

> *September 19, 1944*
> *Dear Virginia,*
> *I still think that I would go to the Mayo as soon as it's arranged. I would not expect miracles. But I would go. When a large group works together, and when the tradition is as high as it has always been there, diagnosis, at last, is apt to be certain. Treatment, of course, is only what it can be with our knowledge [of] what it is. But go, and find out. The very going has a use. Go also with a kind of intelligent hope – that is necessary, and you know what I mean. I imagine that you will be with him. In that case you can see to it that it is you who are to see just how things stand, so that you have the whole responsibility, and make entirely whatever decision, if any especially is to be made. That is better for you, and that is better for your father.*
> *Ask me anything that you think I can tell you, or any help that you see I could give. I wish there were more.*
> *Affectionately,*
> *Gustav Eckstein*

"A month later my father died and I received a telegram from Eckstein that said,

> *November 12, 1944*
> *I am very, very sorry. You were the best kind of daughter to him. I know that you made it as easy as was possible. Try to remember that now. My sympathy to your mother and to your sister.*
> *Affectionately,*
> *Gustav Eckstein*

"When Lucy was a toddler, she had an imbalance in the strength of the muscles of her eyes, so when she was tired one eye would wander. I feared for her vision. I had taken her to Dr. Costenbader, a respected ophthalmologist in Washington, D.C., where we were living. He recommended either an operation or eye exercises. I wanted a second opinion, so I called Eckstein for advice. He recommended a doctor in Philadelphia. Dad, Lucy, Muffin, still an infant, her nurse dressed in a stiff white uniform, and I drove there to see him. He concurred with the diagnosis of the D.C. physician. We opted for no surgery, and Lucy cooperated with effective exercises."

"Wow. Was Dad ever jealous of your friendship with Eckstein?"

"I do believe your father resented the extra time I devoted to what was supposed to be a part-time job. I tested him sorely on one occasion. Eckstein was invited to lecture at a luncheon at Ohio University in Athens, and he asked if I would drive him there because he wanted to be rested for the lecture. I consented, so long as I drove a familiar car, our Ford roadster, because I had never driven beyond the city limits of Cincinnati."

"Mams, that is so hard to imagine!"

"Your dad immediately agreed for me to use our car, knowing I would return in time to pick him up after work and then go out for dinner together.

"Dr. Eckstein's lecture went well and after goodbyes we headed back to Cincinnati. The trip took us through Columbus, Ohio, which at that time was about a two-hour drive north of Cincinnati. When we arrived in Columbus, late afternoon, Eckstein said he was depleted and would like to stop for a cup of coffee. We found a little restaurant on the town square. After coffee, the route around the square would take us back to our highway. Because I was an inexperienced driver, I became confused and turned north from the square instead of south, ending up 180 degrees off course without either of us noticing. As we rolled further and further into the countryside, twilight faded into total darkness.

"Every moment I expected to see the lights of Lebanon, Ohio, just north of Cincinnati, but because we were in farm country, there were hardly any lights at all. At last we saw the glow of city lights in the dark sky ahead. When we pulled into a filling station we learned we were in Xenia, Ohio, which is as far north of Columbus as Cincinnati is south. I called Bob and told him why we would be late arriving home. I felt like such a failure. And I was further embarrassed when Eckstein said, 'Too bad I will miss Arturo Toscanini conducting the National Broadcasting Company Orchestra's weekly radio concert tonight.' Fortunately it reminded me that your dad had a car radio, not a common thing in those days. We rolled south to the heroic tones of 'Beethoven's Fifth Symphony.'

"I dropped Dr. Eckstein at his apartment. It was very late by the time I reached your dad's office. He was waiting in front of his build-ing, hungry and disgruntled. Once he was fed and knew that I ... and his automobile ... were safe, his amiable disposition returned."

"That's fortunate, Mams, for Dad likes his cars second only to his family."

After a long pause Mary spoke again. "Your trip to Ohio Univer-sity tells me a little of what it was like working for Dr. Eckstein, but last night reading *The Body Has a Head* gave me another measure of this unique writer. I had a hard time putting his book down. Dr. Eckstein's teaching must have created the same kind of excitement in his students.

"If someone is trying to decide whether or not to study medicine, I would hand him a copy of this book. The first part is the history of medical science from its origins in ancient Greece to the present and includes information about what is and what is not yet understood about the human psyche. It also includes a discussion of rare dis-eases that still baffle medical researchers. The main portion of the book is like a complete course in physiology, in language a layperson can understand and enjoy."

"When I first went to work for him, Mare, Eckstein was writing the story of Pavlov's experiments with dogs on the subject of conditioned reflexes. Eckstein had just returned from a visit to Pavlov's laboratory in Russia, where he had spent some time gathering material for a book about Pavlov and his research."

As we were talking, Mary and I drove up Mt. Siskiyou, the pass with some of the steepest grades in the Interstate Highway System. We saw Mt. Shasta in our rearview mirror. The scenery had become so entrancing we fell silent. At 2:00 p.m. we crossed the state line into Oregon, one mile below the Siskiyou Mountain Summit (4,310 feet), the highest point on Interstate 5. Speeding down the pass, Betsy overtook a truck barreling along ahead of us. Despite this burst of energy, we felt the jerkiness of an uneven gas flow—*no, not again*! Although the fuel line was still ailing, we were no longer traumatized—at least we knew a technique that seemed to work consistently for Betsy, if only a temporary solution.

At our request, and because we knew it somehow helped, mechanics at Wyman's garage in Roseburg, Oregon, blew Betsy's fuel line backwards and filled the tank with gas along with a can of additive. Mary and I, feeling good, sang and harmonized exuberantly, as we used to do on road trips when the girls were young. We were getting closer, Mt. Hood now standing as a graceful cone to the east, Portland ahead … Seattle beyond …

Mary reflected, "In junior high science, when they tried to teach us how a gasoline engine works, they gave us a mnemonic to remember the four-stage phases … intake, pressure, fuel-burn, and exhaust … of a car piston's action. Teachers' tricks sometimes stick with us! They taught us to say 'Suck-Squeeze-Pop-Phooey!' so as not to forget the four-stroke sequence.

"We are getting mighty familiar with those rhythms … and misbeats. It's been two weeks now and about 4,500 miles … and I'm thinking our destination is just a few suck-squeeze-pop-phooeys away. Let's hope they stay in sync."

CHAPTER 18

Wednesday, October 28
to Sunday, November 1, 1970
Odometer at Portland: 30,456

Portland, Oregon, to
Seattle, Washington
Trip meter at Portland: 4,456

A Devil and a Witch

When the mountain is out–
Mt Rainier above the mist
(original sketch by MABurgess)

I was lying in bed looking through the window, out through the gloom, and spotted a spider web—a web more stunning than any I had ever seen. Each filament forming that continuous structure was covered with dew. Each strand was a string of white oval pearls. I lay still—marveling at the beauty the spider had woven into a home, its sanctuary, so strong that it could support the endless drops of dew.

Mary began to awaken. She rolled over, slowly opened her eyes, and smiled at me. "Are we really going to make it, Mams? There is more high ground between here and Seattle."

She sat up and put salve on her chapped lips, still dry from our drive through the desert. We wasted no time packing and getting to

249

an attractive restaurant where for the third time we split a breakfast—big enough to feed a hungry truck driver. "It is so good that you
two are likely to fight over it," the waitress bragged.

There was so much fog heading out of Portland that we could
hardly see the road, and perhaps because of the fog, we could smell
the foul chemicals coming from a paper mill.

"I wonder how Lucy's neighbors are going to react to having this
old car in their lovely neighborhood."

"Unfortunately, since the Wayfarer is not of pre-World War II
vintage like Dad's old Rolls, it most likely won't receive the respect
it deserves. The early Rolls Royce automobiles with their one-of-a-
kind, custom-built bodies opened doors for us when your dad volunteered to arrange a meet for antique car enthusiasts to visit colonial
mansions along the James River in Tidewater, Virginia.

"Remember Aunt Rina's friend Jack Seeger? Jack's father was a
country doctor who lived beside the James and delivered half of the
babies to families who still had historical houses there at the turn of
the century. Jack introduced us to the present owners of several of
the mansions in that area. With his letters of introduction in hand,
in order to ask permission and arrange for an antique car tour there,
we went first to Sabine Hall, the manor house of King Carter, one of
the greats of the colonial period of Virginia. After many generations
Sabine Hall is still owned by the descendants of King Carter. One
of the Carters had a daughter and no sons, so the Carter name was
lost, but the property stayed in the family. The daughter married a
Wellford and two of their descendants, Carter and Dabney Wellford,
still shared Sabine Hall and its 4,000 acres at the time of our visit.

"Carter and Dabney had divided Sabine Hall through the middle
of the great living room passageway, Carter having all the estate
on the left side, including 2,000 of the 4,000 acres, and Dabney, the
right side with the remaining 2,000 acres. We could look out across
the acreage where it met the bay and imagine King Carter's only son
boarding a ship that would carry him to England to be educated.

"Carter Wellford was a man of the world and had been employed by Dow Chemical in Delaware. Dabney Wellford was a man of the cloth who served the Episcopal Church of Virginia with distinction.

"When Bob and I first arrived at Sabine Hall, Carter greeted us with great cordiality. He and your father enjoyed each other instantly because they could talk business and Washington politics. Carter immediately agreed to having a stream of antique cars visit their estate as part of our tour. After the arrangements were made, he spoke about his forebears. There is one tale I remember clearly.

"King Carter, the first progenitor of the Carters of Virginia, ordered his agent in London to purchase and send him certain items that included pieces of silver. He demanded that his agent pay no tax to the king on this silver. Carter produced a spoon for us to see, a heavy piece of silver, a serving spoon. Engraved on the back of the handle was this message, 'No tax has been paid on this silver,' evidence that King Carter had insisted, along with his fellow colonists, that 'Taxation without representation is tyranny.'

"On the same trip we also met the current owners of the Byrd mansion, the Crane family. They were able to restore and maintain that beautiful colonial home and were also open to a visit by our antique car club.

"The third home open to our group was Mt. Airy, a unique colonial estate that looked like it might have been transplanted from the English countryside. The owner said it would be fitting and very exciting to show off our antique automobiles alongside his collection of antique carriages. As we talked at Mt. Airy, a Black butler descended the stairs dressed in a handsome white uniform, carrying a silver tray bearing one silver pitcher to serve us. The shiny silver was streaked black where the condensation ran in rivulets down the frigid vessel. The vision of this struck me ... the blatant contrasts of history, class, and color ...

"The Rolls Royce car meet through Tidewater, Virginia, was a huge success. Not many are so fortunate as to visit these elegant homes rescued from America's past." [Image 18.1]

As Mary and I drew near Seattle, we rejoiced that Betsy was on the last lap of our journey and rolling smoothly. Blowing the gas line backwards, our repeated trick learned in Tulsa, Oklahoma, we knew was only a panacea; the cause of all our troubles was yet to be found.

We hoped to see Mount Rainier, but it was lost in dense fog. The massive mountaintop quietly emerged like a hovering giant—its base still lost in the gloom. Its snow-covered crest was blinding white in the brilliant sunlight. Too big to be a mere mountain, it is an eminence—unearthly, frightening, but thrilling in its powerful beauty.

"It will be fun to see Baby Michael again. Isn't it great that Lucy and Michael have a girl and a boy now?"

"Yes, how lucky they are to have it work out that way," Mary commented. "After they met as students at Stanford, did they ever date anyone else?"

"Nope, she never dated anyone but Michael at Stanford. At her graduation it sure was a great celebration and family reunion and a time for us to meet Mike's parents when his sister Nancy, Lucy's roommate and future sister-in-law, also graduated. Although Mike was unable to attend the graduation ceremony because of his med school studies, he met up with us later in our travels.

"It was such fun when we three families celebrated Lucy's graduation in Palo Alto: the Ames, the Copasses ... including Nancy C, and the Kroehls, their Seattle friends whose daughter Nancy K was graduating from the nursing school. The three dads got together and sang a song of congratulation for Lucy receiving the Dinkelspiel Award for outstanding academic leadership. Later, when the Ames family was headed back east from Seattle, Michael arrived from Northwestern University and drove Lucy as far as he could to Wenatchee, Washington, before going back to Seattle. Remember our surprise when we all rendezvoused in Wenatchee and she was wearing a new engagement ring!"

In the months before the wedding, Lucy lived with us back in Washington, D.C., working as an assistant to Bill Haddad, associate director at the new Peace Corps office. Lucy and Michael were married at the Seminary Chapel at Immanuel-on-the-Hill. Lucy moved to Chicago until Mike finished medical school at Northwestern. While there, she was an editor at *World Book Encyclopedia*. Immediately upon graduation as a Doctor of Medicine, Michael was drafted into the pre-Vietnam peacetime army and sent for duty to West Germany, where our first granddaughter Clo was born in 1967. When they returned from Germany, they made Seattle their home. Instead of going into private practice, Michael pursued a career as a professor of medicine at the University of Washington, teaching and practicing neurology and emergency medicine at the county-owned hospital, Harborview Medical Center. Michael and Lucy had agreed that with a growing family Lucy would be a stay-at-home mom. [Note 21 – The Copass Family]

I had visited the Copasses when Michael Jr. was born, and again when we wheeled him in a buggy on a visit to Victoria, British Columbia, but Mary had not met either of the children nor had she seen their new home on Mercer Island, so it was a new setting, a whole new ball game, for Mary to visit the Copass family in Seattle.

Betsy rolled us into their driveway for a well-deserved rest, with her trip odometer showing distance traveled from Alexandria to Seattle as 4,629 miles. Turning off the ignition I could sense an audible sigh.

At the Copasses' front door, Baby Mike, barely two, greeted Mary and me dressed as a red devil, complete with tail, ready for Halloween. Cloantha, age three, was disguised as a witch in a peaked black hat, her hair very blonde against a black crepe paper cape. Mike Sr. put down his carving tool, leaving four spectacular pumpkin heads on his work bench. He approached us with a smile. "I am so glad you are here," Lucy said between hugs.

After a much-needed carefree night's sleep we were awakened by a phone call from Mary's friend Chuck Beatley, who had heard she was in Seattle. Chuck, Mayor of Alexandria, had become friends with Mary through her work at the *Alexandria Journal*. He was also a pilot for United Airlines and said that he would be leaving Seattle for D.C. the next day and wanted to have Mary on his flight. "Your scheduled flight goes through O'Hare, and I try to avoid that airport at any cost. It's the busiest and most dangerous, so why don't you fly with me instead?"

At breakfast, we told stories and laughed with the Copasses about our cross-country adventure. Lucy was excited about the hopeful new gift of family transportation, but had to make sure it was dependable. "Let's find out what's wrong with the Wayfarer. We can take the car to the Dodge dealer this morning. This mystery has got to be solved." We dropped off Betsy, as she suggested, and spent the last day before Mary's departure catching up with their lives and rejoicing in each other's company. That was the last time Mary ever saw Betsy.

I spent a short time in Seattle after Mary left, getting to know my grandchildren better. Before I bade them goodbye at the airport, I said to Lucy and Michael, "If that car turns out to be a lemon or if you find it an embarrassment, feel free to get rid of her. She has given us quite an adventure already."

Hugging me goodbye, Lucy said, "Mom, the car is going to be a real help. I can't believe what you and Mary went through to deliver it to us." [Image 18.2]

18.1 Ginny's sketch of a Rolls Royce Owners' Club car meet

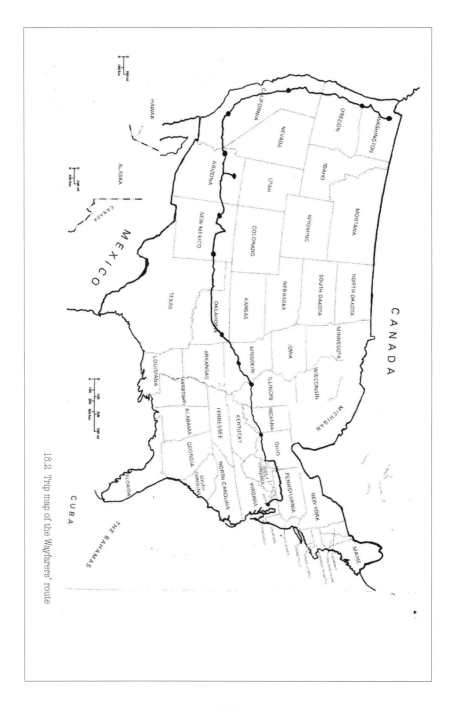

18.2 Trip map of the Wayfarers' route

1950 Dodge Wayfarer Advertisement—
when women were taking the wheel...

CHAPTER 19

Odometer Reading at Seattle: 30,629
Trip meter at Seattle: 4,629

Total mileage from Alexandria,
Virginia, to Seattle, Washington:
4,629 miles

A Letter
from Seattle

Alexandria, Virginia
Thanksgiving, 1970

We had resumed the normal pace of our lives in Alexandria—
Mary at her work with the *Alexandria Journal* and I taking
care of the house again and working with my art—when Lucy's letter
arrived at Orleans Place. I opened the letter with increasing excitement, shaking hands rattling the paper. I hurried to the telephone.
"Mary, will you join us for dinner up here on the Hill?" I told her we
had news of Betsy in Seattle. As we sat around the dinner table that
night, Mary read the letter again aloud.

Dear Oma Ginny, HoHo, and Mary,

When we count our blessings this coming Thursday, we will give thanks for HoHo who sent us Betsy and for the two of you for delivering her to us. We have enjoyed 250 trouble-free miles since you left Seattle. The car has made shopping and getting the kids safely to and from school easier. If any other driver were careless enough to bump us, his car would bounce off of sturdy old Betsy. Her appearance is not an embarrassment as you feared, but an asset. The teenagers in our island community think the car is cool. They call to us and wave as we roll by.

The mechanic returned the Wayfarer a few days after you left for home. "Little wonder no one could solve Betsy's problem," he told me. As he stepped from the driver's seat he announced, "You can blame Betsy's troubles on an empty package of cigarettes."

"An empty package of cigarettes?" I asked. "I can't believe it."

He explained. "When I drained the tank, the fuel was clean, no rust, no dirt. The next day, when the fumes subsided, I opened the tank. Sitting on the bottom of its clean floor was a sheet of cellophane. The size and shape told me it had to be the outside wrapper of a twenty-pack. Somebody—no doubt naughty kids—stuffed the discarded cigarette wrapper into the old lady's tank. Over time the paper would have disintegrated, leaving the cellophane floating free in the tank. On their way out here, whether you were driving up a hill, down a hill, or riding fast or riding slow, or when the gasoline got low, the fuel pump sucked the cellophane up against the gas outlet, interrupting the flow of the gas to the engine."

Happy Thanksgiving!

Affectionately,

Lucy

It appeared that recollections of our trip with Betsy might continue after dinner as Mary eagerly recalled more of our adventures and automobile misadventures for Bob. As for me, I was still reeling from the positive as well as surprising news in Lucy's letter. A *pack of cigarettes* had caused all that anguish, that uncertainty and hazard for us! I escaped into the library to ponder it and simmer down.

Logs in our library fireplace were but embers, yet they still warmed the room. As I sat musing, it astounded me what can be in a name. Emma's moniker "Betsy" for her old car seemed at first a simple way for her, as an elderly widow, to find familiarity and companionship with an inanimate object. Dodge's slick name "Wayfarer" promoted the great potential of this fine piece of machinery during the automotive exuberance of 1950. To us, Betsy had proven both names worthy. Indeed, Betsy, Mary, and I had taken on a familiarity few women and cars are privileged to have. And yes, we had been the ultimate Wayfarers together. But Betsy had somehow become more than that for the two of us.

Betsy had given us some priceless gifts, as might a dear though imperfect friend. It was her inadequacies, in fact, that had given us the greatest gifts—the rare gift of time together, mother and daughter, to elicit important personal stories and to reflect upon their place in the grander picture of history, to reflect on our loves, our beloved relatives and lifelong friends, the curious nature of some people from our point of view, on principles of life that matter so deeply, and on the things that remain constant through the "thick and thin" of time.

Betsy had also presented challenges, hurdles we could now be proud to have met and risen above—alone. By happenstance, and also because of her personality, she introduced us to some exceptional characters whose lives expressed to us the rich diversity of our amazing land, our cherished country.

I rose to join Mary and Bob with thankfulness in my heart, feeling the epic proportions of our odyssey, made possible by Betsy the Wayfarer. [Note 22 – A Note from Betsy]

PART TWO

Ginny and her three girls, 2006.
Left to right: Martha, Ginny, Mary, Lucy

Notes—How It
All Turned Out

Mary once said to me, "Mother, you shouldn't die until you learn how it all turned out."

Many important events occurred after our epic trip in the Way-farer in 1970, so in order to answer Mary's request, several additional happenings are reflected in the "Notes" below. Strands that were only starting to weave themselves in the time of our adventure in Betsy have been followed through their windings. Here they are, tied into interesting ribbons and knots, many still being enjoyed as they twist themselves through time.

You are invited to refer back to sections in Part One via noted numbers for each chapter. For example, in Chapter 9, p.135, where

Mary refers to race relations in the Alexandria schools, there is an elaborating note here in Part Two relating a detailed history of integration in Alexandria after 1970, specifically about the Titans team.

One of the strands that was a highlight of my life was the making and hanging of the reproduced Flags of the Bicentennial. Images of my researched creations, which now reside somewhere in the Library of Congress archives, are presented here. Some of my favorite paintings and silkscreens from my career as an artist are also shared with you here under "Artist's Favorites." You are invited to see many more images of my artwork on our website gallery at www.flordemayoarts.com.

In the picture portfolios to follow, you will find images of family and friends, young, old, or long gone, but all of whom have had a part in this narrative or in the making of us as fellow Wayfarers.

Patriotism (Note 1, page 46, from Chapter 4)

In 1976, we celebrated the 200th anniversary of our country. It was appropriate to feel the flush of patriotism again, and most Americans participated. All seemed right with the world to me for this one brief moment, in spite of the "hippie" generation that continued to question authority. Race relations at the time seemed to be on a positive course.

Cincinnati Union Station (Note 2, page 61, from Chapter 5)

Passenger train service left Union Terminal on October 28, 1972. The fourteen mosaic panels for the train concourse, designed by Winold Reiss, depicted important Cincinnati industries of the time. The mosaics were moved to the Cincinnati/Northern Kentucky International Airport in the 1970s, when the train concourse was removed, and now can be enjoyed by visitors on the airport concourses. The Union Station building was saved and declared a National Historic Landmark in 1977. In the late 1980s, the building was renovated and then reopened as the Cincinnati Museum Center in 1990. Passenger train service resumed on July 29, 1991, when Amtrak began operating at Union Terminal.

The Kassons (Note 3, page 79, from Chapter 6)

Cynthia (Cindy) Kasson's husband, Dr. Curtis Wayne McIntyre, did indeed become head of the Psychology Department at Southern Methodist University, teaching generations of students with his humor. Their son, Wade, continues the comedic legacy as a TV script writer. Their daughter, Sally's, interests include sports medicine, video animae, and homemaking.

Lawyer Hank Kasson and his wife, Belle, have visited me on several occasions in Tucson, when their legal work brought them to the Southwest, and they keep me up to date with the New South. Time perspectives grow more intriguing with age. I am remembering when Hank's daughter Kim was tiny, how Gran-gran adored tending her. Now, Kim has three almost grown children of her own.

Curt and Cindy McIntyre, 2014   Hank and Belle Kasson, 2014

The Sanborns and Jim Sanborn's Career
(Note 4, page 86, from Chapter 7)

Kaye and Sandy Sanborn's son, Jim Sanborn, became an extremely successful sculptor.

In 2010, five of Jim's schoolmates from Burgundy Farm Country Day School and I (mother of schoolmate Martha) attended an opening at Denver's Contemporary Art Museum for one of Jim's "Science in Art" installations of an operational replica of the original atom smasher.

While visiting, since I was the eldest of the group at their reunion, one of his contemporaries asked me, "Do you have any words of wisdom to share with us?"

"Yes," I said without hesitation, "we should all take more time to daydream." As soon as the words left my lips, Jim jumped up and said, "Yes, yes!" His response reminded me of that young contemplative boy who watched the swings so long ago.

From a letter Jim recently sent to me, I've included the following excerpt about his professional journey since the 1970s:

> For the last 30 years I have been making art inspired by science. From archaeology, to cryptography, to physics, my artistic continuum has waxed and waned scientific. At times the allusions to science are subtle, at times obvious, at times the distinction between science and art is blurred and at times some viewers of my work fail to find art in my science. Wide interpretations are fine with me and further the discussion.
>
> In the late 1970s I began working with geological forces, those slow but gigantic processes that formed the Earth we know. My gallery and museum installations included geological cutaways of stone strata that had been eroded in some way. In 1978 I started including lodestones*, a naturally magnetic ore of iron. I collected large numbers of these from the iron mining areas of southwest-

Kaye and Sandy Sanborn

Artist Jim Sanborn at Ginny's 88th birthday

ern Utah. Some of these weighed tons and some were fist sized. I pulled the large highly magnetized ones from the soon to be destroyed mountaintops using mile long cable attached to a bulldozer. I shipped these evocative rocks with the magical magnetic properties back to my studio and included them in both my installations and the public art works. One was destined for a future CIA project.

For millennia lodestones had been considered magical. The ancient Chinese used lodestone spoons in a primitive con game, they were spun by geomancers aka shamans, who knew they would always come to rest in the same orientation and thus they could move the symbols beneath the spoon to falsely predict the "future" of their unwitting Emperor. The Greeks believed that if you sailed a ship too close to a lodestone mountain the nails in the ship's hull would be pulled out and the ship would fall to the bottom of the sea. Tribal chiefs in the mountains of Africa had large, powerful lodestone gates to their villages as the first metal detectors, to locate the hidden iron weapons of their visitors.

267

I liked the invisible forces of lodestones. I liked the invisible forces of the Coriolis force, that force of the spinning Earth that makes whirlpools in the northern and southern hemispheres turn in opposite directions.

Through the 1980s I worked with these forces in all aspects of my art so when it was time for the General Service Administration's Art in Public Architecture panel to select an artist for the CIA commission they made a leap of faith and assumed I could work with the invisible forces of mankind...the invisible work of spies...they were right.

The CIA wanted to embellish their new headquarters building with a work of art. They already had a respectable art collection of largely Color School paintings enlivening the somewhat grim halls. They also wanted to enliven their image, not a simple thing, for an agency with easy targetitis. I think they got more than they bargained for with Kryptos.

Immediately following the dedication of Kryptos, I worked with the subject of secrecy in several exhibitions. In 1991, I exhibited a series of works using the CIA paper pulp as freestanding code rooms and as wall reliefs. These pieces all used coded and or international language texts, mostly in Russian and Arabic.

These shows had titles like "Covert Obsolescence" and "Secrets Passed." Also in 1991 I developed a type of piece that supported me as a public artist for twenty years, the "Projection Cylinder." This device consisted of a bronze cylinder perforated with encoded or international language text. Centered inside the cylinder was a pinpoint light that in a darkened room or on a public plaza projected the text over a very wide area. It was the magic lantern idea with mysterious content. These cylinders are now located in twelve different cities in the US.

All of the coded works related to clandestine tradecraft and covert operations carried out by the various competing sides in a global struggle. The works were inherently beautiful but had a dark edge, the effects were stunning but the message was bleak. I enjoy the beauty and the beast idea and it has been a strong element of my work ever since. I stuck with the coding systems developed during the Kryptos period, only the materials had changed.

Many artists' lives can be divided into stylistic phases. My phases usually last about 10 years, as I mentioned earlier in the 1970s geology was my focus, the 1980s lodestones and invisible forces were the thing and in the 1990s the Kryptos project stimulated a wider interest in secret subjects.

The Kryptos project was intense and fascinating all at once, but by 1994 the project was for me, old work, and by 1998 I began focusing on a very different aspect of secrecy.

Between 1995 and 1997 I took a break and stepped back from the difficult subject matter for a while and completed a series of large format projections in the desert in the western US and in Ireland. I needed to clean the slate, and completed a body of work totally unrelated to secrecy.

In the fall of 1998 during my last projection trip I visited White Sands National Monument in Southern New Mexico. This pristine and surreal spot was just 20 miles south of the Trinity Site, the spot where the first atomic bomb was detonated on July 16, 1945. I grabbed some pamphlets from the Monument store about the test and the implications of that test. After reading the material and studying the subject for weeks, the building of the first atomic bomb became my next stylistic phase. This phase culminated with the exhibition and catalog titled "Atomic Time" exhibited at the Corcoran Museum in 2003 and the Gwangju Biennale in South Korea in 2004.

With the advent of this nuclear phase I began testing the limits of the secrecy establishment. My reconstruction of the atomic bomb laboratory at Los Alamos included the (still classified as "Secret") interior core aka "physics package" of that first nuclear device. It was called "Fat Man" and in order to construct it I needed precise measurements and the design of the device. Since the device was still classified in the US, that info was hard to find, but there were still several sources. The design was not classified in the former Soviet Union and there was a "doomsday" anti-nuclear website run by Chuck Hansen that had the largest repository of Russian nuclear documents. The rationale of the anti-nuclear movement at the time was that nuclear secrets were in part responsible for the arms race. If everyone had the pertinent nuclear info then no one would fight over it, remember this was before 9-11 and the North Korean and Iranian nuclear programs.

*The lodestones on exposed mountaintops are magnetized by repeated lightning strikes over a period of thousands of years. In the historic past the residents of Cedar City, Utah, who would gather to watch the lightning show during storms, have corroborated this visual treat.

Virginia Heights Neighbors (Note 5, page 88, from Chapter 7)

Kaye and Sandy Sanborn remained our closest friends long after our move away from Virginia Heights and shared adventuresome visits with us at our Arizona retirement home and to the charming Mexican town of Alamos, Sonora. Herbert Brown Jr. became a child psychiatrist in Massachusetts. One of the LaHeureuxs' six children overcame her physical disability to become a responsible member of a religious order as a nun. Alan Johnston became an ichthyologist.

Burgundy Farm Country Day School (Note 6, page 89, from Chapter 7)

Burgundy Farm Country Day School was founded by people who wanted to create a progressive environment for their children's education, forward-looking and racially integrated well before that had been enacted into law. Skills brought by the founders and early parents to the Burgundy community were astounding. Worthy of mention are: Lois and Eric Sevareid, he being a news analyst and commentator, when radio was important for news and television was young and visionary; Katherine Stone, delegate from our district to the Virginia House of Representatives in Richmond; Philip Brown, economist and *Washington Post* columnist and his wife, Adel, an art teacher at Burgundy (their daughter Carin served in the Peace Corps and became a gynecologist); Eileen Eddy, genteel community activist and admirer of Eleanor Roosevelt; Tom Harris, lawyer for the AFL-CIO; Knox Kreutzer, a minister and counselor for prisoners; and Rachel Hall, who had taught in the American School in Beirut before coming to teach at Burgundy. Strong and visionary Head of School Agnes Saylor had been earlier blacklisted by Senator Joseph McCarthy for her socialist leanings.

Anne Lanpher (wife of aviator Coe Lanpher, Chapter 5), volunteer admissions officer at Burgundy, had studied at the Sorbonne and worked on Capitol Hill, and later taught high school French with worldly awareness. There is no doubt that the Burgundy experience changed lives of not only the students but their families in exciting ways. Larry Lanpher became a lawyer in Washington, D.C., Gibson Lanpher attended Brown University, overlapping with Martha, and enjoyed a career in the State Department, serving two terms in Zimbabwe.

Lucy Ames, being in Burgundy's seventh grade taught by Anne Ickes, daughter of Harold Ickes (better known as the "Old Curmudgeon" and Secretary of the Interior when F.D.R. was president), went into international relations and served in the Peace Corps office. Martha's appreciation for geology, natural sciences, and Native culture stems directly from second and third grade teacher Maxine Ropeshaw's use of the outdoors as their classroom (a major innovation at the time) and from having her whole class become a band of Algonquin Natives to learn skills of, and for, the land. Mary had inspiration and impetus for a career of articulate writing from her first grade teacher, Camay Brooks, daughter of musician Cab Calloway.

During this postwar time of economic development and social unrest, as our country attempted to change racism-perpetuating laws, strong citizens rose to the occasion and Burgundy Farm Country Day School was a mecca for these dedicated, progressive movers and shakers.

Luvenia (Note 7, page 95, from Chapter 7)

In 1983, when we retired to Tucson, I wrote Luvenia to say that Bob and I would be coming through The Plains in Fauquier County, Virginia, on our drive to Tucson for our permanent retirement in the West—we wanted to see her once again. She gathered all her family together to bid us farewell, those whom we knew and those whom we had never met. As I looked on their warm smiles my heart ached with emotion—pride in their friendship, and humility too, joy because of Luvenia's affection, and pain at our parting from her, leaving the life I had always known. That was our last visit, but we kept in touch with letters. Luvenia's daughter Molly has continued to keep in touch after her passing.

Virginia's Art Career (Note 8, page 98, from Chapter 7)

I did in fact land the commission to reproduce the Flags of the American Revolution, which I completed at the Torpedo Factory in time for the 1976 Bicentennial celebration at the Library of Congress. This experience is described in detail in Note 11. After leaving the exciting Torpedo Factory Arts Center when we retired to Tucson in 1984, I had many adventures that inspired my art over the ensuing years. Here are some of the highlights:

Cook Islands

For several seasons, I and a group of my fellow Tucson painters, who needed experience in drawing-from-life, hired a model and convened every month to improve our sketching. We seldom socialized because we were eager to sketch the model and too tired after sketching to feel very sociable before we went home. Out of the blue one day, John Jefferies asked, "Who would like to go paint in the South Pacific? I can make it happen for us." It came like a bomb. Four of us were able to take him up on his offer to make all the arrangements for a trip to the Cook Islands.

John is an astronomer from Australia who established one of the observatories in the Hawaiian Islands. Since he retired to Tucson he has used his great energy to become an excellent painter. He chose Roratonga, the largest of the Cook Islands, to start our art adventure. An American artist friend of John's living on the island guided us to the right places to paint.

No sooner had we set up our easels, when a young Polynesian lad happened by with a beautiful cock nestled in his arms. We asked him if he would pose for us as soon as he was free. Agreeing, he found us a fitting place to work in the shade of a large shed and went away with his chicken. Another islander saw the four of us painting and said, "You must be thirsty." He shinnied up a palm tree and came back with a coconut. With a hatchet, he deftly peeled away the rough bark of the nut, made a hole in the hard shell, and poured sweet coconut milk into four containers for each of us. He said, "Here, drink this. It will quench your thirst." When the young lad returned with the chicken, we congratulated him that his cock won the fight. He and his rooster proved excellent models, and the result was one of my best large pastel works. [Note: see Artist's Favorites.]

While in the Cooks, someone suggested that we hop a plane to Aitutaki, an island with the most beautiful lagoon in the world. It was. We motorboated out to be dropped off at one of the smaller atolls in that shallow lagoon, where we had a whole day to paint in this piece of heaven occupied only by chickens and feral cats.

Back on Aitutaki for a week, every evening as the sun went down I met three little native girls on the beach. They would dance the dances that the women were famous for performing. I asked the girls who had taught them. They said that all the girls on the island learned from their schoolteachers. I was so enamored with their personalities and endearing charm that each evening I asked these lovely girls to sit and pose while I sketched them. Even with their constant wiggling and giggling, I was able to get a number of sketches that I eventually used for a pastel painting. [Note: see Artist's Favorites.]

One day I sent my fellow artists off to paint in the mountains so I'd have a day to work alone. Beyond the high fence of the motel I heard the squealing of pigs. Two friendly cleaning women from our lodging told me a feast was being prepared for the installation of a new island chieftain. They said, "We'll take you to see what they are doing behind the fence." Many women were sitting on the ground preparing breadfruit and other delicacies to be served in hand-woven palm baskets. They introduced me to the few men there, first to the head of the ceremonies, from whom I asked permission to take photographs. He replied with great authority, "If I say you can make photographs, you can make photographs ... and I say you can make photographs." He then turned and introduced me to the new chieftain. Being so honored getting to know the true Cook islanders, I was sorry my artist friends had not been with me.

With Clo in Italy

My art experience was enriched when my granddaughter, Clo Copass, outlined a trip for me in Italy, a country she became familiar with while studying abroad her junior year at Stanford. Because Italy is so rich with works from the masters, it can be overwhelming. Clo knew this and, while visiting the many museums and churches throughout the country, guided me by pointing out one or two of the most significant masterworks that I should not miss.

To Italy with Muffin

I heard that well-known Tucson artist Sarah Schmerl was teaching a class in Italy. Without hesitation I signed up and invited my daughter Muffin to take the course with me. She hesitated, saying, "I know I can draw, but I've never painted." We purchased the art supplies she would need, practiced together a few times, and set off to the LaRomita Art School, located in a de-sanctified monastery in Terni, Umbria, Italy. For two weeks we painted in charming little hilltop towns, bringing picnic lunches provided by the school. Each day, Muffin and I explored these quaint villages before settling down to paint. These small towns revealed ancient houses and buildings that had been preserved through generations and provided us delightful subjects for our art. Muffin's skill burgeoned in Italy, and she returned to Tucson with more paintings than I.

Back and forth to Tucson

Long road trips after the "Betsy" journey became habit-forming, as my husband loved car travel. Bob and I took five road trips across country to Tucson and the Southwest before settling there in the early 1980s. Along the way, I would travel with my art supplies—a board with watercolor paper leaning on the dashboard, my water can in the cup holder, my travel tin of pigments on my lap. As scenery sped by, I learned how to get something on paper quickly. When we passed through farm country, I found if I didn't finish one farmhouse

275

before it disappeared, a similar one would soon come into view to aid me in completing the image. The speed with which I had to complete a composition was better training than many of my formal classes. The end result was a series of more than a hundred miniature watercolors that I enjoy having in my home today as reminders of great adventures. [See Chapter 1, header image.]

Once Bob and I made the decision to land in Tucson, I found it to be the perfect place for painting, mainly because of the light, but also due to the "exotic" vegetation and wonderful rugged landscapes. Wherever I went I sketched or painted. I became a member of the Southern Arizona Watercolor Guild, participating in their exhibits, and later taught drawing and pastel painting for SAGE, a continuing education organization full of interesting retirees and associated with the University of Arizona, now known as OLLI.

With Mary in France

I was able to visit Cezanne's countryside in Provence, France, with my daughter Mary Ames and her partner, John Stubbings. The scenes we passed brought so many of Cezanne's paintings to life, particularly around Mont Sainte-Victoire. We traveled down to the Mediterranean to see the work of Matisse, particularly to see his cut-out assemblages.

Being able to stand in front of original artworks of these masters rather than seeing them printed in an art book was tremendously inspiring. I returned from these trips re-energized, my own creativity rekindled.

Lichen Rocks on the Snowy Range

On our second trip west in our low-slung, long-wheel-based '61 Ford Galaxie, Bob and I decided to spend the night in the happy spot where we had stayed years before in the Snowy Range of southern Wyoming. After a long day of driving, we rested over a cocktail, felt revived, and decided to explore in the car before supper. Bob took the idea of exploring literally and turned off the main highway onto a two-track fire road meant for jeeps. The road kept rising and we kept motoring until we realized that we couldn't turn around. Soon we emerged above the tree line onto a meadow where we could see the fire lookout still higher up the meadow. We figured we were about 10,000 feet high and found ourselves really tipsy from our one cocktail. We stopped and got out of the car, seeing the world as we normally wouldn't have, looking down at the sun setting behind a mountain below us. The sun lit up a lichen-covered boulder nearby. At that moment, I thought I had never seen anything so beautiful as the colors of the lichens on the rock. That memory remained so strong that later, back in my Alexandria studio, I recreated those lichens on canvas with acrylic paint and a roller. I will never give that painting away!

Sputnik (Note 9, page 112, from Chapter 8)

For many years after Sputnik's first pass, we unexpectedly saw it two other times, once while gazing at the Big Dipper from our patio in Tucson on a pleasant summer night and another by chance through the back window of our car as Bob drove us from Washington to New York. Viewing it did not engender the Cold War fears that it brought when we first saw the strange moving star in the sky. Those subsequent sightings were a sign of our new Space Age and its positive boost to technology.

John Hubbard Ames, the Younger (Note 10, page 113, from Chapter 8)

Martha was living in the house Bob and I purchased in Tucson in 1978 for our later retirement. Bob's nephew John Hubbard Ames moved from the east to Scottsdale and often drove down to Tucson to celebrate holidays or help Martha finish landscaping the garden. In 1979, we flew west for a visit in time to have Christmas dinner with Martha and her friend Sandra Turner. Sandra brought her sister,

Wendy Thompson, with Wendy's little daughter Amy. Cousin John came to join us. All evening, John snapped pictures of everybody present, but his camera became heavily loaded with shots of Wendy and Amy. John and Wendy married on July 18, 1981. They are the beloved grandparents of Amy and Glen Masuhara's children.

John and Wendy Ames,
Ireland 2013

Amy and Glenn
Masuhara and family

Flags of the American Revolution (Note 11, page 122, from Chapter 8)

Soon after delivering the twenty-year-old Wayfarer to Seattle and returning to Alexandria, I learned that I had been awarded the commission to create the flag exhibit that the Library of Congress envisioned to celebrate the Bicentennial of the American Revolution. The first skill required for this project was experience in sewing, which included pattern-making and embroidery work. Additionally, painting on fabric was necessary. I fit the bill perfectly! The assign-

278

ment was to replicate in giant size, as close to the originals as possible, the flags that were known to have flown in battle during that war, either on land or sea.

Another skill necessary was the ability to do research. For the project I uncovered references to ten flags, presented my findings to Associate Librarian Elizabeth Hamer, who was overseeing the Library of Congress's participation in the big celebration. She subsequently presented my ideas to the two historians appointed by the Library committee in charge and they said, "Yes, full steam ahead." In 1974, the Library of Congress published the booklet *Twelve Flags of the American Revolution* to accompany its exhibition on the Bicentennial of American Independence, in which they added two flags to my ten.

I worked on the flags during the impeachment proceedings of President Nixon. Watching the drama unfold on television, I wondered how *this* was going to turn out. Would the government survive the impeachment of a president? I consoled myself by remembering the American Revolution and the people who made a positive outcome possible—men like Adams, Jefferson, and Washington.

The Betsy Ross Flag was not among the ones assigned to replicate. If you believe, as our history books told us, that Betsy Ross made the first national banner and three great leaders of our country called on her and ordered a flag to be made with thirteen red and white stripes with a circle of thirteen white stars on a field of blue, you are into mythology. True, Betsy Ross might have had something to do with Revolutionary War battle flags, but whatever she fabricated is a conjecture. The only documentation historians have at their command is a single invoice submitted to the Continental Congress by "Betsy Ross, seamstress."

What *is* certain is that at the time when the colonists were protesting to the king, a hot-headed patriot sewed six white stripes on the red field of the British Red Ensign flag to speak for thirteen protesting colonies still loyal to the King. In 1775, when war seemed

279

inevitable, George Washington was in New York putting together an army. He proposed that there be a banner to unite the colonies and that it should have thirteen red and white stripes with a field of blue and thirteen stars in the upper left quadrant. Silk was ordered from France to make such a flag, but the silk was still in a warehouse at the end of the revolution. The British Ensign's Cross of St. George and St. Andrew remained on the flag in the upper corner and was later referred to as the *Grand Union* flag. This one was the prototype for our National Banner today.

Described and illustrated below are my reproductions for the Library of Congress Bicentennial:

Grand Union – This flag was first seen flying from the masts of the colonial fleet on the Delaware River late in 1775, before it was raised at Prospect Hill. On January 1, 1776, General George Washington's troops raised the *Grand Union* on the liberty pole at Prospect Hill near the American general's headquarters in Cambridge, Massachusetts. For almost the entire first year of the American Revolution, the Grand Union Flag was the ensign of the struggling new "United States."

Grand Union Flag

Pennsylvania Regimental Banner (and Harrisburg Trial) – In 1972, I went to Harrisburg, Pennsylvania, to research this banner. It was brought out of archives so that I could photograph it, make color sketches, and measure it. The Pennsylvania flag I fabricated was based on this research.

Mary came along with me because she had heard about the Harrisburg Seven Trials and was interested in attending this historical event scheduled at that time. She managed to get in on one of the

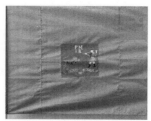

First Pennsylvania Flag

first days of the trial. U.S. attorneys charged the Harrisburg Seven with conspiracy to kidnap Kissinger and also to bomb heating tunnels under Washington government buildings. They filed the case in the City of Harrisburg. Activist attorney, former Attorney General Ramsey Clark, led the defense team for their trial during the spring months of 1972. Unconventionally, he didn't call any witnesses in his clients' defense, including the defendants themselves. He reasoned that the jury would at the outset be sympathetic to his Catholic clients but that sympathy would be ruined by their testimony if it were disclosed that they had burned their draft cards. After an extraordinarily long deliberation, the jury remained hung and the defendants were freed. Although the government spent $2 million on this trial, it did not win a conviction. This was one of the first reversals suffered by the U.S. government in such cases.

Texel Flag – This flag was flown by John Paul Jones on the ship *Bonhomme Richard* during his successful defeat of the H.M.S. *Serapis* in a battle in the English Channel on September 23, 1779. The flag name is from the Netherlands island port of Texel. When Jones sailed into the Dutch harbor, the English accused the Dutch of harboring pirates under the flag of an unrecognized country. To protect themselves, the Dutch commissioned sketches of the flags on both Texel and on the captured *Serapis*. It was from these paintings I designed this flag.

Texel Flag flown
by John Paul Jones

The Flag of the Third New York Regiment – This flag is alleged to have been carried by soldiers in the Battle of Yorktown in 1781. I reproduced my flag from a photograph of the original, which is pre-

Third New York Flag

served in the Albany Institute of History and Art.

Rhode Island Regimental Banner

Rhode Island Regimental Banner – This flag may have been the first with thirteen stars to represent the colonies. This was one of the flags I miniaturized for needlepoint design, later duplicated into kits to be sold in the Smithsonian Institution Museum Shop. The original finished, framed needlepoint reproductions that I made hung in the Lyceum Museum in Alexandria, Virginia, during the Bicentennial celebration.

Gadsden Flag–"Don't Tread on Me"

The Gadsden Flag - Don't Tread on Me – Col. Christopher Gadsden, a delegate to the Continental Congress and a member of the Marine Committee, designed this flag to be used by the commander-in-chief of the American Navy. He brought it to Charleston and presented it to the Provincial Congress of South Carolina on February 9, 1776. As described in the congressional journals: "... an elegant standard ... being a yellow field, with a lively representation of a rattlesnake in the middle, in the attitude of going to strike, and these words underneath, 'Don't Tread On Me.'" I had to design the Gadsden flag based on this description because there were no historical drawings to guide me. The drawing of a striking snake lost nothing in the translation and I found it easy to create a "lively representation." This was also one of the flags that I miniaturized for needlepoint design. In fact, the snake was so lively that some young "enthusiastic patriot" could not resist removing this framed needlepoint from the Lyceum and taking it home with him, never to surface again.

An Appeal to Heaven – The Pine Tree, a longtime symbol of New England, was chosen as the emblem on the flag of two floating batteries on the Charles River during the siege on Boston in September 1775. It was later adopted by "Washington's Navy" in order to distinguish the American ships from the enemies' ships. It seemed likely to me that because of the rush of 1775, in fabricating this flag, the bunting used for these flags might be like today's homespun. I could easily imagine a soldier's loving wife or mother embroidering this green pine tree on the white background. With no illustrations to follow, I used this assumption in creating the flag.

An Appeal to Heaven—the New England Flag with pine tree symbol

Guilford Courthouse Flag—North Carolina

Guilford Courthouse Flag – Although it is not confirmed that this flag was used in the revolution, it has been associated with the Guilford Courthouse battle. It is also believed to originally have had fifteen stars and fifteen stripes. A surviving flag is displayed at the North Carolina Museum of History in Raleigh, North Carolina, and was the design I used, with the eight-pointed blue stars on a white field, seven blue stripes, and six red stripes.

Second New Hampshire Banner

The Flag of the Second New Hampshire Regiment – During the British invasion of New York from the north, led by General John Burgoyne in the summer of 1777, the British Ninth Regiment of Foot encountered a small band of retreating American troops from the Second New Hampshire Regiment at Fort Anne in New York. In July, an unknown British officer recorded in his journal: "The 9th took 2 stands of colours, and some prisoners," meaning two of the prisoners' local militia flags. A few months later, following the surrender of the British, Burgoyne hid the British flag of the Ninth and the two from New Hampshire. All three flags traveled to Britain. The British Ninth Regiment flag was presented to the King, but it wasn't until 1912 that the two New Hampshire flags were bought and returned finally to the United States. They are in the archives of the New Hampshire Historical Society. It took me days to replicate the interlocking rings of the thirteen circles, and I liked this image so much that I actually painted it onto a table at my studio.

Bennington – The historians I worked with on this project doubted it was used in battle because of its enormous size of 5.5 feet by 10 feet. They projected that it was more likely to have flown over the American encampment near the battlefield at Bennington. It is the earliest stars and stripes flag and the first to be used by land forces in the United States.

Bennington Flag

I think the most humorous and sexy revolutionary flag story originated at Fort Schuyler (present site of the Bronx) when it was under siege by the British. The British kept Fort Schuyler under siege for so long that rations and morale were dangerously low. A contemporary newspaper had written of their hunger also for a national banner. Legend has it that this newspaper article might have been slipped into the fort and became the inspiration for the making of a flag. Such a flag was supposedly fabricated from an officer's white shirt, the blue cloth of a captain's cloak, and the red petticoat of a camp follower. The emblem of red, white, and blue was pieced together by the women of the fort. It is said that when the last stitch was taken, a soldier drummed for an assembly, an officer read the congressional resolution, *BANG!* went the cannon, up went the flag, and amid the cheers of the men, Fort Schuyler first unfurled the Stars and Stripes in the face of the enemy. All we really know is that an officer at Fort Schuyler sent a bill to the Continental Congress to repay him for his white shirt. So much for the unsung contributions made by "fellow" revolutionaries.

Notes for flags are based on research by Virginia W. Ames in addition to research by historians from the Library of Congress in *Twelve Flags of the American Revolution*. Washington, D.C.: 1974

Engraving of Smithsonian "Castle on the Mall"

The Emperor's Visit to "The Castle on the Mall"

Shortly after the Bicentennial flag experience, the head of purchasing for the Smithsonian shops asked me to design another needlepoint kit—one for the Francis Scott Key flag. She said, "I will give you enough postcards of the flag on display to include one in each of these kits. The box of cards will await you at the information desk of our Natural History Museum entrance on Constitution Avenue." My trip to pick up the postcards of this flag is worth telling.

The Smithsonian Castle on the Mall in our Capital City looks exotic in the company of the neoclassic memorials to Lincoln, Washington, and Jefferson. The castle is headquarters of the Smithsonian Institution, whose offices were at that time on the ground level where some rare items are also exhibited. On this day, my friend Kaye Sanborn and I arrived at the castle and entered through a lower level rear door to the business department. Our intent was to leave our coats in the office of a fellow researcher with whom Kaye had worked, to mount the flight of stairs to the main floor, and go through a double door and across the lobby to the dining room to enjoy a luncheon, a privilege extended to Smithsonian members.

A huge sign stopped us short, "**Dining Room Closed**." A guard in uniform stood stiffly by the entrance, and when we inquired why the sudden closure, he answered curtly, "Today the dining room is closed to outsiders." A little chagrined, we turned to leave but were stopped by another guard at the double door through which we had entered. "Sorry, you will have to exit by the main entrance." How weird, we thought, as we walked down the front stairs around to the back entrance where, fortunately, we were able to get our wraps and leave.

"Let's pick up the postcards first and afterwards treat ourselves to lunch at the Hay-Adams. I will drop you at the Constitution Avenue entrance to the Natural History Museum, wait for you if I can, circle around if I cannot, and pick you up right here, as your box will be heavy."

The bulky box would contain hundreds of copies of the postcard depicting the battle-torn Star Spangled Banner, now hanging on display in one of the Smithsonian buildings, the same flag that had flown over Fort McHenry in Baltimore during the War of 1812 when the fort was under siege by the British. Every school kid in America has heard the story of how Francis Scott Key was inspired to write the national anthem while watching that flag in the rockets' red glare during this battle. By the time of the Bicentennial celebration of the American Revolution, the Fort McHenry flag had at last been put on display for all to see.

When Kaye pulled up close to the back entrance of the Natural History Museum to let me off, we were rushed by three D.C. police officers flailing arms and shouting, "*Move on!*" Heavy traffic on Constitution Avenue held us captive against the curb. Did those officers volunteer to stop the traffic so that we could move on as they demanded? No! With voices strident, they ordered us to get going. At last, a break in the traffic allowed us to escape and as we pulled away, a big, black limousine rolled into the spot we had vacated. I could see in the rearview mirror that an American flag flew from one of the front fenders of that machine and from the other, the red circle flag of Japan. So *this* was why the Secret Service had thwarted us at every turn. Emperor Hirohito of Japan, who was forced out of his protected isolation following World War II, was now in Washington, D.C., on his second trip to the United States. We learned from the following morning's *Washington Post* that he'd visited the Smithsonian because he had a profound interest in mollusks.

But my encounters with the emperor were not over. The next day, while picnicking with a friend on the wharf beside the Potomac River at the foot of King Street, Alexandria, we saw the president's yacht cruising by. Between us and the yacht were two small boats populated with Secret Service agents, their guns drawn and pointed at *us*. Heavens! I turned away quickly. Maybe the Secret Service agents wondered why I was always present when the emperor was passing near. For a moment, I felt vulnerable, and was relieved when I read thereafter of his return to Japan. I never did finish those needlepoint kits of *The Star Spangled Banner*.

Immanuel-Church-on-the-Hill Community (Note 12, page 123, from Chapter 8)

In addition to those Immanuel parishioners, like the Sanborns discussed elsewhere in this writing, other friends from the Immanuel congregation have gone their separate ways over the years and their children continue to make the world better.

Bill and Emily Bobbitt retired to their Appalachian mountain home at WEB Hill Farm. Buzzie and Vernie Knight took their retirement in Tidewater, Virginia. Their son John, a pal of Muffin's, became an admired lawyer in Richmond, Virginia. The Cartens' daughter, Beth, married a physicist, now involved in super collider research in Switzerland. Bob and I escorted Johnny and DeeDee Walker in Bob's 1936 Rolls Royce to their 50th wedding anniversary celebration.

Soon after we settled in Tucson, Ivan Winterberg visited us by bicycle, en route from California to the East Coast. Julie Winterberg hasn't missed sending an annual Christmas card to me for decades.

Bob's ashes were interred in a 1993 ceremony attended by many Immanuel friends in the Memorial Garden that Bob and I had helped design and plant behind Zabriski Chapel and the Parish House, with our azaleas and other flowering shrubs under the oaks.

Celestine Sibley (Note 13, page 126, from Chapter 8)

Celestine wrote twenty-five books, some of them mystery novels. I read one of her novels, *Jincey*, a story about the people she knew around her in her Georgia home. She received the McGill Award for Outstanding Journalism, so I believe that her thoughts about racism were compatible with Ralph McGill's. I tried to reach her at her office, which McGill had set aside for her use until her death. Sadly, I never heard from her. She died at 85 in 1999 with three grown children whom I would enjoy meeting.

Backstory for *Remembering the Titans* (Note 14, page 135, from Chapter 9)

In 1971, the schools of Alexandria, Virginia, were at last integrated. Because the entire city would judge the success of the racially-mixed school system on the success or failure of the newly integrated football team that first fall, the news was much more significant than results of a sporting event. Thankfully that same year, the Titans, the T.C. Williams High School football team, won the state championship.

Twenty-eight years later, in 1999, these events were interpreted as a movie, *Remember the Titans*. President Clinton, Denzel Washington (who played Coach Herman Boone), Herman Boone himself (the Black head coach who came from North Carolina), the Titans' Coach Yoast, and many of the players and people originally involved in the events came to the kickoff showing of the movie.

At this premier, Mary gave a copy of the tape of the original radio broadcast of the state semi-final game and copies of her original articles to the players present. Mary had covered the 1971 football season in the *Alexandria Journal*. Two years after the movie, in 2001, the Alexandria Human Rights Commission held a thirty-year anniversary celebration of the integration of schools and the Virginia state football championship that had resulted.

Mary served as a news reporter for the *Alexandria Journal* from 1969 to 1975, assigned to cover the City Council, the schools, and the courts. In this account, she intentionally uses the terms that were in regular use at that time. The following is the text of the document:

> ### The Role of the 1971 T.C. Williams Titans' Football Team In the Bigger Picture—Recollections of Mary E. Ames for the Alexandria, Virginia, Human Rights Commission's 30th anniversary celebration of secondary school integration and the state football championship, December 3, 2001:
>
> It's always difficult to imagine what an event was like if you weren't there, or what a period of time was like if you didn't live through it. Just think how many people at the scene of the collapse of the World Trade Center buildings this September mentioned what a difference there was between seeing the devastation in person and seeing it on TV. And, if you weren't alive during an important period in history, like the
>
> Great Depression or the Civil Rights Movement, it's that much harder to imagine.

Even folks who are present and deeply involved in these sorts of life-altering events don't recall them the same way. Details–often the painful ones, thank goodness–get deleted from memory. Our personal roles are rewritten in our imaginations so that we end up believing we played a larger or smaller part than we really did. Historians alter facts inadvertently, movie screenplay writers, on purpose, for dramatic effect.

So it should come as no surprise if each of us, today, has a different idea of how the events of 30 years ago unfolded in Alexandria–or, if people who wanted a different outcome then, recollect those days far differently than we who were pleased.

Nevertheless, we now celebrate. And we do so, not because we believe the upheaval that accompanied the integration of schools those decades past has solved the problems of human rights in our city. We celebrate because we can see, looking back from this distance, that in 1971, the course of human relations in Alexandria was altered for the better. We want to show our gratitude to the host of people who helped dismantle the long-standing system of racial segregation in our public schools. And, in particular, we wish to thank the young men of the 1971 T.C. Williams High School football team and their coaches for demonstrating so clearly that the notion of providing everybody an equal opportunity to excel is beneficial in practical ways, and not just correct in theory.

Yet we also feel we must remember, or try to imagine, how tense those times were, in order that neither we, nor future generations, repeat any of the long series of injustices that began with that enormous injustice: slavery; so that we never again get mired in a system that gives one group of people unfair advantage over another.

290

So we ask: What were the forces that divided our community along racial lines in 1971 and what enabled us to begin in earnest to break them down that year?

Background: Segregation in Virginia and in Alexandria

Most amazing to recall, now that the Alexandria schools are filled with the colors, races, beliefs and languages of the whole world, is that all but two percent of the people in the city during that era were considered either black or white. Throughout the South, a person's race, far more than gender or religion, and leagues more than talent, brains, or even wealth, had come to define his or her status. More than 100 years after fighting the bloodiest war in U.S. history over the issue, race was still the characteristic that, more than any other polarized us.

Whenever I refresh my memory on this subject by doing the necessary digging into legal documents and my own news accounts, I become acutely aware of just how organized and determined the opposition to racial integration had been, for decades, throughout Virginia and still was, in 1971; and how well disguised it often was beneath a facade of gentility or concern.

The Commonwealth had persisted, longer than most states, in passing laws to resist any change to the old system of segregation which, since the Emancipation, had preserved for white people privileges—real and imagined – in every facet of life, not only in education, but in work, housing, travel, even in the choice of a spouse. For a very long time after federal law required the integration of public schools throughout the country, Virginia schools were not, in fact, fully integrated.

Alexandria had long been segregated by patterns of housing—a situation that persists today. In 1971, even more than now, black people were concentrated in the extreme eastern part of town and white folks, in the central and western parts. That meant people of different races remained ignorant of each other's daily lives and habits, a sure recipe for perpetuating fear and mistrust. And, because a child generally attended the school closest to home, most children didn't have the chance, even in school, to play with, or exchange ideas with, children of the other race. And this was in a city that had almost 18,000 students, 28 percent of whom were black. If exposure to each other didn't begin at a young age, how were people of different races ever going to get along?

When the federal courts finally forced the issue of public school integration in the South, early in 1971, the changes that had to be made in Virginia, and in Alexandria, were far more extensive than in states or school districts that had gradually complied with the law. And the daily lives of many citizens–black and white–were abruptly altered.

In hindsight, it appears to me that the extent of the disruption required to integrate the Alexandria secondary schools in 1971, and the elementary schools two years later, may have been a blessing in disguise. But it didn't seem so then. Just as the recent, shocking events in New York and neighboring Arlington County have brought people together, the wholesale desegregation of the Alexandria schools caused many people (including teenaged boys who thought they had little in common but the game of football) to find common ground with strangers and new strength within themselves.

Race Relations in Alexandria and its Schools, 1970-71

In the summer of 1970, with the demands of law enforcement fast outpacing the training and resources of Alexandria's police department, twenty-seven officers left their jobs. By November, major crime in the city, as reported to the FBI, had increased about 41 percent over the same period the previous year, propelled by a huge rise in cases of burglary and larceny. Law enforcement professionals knew that most of these crimes were motivated by drug addiction and poverty, not by hatred itself; and they said the number of cases would diminish once more police officers were trained and back on the streets. But people weren't so sure. Molotov cocktails had been hurled into the window of the boyhood home of Confederate General Robert E. Lee and a couple of other buildings around town. Before police could figure out that the perpetrators of those acts were few in number, white folks feared that widespread rioting was underway and black people were afraid of the possible backlash. Also by November of 1970, a trial was underway in the case of John Hama, a 24-year-old white, 7-Eleven-store employee who had apparently shot a 19-year-old black youth, Robin Gibson, and then planted a knife to make it appear the killing was in self-defense. White people were clinging to the hope that the motive was self-defense. Blacks were afraid justice would not be served because the jury consisted of 12 white men.

Tensions in the larger community, naturally, reverberated through the schools and back out. The city had three high schools, each of them serving students from ninth to twelfth grades. Of the three, George Washington High School, in the east end of town had the largest black student population–48 percent. More than 85 percent of teachers and administrators at the school, however, were white. The principal, nearing retirement age, was the living image of George Washington, the man. He was a particularly kind soul with a reputation for being good with kids, but he was definitely not someone with whom the students could identify, nor did he succeed, that year, in holding their respect. At the school's homecoming football game, on October 3, 1970, the white senior class president made an insulting reference to a black girl who had just won the homecoming queen title. Tempers flared; epithets flew. School administrators responded by enacting new disciplinary measures and strictly enforcing the old ones. But it was the students who eased the situation by calling for a new election in which a black football player, nominated by a white student, became senior class president.

Three weeks later, at an assembly at midtown T.C. Williams High, held as part of the school's Community Affairs Week, students there voiced various grievances and asked pointed questions of Superintendent of Schools John Albohm about the possibility of change. They later complained of "the lack of seriousness" with which the superintendent answered those questions. Then, in late November, the very same week the trial of the 7-Eleven-store clerk began, the T.C. Williams football team beat George Washington to put T.C. first, Hammond High second, and G.W. last, in a hotly contested intra-city competition.

Just before Christmas, the Parent-Teacher Association Council held a meeting to elicit the views of recent high school graduates on their educational experience, including race issues in the schools. Students of both races said that black kids hadn't been encouraged to excel because of a pervasive attitude, among faculty and guidance counselors, that black students were headed for jobs rather than college.

In addition to reporting these events, The *Alexandria Journal-Standard* (now, *Journal*) ran a front-page editorial, posing as a letter to Santa. The "letter" wished for certain "presents" for various public officials. Because its message was cloaked in humor, rather than the usual serious, high tone of opinion, the editorial was able to advocate change without causing much offense. And, indeed, that editorial has always seemed to me to stand out–like an arrow on the pavement–marking a shift in direction then taking place, not only in the newspaper's back office, but also among large numbers of Alexandrians who had long been riding comfortably down the middle-of-the-road.

The *Journal*'s Christmas wish for traffic director Ken Smith was "a memorial statue to the Union soldiers [to be placed] at the other end of Washington Street." (The Confederate statue at the south end had become both a traffic hazard and a symbol of the city's recalcitrant southern leanings.) The editorial begged Santa to bring fire chief Milton Penn "six qualified black firemen, before the fire starts," and, for superintendent Albohm, "a gross of birch rods, so he can stick to his new educational philosophy."

Here was a Republican-owned newspaper–one of its owners, a member of the Nixon White House staff; its publisher, a proponent of the increasingly strict measures in the schools–admitting publicly that a whole lot more than tight discipline would be needed to improve race relations in Alexandria.

On the first Monday of spring, instead of going to classes, 50 or 60 black students, and some non-students, assembled in the G.W. cafeteria demanding to discuss with school officials a list of changes they wanted to see at the school. The demands covered items ranging from the racial make-up of the faculty and the lack of black culture courses to the quality of food and the desire for a jukebox in the cafeteria. The list, they said, was compiled from a survey of fellow students. Dick Hills, the principal, promised to meet with the students in two days, "if," he said, "it could be done in an orderly fashion," before or after classes. After lunch, the group grew to about 300 and reassembled in the auditorium. Some students were suspended for encouraging attendance at the unauthorized assembly and two non-students were charged with trespassing.

On Wednesday morning, the principal announced he had not yet arranged the meeting he had promised. By then, angered over one of the suspensions, the group of black students, joined by some from T.C. and from Parker-Gray Middle School and others, beyond Alexandria, had grown to 350 and had moved into the gymnasium. There, the principal told them he had reached the superintendent who was willing to meet with them. Minutes later, smoke from a fire set in the gym could be seen billowing out of the generators. Five minor fires were discovered elsewhere at the school that day, and classes were dismissed early.

As racial tension in the schools had been mounting that year, elsewhere in public life, fortunately, it seemed to be lessening. The face of city government itself had been changing, and that was a major factor. The seven member City Council, newly elected the previous summer, featured a bright, young crop of lawyers and businessmen, including Ira Robinson, a corporate attorney and the town's first black elected official since post-Civil War reconstruction. John Holihan, a new police chief, far more open to change than his predecessor, had taken the reins of the department, also in the late summer of 1970. Of 12 new officers he hired that autumn, two were black, an increase of 33 percent in the number of black patrolmen. Wayne Anderson, a new city manager from the Midwest, arrived in December and quietly but swiftly altered the way things were done at City Hall. Anderson's professional attitude and even-handedness raised spirits all over town. One of the many changes he made was the appointment of a black assistant city manager. And, finally, in July of 1971, following the troubled school year, the school board selected Ferdinand Day its first black chairman in memory.

School Integration and the Law: The Titanic Struggle in the Courts

By 1971, racial integration of public schools had been the law of the land for 17 years, having been mandated by the Supreme Court in 1954 after 13 Negro parents (as the Court then called them), led by railroad worker and part-time preacher Oliver Brown, brought a case against the school board in Topeka, Kansas. It could be said truthfully that Alexandria schools were no longer legally segregated in 1971. Black and white children attended school together in our city, but only to the extent that the neighborhoods around the schools were integrated.

In practice, Virginia was one of the last frontiers in the movement of non-white citizens to attain the equal protection of the laws, mandated by the Fourteenth

Amendment to the U.S. Constitution. So powerful were the forces for segregation, including some of Virginia's most influential lawyers, that—even after the Civil Rights and Voting Rights Acts became law in the mid-1960s—the Commonwealth instituted a system, backed by provisions in the state code, that flew in the face of the Supreme Court by allowing parents to choose what school their children would attend. The system was called "freedom of choice."

Rural New Kent County, between Richmond and Williamsburg, for example, had only two schools, one traditionally black, and the other white. The school population was roughly half and half, and the homes of people of both races were scattered throughout the county, not segregated geographically, as in Alexandria. Complete integration of the schools, therefore, could have been accomplished in accordance with the 1954 court rulings without complicated zoning plans or cross-county busing. Instead, bolstered by state law, the school district allowed parents to choose which school their children would attend. From 1965 to 1968, the year the Supreme Court ordered a change to the "freedom of choice" practices in New Kent County, the justices noted that not a single white student had chosen to attend the county's "all-Negro school, although 115 Negro pupils [had] enrolled in the formerly all-white school."

It's instructive to remember, also, that, until the Supreme Court ruled in a Virginia case in 1967, interracial marriages were illegal in our state. A white person could only be married to someone who had (and this is a quote from the statute) "no trace whatever of any blood other than Caucasian." The law went to great lengths, however, to make an exception for anyone with one-sixteenth or less of American Indian blood—on the chance that such a person might be a descendant of the hallowed union between Englishman John Rolfe and native-American Pocahontas.

Against this backdrop of persistent and successful efforts to perpetuate a system of separating black and white people in opposition to its decisions, the Supreme Court, in October of 1970, heard arguments in an appeal of a Charlotte, North Carolina, school integration case that had been going on since 1965. The ruling, which came the following April, established a high standard of compliance for the dozens of districts in the southeastern United States that had not fully dismantled their formerly segregated systems. Alexandria was one of these.

Though the court did not mandate any precise formula for achieving full integration, the school districts subject to the rulings in the Swann case, could only be certain of complying if the racial mix in each of its schools approximated the racial composition of the district's total student population.

Well before the case was decided, John Albohm, the Alexandria superintendent, could see the writing on the wall. He had served here for eight years and in Pennsylvania for many years before that. Even his toughest critics had little doubt the superintendent believed school integration was morally right, legally just, and could be accomplished in a way that was educationally sound. But Albohm was a man who understood political power and sought political approval. For years, he had not pushed for changes that he, himself believed were right and knew were inevitable.

Albohm was aware of the details of a plan, devised by a court-appointed consultant to the Charlotte-Mecklenburg County school board, for grouping each in-town black elementary school with two or three suburban white ones and busing children between the outlying and inner-city schools. That plan had been approved by the court the previous year but rejected, in large part, by the Charlotte board of education. The superintendent knew such a plan would suit Alexandria, considering its segregated housing pattern. But he was more influenced by the political opposition to massive busing and not inclined to initiate such a sweeping reorganization of the elementary schools until he was convinced the federal courts would leave Alexandria no other option.

The superintendent's persistent lack of action was a great frustration to proponents of school integration. On April 25, 1971, at a meeting of the local NAACP, City Councilman Robinson delivered a speech citing certain deficiencies in the schools that could be documented with the administration's own figures. Primary among them were that black children were being advanced through most of the elementary schools without having been taught to read adequately, and that qualified black educators, guidance counselors, and athletic coaches were not being promoted or hired in sufficient numbers to achieve integration of the staff or to provide role models for black students. None of the six secondary schools, he pointed out, had black principals or head coaches.

Robinson laid these deficiencies directly at Albohm's feet and called for the superintendent's resignation. It was a decision, Robinson said, that had taken him "a good many months and years of thought." No wonder, considering the factors that must have entered into his calculus. One of these was that Alexandrians on the other side of the integration issue, notably a group called

Citizens for Quality Education, anticipating that Albohm would further integrate the schools, had been calling for the superintendent's ouster for months. Another was that black parents were no more thrilled than white ones at the prospect of sending their children across town to school in an unfamiliar, perhaps unfriendly neighborhood.

Helping to tip the balance, however, was the Supreme Court's decision in the Swann case, written just five days before Robinson's speech. In addition to the thorny questions of student assignment and busing, the Court had reiterated that "policy and practice with regard to faculty, staff, transportation, extracurricular activities, and facilities are among the most important [indicators] of a segregated system, and the first remedial responsibility of school authorities is to eliminate invidious racial distinctions in those respects." Robinson keyed on the system's well-documented disparity in the hiring and promotion of black educators, and its below-level reading scores—disparities that Albohm could have eliminated over the years—and he pressed.

Though Robinson was preaching to the faithful (only a few white people, and none of them his fellow councilmen, attended the meeting), a full summary of his speech appeared on the front page of that week's *Journal*. Elected officials reacted quickly to the story, saying they agreed with Robinson about everything except Albohm's removal.

The Plan for Integrating the High Schools

Under the mounting legal and political pressure, the superintendent shifted into high gear his search for the most acceptable and educationally sound way to in-

301

tegrate the city's three high schools and three middle schools–a task the Charlotte, NC, school board had also tackled first. Albohm and his staff soon developed a plan for reorganizing those schools by grade-level, modeled on a school district in Bucks County, Pennsylvania. There, secondary school students moved up to a different school every two years, rather than spending four years in the same high school as was the case in Alexandria. By reorganizing in that way–by having every eleventh-and twelfth-grade student in the city attend T.C. Williams, Alexandria's newest and most centrally located high school–full integration would be achieved in a single stroke at that school. In addition, with so many students of the same age in one place, it was likely that age-specific educational and extracurricular activities could be enhanced. The same would be true for the city's ninth-and tenth-graders who would then be split between the two remaining high school buildings in the east and west ends of town, many transported across town to achieve racially mixed student bodies at each school. Seventh and eighth-graders would remain at the three existing middle schools, though some of them, too, would have to be reassigned to achieve more complete integration than in the past.

Before presenting this K-6, 2, 2, 2 plan, as it was called, to the school board for official action, the school administration wanted the board and the City Council to see for themselves how the plan worked in actual practice. So the administration arranged for the policy makers to visit the Pennsylvania school district on which their plan was modeled. Local news reporters were invited to come along. Upon arrival at the two-year high school, its educational and extracurricular advantages were immediately and everywhere evident. During the course of discussions with school officials there, it became particularly clear that, due to the larger pool of students at each grade level, a broad variety of offerings not previously available in Alexandria–like classes in Russian or advanced German, instruction in the performing arts, college level science courses, and intramural sports–could be introduced without net budget increases.

The Pennsylvania trip raised the hopes of school and city officials that an emotional, negatively charged situation could be turned into a positive one. And it had the effect of lining up community leaders of both races behind a single plan for the reorganization of the secondary schools. That was critical. Though opponents of school integration in Alexandria did not crowd the streets with placards as depicted in the Disney movie, opposition voiced at public meetings was strong, as was the quieter opposition typical of those who already had the ear of policy makers. If supporters of integration had not found a worthwhile plan to rally around–or had they put forward more than one–they would have been hard pressed to generate sufficient public backing.

By summer, the board had adopted the administration's plan for the secondary schools. The huge tasks of redesigning the high school curriculum, reassigning staff and students in the secondary schools and arranging new bus routes for several thousands of them consumed administrators right up until the opening of school in September.

Because of parental reluctance to send young children a long way to school on a bus, the administration and the board kept a lower profile about various plans under consideration for elementary school integration.

(Two years later, the board did adopt a plan that paired 10 elementary schools and divided their student populations by grade level–in somewhat the same way the consultant's plan in Charlotte, NC, had grouped inner-city black and suburban white elementary schools.) Meanwhile, school officials tasked with the responsibility of desegregating the elementary schools, and others who favored early childhood integration, were counting on the success of the high school reorganization to reduce public friction and smooth the way for the next step. They were betting heavily that concrete signs of success would emerge to quiet the critics, like higher test scores or more college acceptances–or more victories in competitive sports.

The 1971 Titans

First up, when school opened that autumn, of course, was the football team–a team that would finally have a chance to be competitive in its league due to the combined talent from the three former high school teams. But, first, those three former rivals would, somehow, have to be forged into a single unit.

As anyone with a video tape player now knows, Herman Boone, previously an assistant at T.C. Williams, was selected to make it all happen. He was named head coach while Bill Yoast, formerly the head coach at Hammond, was assigned to be his assistant, despite Yoast's seniority in the Alexandria system. There was, no doubt, some serious back room wrangling over that decision; but there also must have been some divine intervention. For a man like Boone doesn't come along every day, with a fire burning in his chest; nor does a man with Yoast's quiet endurance and strength of character. In effect, these two were thrust into a situation where they either abandoned their careers and their young charges or swapped the traditional roles so long imposed by race. The adjustment wasn't easy. Each paid the considerable personal price exacted, in their day, for stepping that far out of line. Yet, if they hadn't, imagine how much longer the old stereotypes would have persisted in our town, how much deeper they'd be embedded.

Under the circumstances, it would have been of little help in pulling the community together if the T.C. Williams football team had simply done better than previous teams. If the team had lost even a single game, people would have been free to speculate that a white coach could have done better, or that any one of the former teams might have done better; that integration wasn't so great, after all.

In an interview just days before the championship game, I asked Coach Boone if his team realized what was at stake. "Nobody in the country," he replied "knows what this game means to the city and the area more than they do." But even after that game, after the championship trophy was in hand and the last piece of confetti was out of our hair, none of us—not the coaches, not the players, not the reporters, not one parent, administrator, school board member, or city councilman—knew that the story of the 1971 Titans would someday inspire people across the country and around the world.

And here is the irony: Those of you who were trying out for the team and busy vying for starting positions earlier that season probably didn't realize how great a challenge the '71 Titans were up against; didn't fully understand the frighteningly familiar pressures your black coaches were under, or the frighteningly unfamiliar circumstances your white coaches found themselves in; did not really comprehend, until close to the season's end, the strange, new bet an entire community had placed on you.

And it was good that you didn't know the enormity of it. Because without knowing, you were free to work things out one-on-one. You were free to resolve your differences the way all truly important issues are resolved, no matter how large in scope they may be. And no matter how large they may appear, as we look back through the distorting lenses of history and our own proud memories. [end of Mary Ames' document]

Mary Elizabeth Ames went on to run several businesses in the Outer Banks of North Carolina and Key West, Florida. Her poetry and prose have flourished, and she's presently writing an historical novel about Ira Robinson's innovative family.

Connections with the Death of John-John (Note 15, page 148, from Chapter 9)

While I was watching television one morning in 1999, the cameras were focused on the ill-fated Kennedy family as they gathered on a naval barge to be transported to the battleship *Briscoe* for casting the ashes of John Kennedy Jr. into the sea where he had perished. Like most Americans, I was remembering the poignant picture of little "John-John" saluting his father as the bier rolled by, and now here was another ending.

Then the name of the ship rang a bell for me. I was wondering if the S.S. *Briscoe* that I was watching on television was named in honor of Kate's midshipman from my youth in New Orleans. I called the information officer of the Navy in Washington, D.C., and learned the following: Robert T. Briscoe was a four-star admiral who served with distinction in World War II and the Korean War and retired in 1959.

At the time we had seen him, he was living in the Navy yard next to the Anacostia Naval Station. When the Briscoes occupied Quarters One, Briscoe had been Deputy Chief of Navy Operations. The S.S. *Briscoe* was indeed named in his honor, and he was indeed "our policeman" midshipman-become-admiral over a dedicated career.

Oswald Hermann Hartmeyer (Note 16, page 153, from Chapter 9)

While doing research for these memoirs, I found Oswald Hermann Hartmeyer. He was born around 1903 and died in Hamburg in 1936. Apparently, he was the grandson of Dr. Emil Hartmeyer, a well-known German reactionary, a pan-Germanist. Oswald's grandfather was the owner of the *Hamburger Nachrichten* newspaper, which was in his family for generations. Dr. Hartmeyer was very active in spreading German propaganda—a great admirer of Otto von Bismarck. He was among the first to place his newspaper at Bismarck's disposal. In researching it, according to a *New York Times* article from 1921, I found that in 1920/1921 a German newspaper syndicate had begun purchasing many Austrian newspapers to be the voice of propaganda for the Greater Germany Party. Possibly Dr. Hartmeyer became the syndicate's managing editor. When I learned what an arch-conservative Oswald's father was, I wondered why Oswald died in 1936, so young, and wondered why he had a grave marker of wood rather than stone. I wanted to keep my memories of that urbane young Oswald as he had been when he taught us to tango in Cincinnati. I decided I didn't want to know.

What Happened to Jimmy McLemore's Ring (Note 17, page 155, from Chapter 9)

My friend Jimmy had received a class ring from his beloved grandmother on his high school graduation. When I graduated a year later, he placed this ring on my finger to show that we were special friends. Although I was not romantically interested in Jimmy, he was a very dear pal. As related in my conversations with Mary on our trip in Betsy, I had previously attempted to return the ring to Jimmy but failed to locate him in Mobile. In later years, my best friend from high school, Helen Croft, offered to look him up again. Helen discovered that Jimmy had retired to a Florida key which was next to Key West, where Mary had a craft store.

Mary and her partner, John, who were both dying with curiosity about this whole incident, went to see Jimmy, and this is how she reported the meeting: "Jimmy, with his wife, greeted John and me in front of their well-kept mobile home. Jimmy seemed nervous. His wife was hostile. Visiting them at the time was their daughter and her husband. Everyone was a bit uncomfortable. Jimmy shifted his weight back and forth from one foot to the other and said that he'd forgotten ever having such a ring. His wife gazed away from the group as though she was uninterested, but the son-in-law and John leaned forward so as not to miss a thing.

"John and I worked at putting them at ease, got them talking and laughing. Relaxed now, I placed the 1930 class ring that his beloved grandmother had given him into his hand, and he responded, 'Mary, your mother was the first girl whose hand I ever held.'

"I now knew it was all right to tell them of the time, years before in Mobile, when he failed to *be there for you*, as he had promised when you left Mobile for Cincinnati. Even his wife laughed.

"Jimmy was pensive for a while. 'I guess when your mother came to our house in Mobile we were at church and the boys were home, grubby, tinkering with their motors. No bevy of females could have invaded their territory.'

"Before we left Jimmy and his family, I told him about Muffin being in Arizona, to which he responded, 'To celebrate my last umpteen birthdays, I have hiked to the bottom of the Grand Canyon and back up again.'"

When Mary reported back to me, she said, "Well, Mom, I closed *that* chapter for you. For one, I'm glad it was *Dad's* ring you kept on your finger."

I thought there was a lot of satisfaction living beyond one's life expectancy. You do get to learn "how it all turned out!"

La Posada, Winslow, Arizona (Note 18, page 201, from Chapter 13)

Once a stately hacienda-like railroad hotel, La Posada property was designed under the direction of architect Mary Jane Colter, who had been contracted by the Fred Harvey Company. It served as an elegant way station for the Santa Fe Railroad, opening to train passengers and Route 66 tourists in 1929, just before the crash of '29. Later, as the age of passenger trains declined, so did La Posada Hotel. The railroad company closed the hotel in 1957, gutted the building, and used it for administration and rail traffic control. The Santa Fe Railroad abandoned La Posada in 1994 and announced plans to tear it down. After the city of Winslow declined to accept the property for a fee of $1.00, in 1997 it was purchased and renovated by four dedicated citizens. Their hotel and restaurant once again have the same allure as the old Harvey Houses. Martha and I have visited it in recent years, as Martha knows the chef of the Turquoise Room dining room, who specializes in gourmet dishes made with native and local foods. La Posada continues to draw tourists attracted to its history and charm even more today than in the past.

The Harvey House restaurant where we ate in 1919 was probably the earlier Harvey House at the old Santa Fe station, no longer standing, on the other side of the tracks from La Posada. Winslow, Arizona, no longer a large city since the building of Interstate 40 and the decline of rail use, was an interesting stop for us Wayfarers when we got off onto historical Route 66 through town. Hearing the famous song from 1972 "Take It Easy" by the Eagles, Mary and I always are reminded of our visit to Winslow in Betsy.

Professors, Mentors, and Scientists (Note 19, page 203, from Chapter 13)

On an interesting note related to Martha's 1970 excavation at Stanton's Cave mentioned in Part One, after years of effort by concerned biologists to save the California condor from near extinction, condors have now been re-introduced to the Grand Canyon.

Regarding scientist mentors, Antarctica explorer Dr. Lawrence McKinley Gould (known to us as Larry) and author of *Cold*, a book about his experiences in the 1957 International Geophysical Year in Antarctica, became one of my champions. He and his wife, Peg, enjoyed my artwork and purchased some of my best collages and paintings. Larry had been second in command of Admiral Byrd's expedition to the South Pole by dogsled in 1929. On the later 1957 IGY expedition to Antarctica, the science team made it possible for Larry to sample rock from a mountain emerging above the ice by supplying him access with an aircraft and pilot. After landing near the mountain and securing the airplane, they set up camp. During the night the winds got as high as 150 mph and the plane broke its tethers in the ice and blew away from camp. They reported what had happened later over the intact radio when they found the plane. When he learned that U.S. newspapers reported a famous geologist had gotten lost on Antarctica, Larry was irate about the false claim and said, "I wasn't lost, *I* knew where I was!"

Professional geological photographer and friend, Tad Nichols, in one of his many stories, told of an Indian farmer in Old Mexico who, while cultivating his crops, was terrified at steam and smoke belching out of his quiet cornfield. The village people realized that they were witnessing the birth of a new volcano. When heavy lava began to flow, Tad went to document it with camera in hand. He also took pictures of the local people, including one shot of a foolish observer lighting a cigarette on one of the glowing hot stones that had just landed at the base of the hot cinder cone after being jettisoned from a steam hole. This was indeed the birth of Paricutin Volcano in 1943.

Peter Kresan, also a professional photographer, became a geology professor at the University of Arizona, inspired by faculty members Larry Gould and Don Sayner. Peter and Tad once hiked from Cusco in Peru, in the Andes, until they stood on a high vantage and saw Machu Picchu for the first time. In multi-media presentations in Tucson, which some of us have been privileged to see, he has shared with us dual-screen extravaganza shows of his worldwide geo-expeditions accompanied by heroic symphony music. His artistic photographic perceptions can be seen at Davis-Dominguez Gallery and on www.peterkresanphotography.com.

Dr. Paul Martin was chief scientist at University of Arizona Desert Laboratory at Tumamoc Hill, studying the impact of humans on the Ice Age beasts that once roamed the Southwest. Muff attended many of his field trips throughout the Sonoran Desert and the relatively unknown northwest extension of tropical Mexico. Paul Martin and Dr. C. Vance Haynes inspired her to lead Sonoran Desert expeditions herself later for the Arizona-Sonora Desert Museum.

Dr. Raymond Turner became a good friend of the Ameses. Working in the Water Resources Division of U.S. Geological Survey at the University of Arizona Desert Laboratory on Tumamoc Hill, Ray has documented generations of saguaro cactus and other desert plant populations. Muff was privileged to be on some of Ray's saguaro measuring expeditions to the Pinacate Volcanic Field and other desert places.

Tree-ring and heirloom bean expert Dr. Barney T. Burns was one of the founders of the seed conservation organization Native Seeds/ SEARCH with his wife, Mahina, in Tucson. Through the years they have been great friends with the Ameses and fill any gathering with priceless stories of archaeological adventure and native seed discovery. They know me as "Mamsie."

Desert ecologist Dr. Tony Lambard Burgess returned from Vietnam to earn a master's at Texas Tech and his PhD at University of Arizona in ecology and evolutionary biology, where he re-united

311

with Muff. In matrimony, with the addition of son, Beauregard Ames Burgess, they purchased a farm in Colorado as an economic parachute, while helping to design and study BioSphere 2 in Tucson. Tony designed the rooftop desert gardens and interpretive dome for the Caravan of Dreams Perform-ing Arts Center in his hometown of Fort Worth, Texas. He became an admired voice for the desert and ace field ecologist at the University of Arizona's Desert Laboratory, Tu-mamoc Hill, with the U.S. Geologi-cal Survey's Water Resources sec-tion. He helped design and taught innovative field classes for Colum-bia University's Earth Semesters using BioSphere 2 as the impetus and base camp. Tony retired from Professor of Environmental Sci-ences at Texas Christian University in Fort Worth in 2013, from the de-partment which he founded. He now resides in a new Boreal biome with son, Beau, in Homer, Alaska. I have written about an exciting chapter in Tony's life, a biology and archaeol-ogy project he worked on in Canyon de Chelly National Monument, in a chapter in my upcoming book, *Inno-cent Intruders* (in press).

Professor Tony Lambard Burgess, circa 1998

Papa Tony and Baby Beau Burgess, November 1985, Puerto Libertad, Sonora (photo by Mama Muff Burgess)

Beauregard Ames Burgess, Muffin's and Tony's son, is now creator-owner of several burgeoning businesses in Homer, including HomerBookkeepers LLC, which keeps several businesses solvent, documented, and transparent; and Southern Exposure LLC, a construction company building sustainably efficient homes and designing wind generation for the Kenai Peninsula. He serves on the Homer City Council, where he is bringing energy-saving infrastructure and high-speed internet to the end-of-the-road.

Beauregard Ames Burgess, age 6, pastel portrait

First coming to University of Arizona for a master's degree in dendrochronology, Martha (Muffin) Ames Burgess founded the Desert Museum's members' field program in the '70s, where she initiated the Desert Harvest Bazaar, the speaker series, nature photography competitions, and one-of-a-kind study tours. Her expeditions introduced novice adventurers to remote places in the Sonoran Desert region— to raft Sonoran rivers hung with inverted agaves and strangler figs, to seek belly flowers on the Pinacate lava flows, to kiss whales in the lagoons of Baja California, to explore landmarks like Nacozari (where Jesus Garcia, the "Casey Jones of Mexico," sacrificed himself and his train to save the town from a dynamite explosion), to study earth history and desert plants via pontoon on the Colorado River. With Beau an infant and Tony away for BioSphere 2, Martha became a stay-at-home mom.

When Beau started school, she returned to work with Native Seeds/SEARCH to run a diabetes-prevention project on the Tohono O'odham Nation, using traditional foods as medicine. In order to raise awareness of our desert agricultural heritage, she founded La

Fiesta de los Chiles, the San Juan's Celebration, and other seed celebrations for Native Seeds/SEARCH. Mentored early by Tohono O'odham elders Juanita Ahil and Frances Manuel about harvesting of traditional plants, Martha continues to teach classes in desert foods, medicinal plants, and desert gardening, and to advocate for sustainable living in the desert through her company, Flor de Mayo, www.flordemayoarts.com. Her informative articles appear in the magazine *Edible Baja Arizona*. She now serves on the boards of Native Seeds/SEARCH and Baja Arizona Sustainable Agriculture. She can be found with her partner Rod Mondt at farmers' market events in Tucson, Phoenix, and western Colorado expounding upon native food nutrition, sustainable agriculture, and plant lore. Rod was one of the founders of the conservation organization, Sky Island Alliance, and is working creatively to assess and protect wilderness in the island-mountains of the Borderlands. He and Muff share their volunteer time also at the

Bob and Ginny Ames' church photo, Grace-St. Paul's, 1991

Roderick Mondt and Muffin Burgess at a Desert Botanical Garden event, 2013

living history Mission Garden where Friends of Tucson's Birthplace displays the heirloom fruit trees and vegetable plants of the community's colorful prehistoric and historic past.

Dubbed "HoHo" by Baby Clo for his Santa Claus act, Bob (Robert Hyde) Ames became HoHo to the rest of the family ever after. He and I enjoyed ten wonderful years together in active retirement in Tucson, Arizona, where we came to know the exciting university professors, scientists, and mentors Muff had first introduced to us. We celebrated our 50th wedding anniversary with many lifelong friends and relatives in attendance and a view toward the future at the yet-to-be-sealed BioSphere 2 site. After Bob passed in 1993, I dove into my artwork, exploring many print media in my Tucson studio, adventuring to far-flung places like the Cook Islands and Italy's Hill Towns to paint, and sharing my love of art by teaching classes at the University of Arizona's SAGE/OLLI society for life-long learning

Now, in an attempt to keep my neurons firing successfully after ninety-nine years and diminished eyesight, and with the help of an inspiring younger musician-pal Boyce McClung, I have taken up learning the stand-up bass. It is one of the most rewarding activities of my life, bringing back the pleasure of old songs, but also for bringing out smiles and laughter among friends.

Ginny Ames at the bass fiddle, 2013
(photo by John H. Ames)

Dr. Gustav Eckstein (Note 20, page 241, from Chapter 16)

About four years before he died, Dr. Gustav Eckstein was interviewed by *the Cincinnati Inquirer* and recalled being asked by Dick Cavett if he was afraid to die. Eckstein's response was, "I told him, 'If you mean gasping my way out, the pain, the agony, of course I wouldn't like that. But I hope to be present at my own death. Regardless of what happens, I want to be there and see it. There are two things I'd like to do before I die and that is to finish my autobiography and the other is to finish my book on Pav-lov.'" Neither one of those goals was actually accomplished before he passed, and although I've tried to find the research notes Eckstein made of Pavlov's experiments and his notes on his autobiography, where they went after his death remains a mystery. The most hope I've had is through the librarians at the University of Cincinnati's College of Medicine Library, who continue the search.

Eckstein had two opportunities to have a bust sculpted of him. The first request was by chance while the Russian artist Konenkov was visiting New York City around 1935. Konenkov asked him if he might create a sculpture of Dr. Eckstein's head. He wanted to do this while visiting in America, because his own studio was in Moscow. Af-ter some resistance, Eckstein agreed and happened to encounter Dr. Albert Einstein on a few occasions while going for his sitting appoint-ments, striking up brief conversations with him in their native Ger-man tongue. Before the sculpture was completed, when Dr. Eckstein left Konenkov's studio once more, he was delighted to see that Albert Schweitzer was also having his head sculpted by the same man.

The second sculpture was created when a group of doctors from the University of Cincinnati commissioned Mike Skop of Fort Thom-as, Kentucky, to do Dr. Eckstein's head for display at the University of Cincinnati College of Medicine in the '70s, when Eckstein visited his friend Dr. Clay Crawford at the historical home of deceased no-table sculptor, Julian Bechtold, where Skop now resided. The unveil-ing of this bust of Eckstein took place at a celebration in honor of Gus, as everyone affectionately knew him, on his eighty-ninth birth-day at the University of Cincinnati College of Medicine, where his peers offered accolades for Eckstein's worthy contributions.

Michael and Lucy Copass and their family (Note 21, page 253, from Chapter 18)

Lucy Ames Copass graduated from Stanford *magna cum laude* and also received the highest award at Stanford given to a man or woman for his/her greatest contribution to undergraduate education.

While raising their family, Lucy was an active member of the League of Women Voters, which published her study on the availability and use of energy in Washington State. She was also on the planning commission for Mercer Island. When their children were grown, eager to use her education from Stanford, Lucy started her own public affairs consulting firm in the Seattle region.

Michael Copass graduated from Stanford University and received his medical degree from Northwestern University in neurology. He became a neurologist and taught at the University of Washington, School of Medicine. His work also included the training of paramedics for Seattle's pioneering Medic One emergency response system, which has profoundly changed the industry worldwide. Medic One was founded in 1969 as a collaboration between Dr. Leonard A. Cobb, a University of Washington cardiologist, and the Seattle Fire Department. A few years later, when Michael was in charge of the training, he taught the medics to think and act like doctors instead of just as an emergency crew. He kept in touch with the emergency vehicles by phone and also prepared the emergency room for the patient prior to arrival. Sometimes he rode with the paramedics to see how to improve the service.

Michael tells the story about the time when he rode in an aid car and a call came in from a man who said his wife was in labor. When they arrived, the husband was sitting at the dining room table with friends—playing poker, smoking, and drinking. The wife was lying on the living room sofa groaning with labor pains. When a paramedic said, "We'll never get this lady to the emergency room before the baby is born," Michael said, "Then you're in charge of the delivery." After the paramedic delivered the baby, wrapped it in a blanket, and arrived at the emergency room, he was reluctant to hand the baby to the nurse, the first baby he had ever delivered. It was as though he felt this baby were his own.

Medic One has an international reputation for innovation and excellence. It is said of Medic One, "If you are going to have a heart attack, have it in Seattle, where the average time of arrival at the site is four minutes."

Michael served as director of emergency services of Harborview Medical Center for thirty-five years. To honor him for his outstanding accomplishments, the Medic One Foundation established a named endowment at the University of Washington in honor of Dr. Michael Keys Copass. He has become world-renowned for his pioneering paramedic training programs and pre-hospital emergency care. Interest generated by an endowment in his honor helps today to cover paramedic training costs and equipment, plus honorariums for guest lecturers and physicians, as well as support for instructors.

Their first daughter, Cloantha Wade Copass, graduated from Stanford in the next generation, having concentrated on city planning and historic preservation. She and her husband, Douglas Fleming, gave me my first two great-grandchildren, talented athlete Nicholas and dancer Catharine.

Their son Michael Keys Copass Jr. studied cell biology as an undergraduate at Stanford and stayed for a master's degree. After two years working for a pharmaceutical company in Italy he returned to earn a second master's at Harvard. He was instrumental in founding a training school for young athletes in a poor part of Brazil and con-

Lucy Ames Copass and Dr. Mike Copass in their treehouse,
Mercer Island, Washington

Mike Copass Jr. with Oma Ginny and HoHo,
Tucson, March 1989

Cloantha Wade Copass and Douglas Fleming
family with Catharine and Nicholas

Catharine Dean Copass with
HoHo's 1972 Rolls Royce

Mike Copass Jr. with nephew Nicholas,
San Diego, 2005

Dr. Catharine D. Copass, 2005

Zephyr and Finn Thompson,
Catharine Copass' sons, July 2013

319

tinues his teaching and fitness training career in the Port Angeles area.

Their second daughter, Catharine Dean Copass, also graduated from Stanford, majoring in biological sciences, and works as a planning ecologist for the National Park Service in the Pacific Northwest Region. Her two charming sons, Finn and Zephyr Thompson, are my other two admired great-grandchildren.

A Note from "Betsy"—how it turned out for me ... (Note 22, page 259, from Chapter 19)
June 1994, Mercer Island, WA

I got a positive charge out of my years shuttling bouncing Copass kids to school, soccer practice, dance recitals, and swim teams, and always felt a thrill to see children hail me, or even laugh or gawk at my old-fashioned streamlined body. When the family purchased its new second car, teenagers no longer waived at me; I was different. Useless, I sat just off the driveway in the shade of a stand of northwestern conifers. My finish felt rather dull.

One day the mail delivery man stopped and asked if he might purchase me. Happy that I would have more adventures, the family parted with me. I knew I would miss the Copass children, whom I enjoyed. But life continues for me, nonetheless. Now, little kids and friendly dogs rush to greet me as I put mail in their mailboxes on the street. I'm of service once again. Neither snow nor rain nor heat stays me "from the swift completion of my appointed rounds."

I hope each of you relishes wherever life takes you on *your* wayfaring journey.

Sincerely, Betsy, the Wayfarer

Virginia Ames at Rancho Linda Vista art show 1998
with her pastel, *Polynesian Children*

The Artist's Favorites – Virginia Ames' Own Favorite Artworks

Special places and adventures, mentioned either along the way on our Wayfarers journey or in Part Two, made deep impressions on me and became subjects in my art. Here are a few images of my creations:

Polynesian Children, Cook Islands – pastel

Woods at Orleans Place in October – paper collage

Fishermen on the Outer Banks, NC
– watercolor

Opening Night at Kennedy Center
– 1971 watercolor

Cook Islands Coconut Palm – watercolor

Canyon de Chelly – mixed media pastel and acrylic

Baboquivari from Kitt Peak – acrylic on canvas

Corral at Rancho Linda Vista – pastel

Aloe Forest – pastel

Desert Lace – collograph

Pueblo Women – silkscreen print

Gary, Indiana – acrylic on unprimed canvas

Polynesian Boy with His Fighting Cock – pastel

Some Things
I Have Learned

For most of us, a will brings to mind a legal document declaring how a person's possessions will be distributed after his death—his money and his property and any other valuable things he owns. Recently, a thoughtful man declared that what a person has *learned* may be more valuable than what that individual has *earned*. He proposed that each of us have a second will in which we pass along some insights that have added depth to our lives. This he called an "Ethical Will," but I prefer to think of this second document as "Some Things I Have Learned." I share these thoughts below.

We should take more time to daydream.

Americans are battered by the hectic pace of life. Daydreaming can restore tranquility, but it can do much more. When did you last lie on a green grass slope and watch the white clouds billow into the blue sky creating ever-changing images as they move, perhaps seeing the head of a woman evolve into the face of a rogue, or an angel become a swan in flight? Do you, the breadwinner, read the *Wall Street Journal* at the beach when you could be lulled by a breeze from the sea or by the rhythm of waves breaking on the sand?

Tranquil moments such as these foster creativity. Some idea generated by your unique quiet mind may be sparked by one of the myriad facts stored in your brain and at that exciting moment, a totally new concept may come to life, one that could change our world. Think for a moment of the chip that revolutionized electronics, or of the electron microscope that moved medicine ahead immeasurably, or of the revolutionary telescopes and cameras that have taken us deeper into the cosmos.

Another bit of wisdom contemplated seriously by many but seldom made a practice in our thinking has great appeal to me:

We should re-examine our assumptions from time to time, re-assessing our values, our beliefs, and our habits.

We change slowly, while knowledge expands rapidly and the world continues to change and evolve. Any values that are really important to you can survive such a re-evaluation. Ernest Hemingway expressed this idea with humorous suggestion, "A man should repot himself every ten years."

Speaking at a graduation ceremony at Stanford University some years ago, Edwin H. Land, CEO of the Polaroid Corporation, advised the graduates to take an "a-polar view" of all their plans, beliefs, and procedures. The substance of his lecture was that if you see things from an entirely new perspective, you will see more clearly what course to follow.

Years ago, when I was secretary to Dr. Gustav Eckstein, professor of physiology and later psychology at the University of Cincinnati College of Medicine, he shared with me one of his great insights:

When things go wrong, STOP—THINK—<u>THEN</u> ACT.

In the ensuing years, thinking of this piece of Eckstein's wisdom has kept me steady through moments of panic.

Now in the twilight of my life it seems to me our self-governing country is beset by more serious problems than it can solve—poverty in the midst of plenty and jobless citizens who need a helping hand out of hopelessness. A good educational system, in time, could solve both of those problems. We blame our representatives for refusing to resolve their differences in order to get the job done, but responsibility lies on the shoulders of *all* Americans, yet only half of our countrymen even go to the polls to vote.

We citizens have the power to take control!

Negligence could threaten our freedom, even our democratic form of government. This may sound unlikely, even bizarre to anyone who did not live through the McCarthy era. Joseph McCarthy, a member of the Senate, took unto *himself* the power to bring a person to trial, accusing him or her of being a member of the Communist Party. Without counsel, the accused could not see his accuser face to face.

Reputations were ruined, jobs were lost, and influential men feared their companies or publications would be blacklisted. No one would call McCarthy's bluff. At that time, Edward R. Murrow, a respected newspaper reporter, was the only one brave enough to expose McCarthy's abuse of power. Relief ran through the country like falling dominoes when the first key tile lost its balance.

This is no time for negligence in our country when millions around the world are fighting to rid themselves of tyranny. We must be watchful, clear in fact-finding, and *active* in voting and expressing our opinions.

When major disaster strikes somewhere in the world, our country is often the first to be there with aid—food, medicine, and money. This makes me proud to be an American.

But are we not able at the same time to see that
no American goes to bed hungry?

Our middle class is shrinking—many new families falling below the poverty level while a very small percentage control almost all of the wealth. *Now* is the time for all smart men and women "to come to the aid of their country."

When I am overwhelmed by our problems, I find it helpful to do two things.

I think of some small task I can do
toward solving just one problem.

Some people think, "What difference does my one little action make?" But joined with similar actions by more people, change can and does happen. Courage and energy are increased even when incremental progress is made in the right direction.

Next, I ask myself to consider the unbelievable *number of things for which I am profoundly grateful.*

I am grateful that we have curiosity, which makes us explore and learn new things.

I am grateful for our capacity for speech and language, so we are able to share our knowledge and feelings with one another.

I am grateful for compassion that makes me mindful of the needs of our fellow man and all living things.

I am grateful that life began at all. We may be interested in the *when* and the *how* of the beginning of life on our planet, but while we argue among ourselves over who has the truth about the when and how of the origins of life—in a muddy pool on our planet, or in the hot depths of the Pacific where there's no sunlight, or riding in from space on a dirty snowball, or from Adam's rib—we lose sight of the unbelievable miracle that life began at all.

I am grateful that I am conscious of existing, that I can enjoy and share what I have learned with others, that I can learn from the past, and that I can plan for the future.

I am most grateful for the capacity to love, for love keeps us from being lonely in this crazy, wonderful old world.

And now, with gratitude, I turn over responsibility to you to keep this crazy, vibrant, old world going.

A FAMILY ALBUM OF
ANCESTORS

Sally Louise Powers Wade (Bigmother), b.1858 Florence, AL,
married Alex Corson Wade, d.1941 Birmingham, AL.

Ginny's father, Albert Thompson Wade, in Louisville, KY, 1940s

Albert Thompson Wade (standing left) on Florida
fishing trip for L&NRR executives

Harriet Guscott Forbes
(Virginia's Aunt Hattie) raised
younger sister Pearl Guscott (Wade)
after their mother died

Pearl May Guscott Wade
(b. Sept.11, 1892), in trousseau
gown 1912 awaiting first child

Bob Ames' Aunt Rina, Catharine
McEwen Ames, in her maturity

Bob Ames' mother, "Bessy,"
Elizabeth Atwater Butler Ames,
as a young matron

Bob's maternal grandparents: Elizabeth Atwater Barker
1784-1866, and John Barker 1792-1833

Bob's maternal great-grandparents: M. Rachel Barker
1764-1823, and Edward Barker 1747-1825

Bob's paternal
great-grandfather,
William Ames

Bob's paternal
great-grandmother,
Catharine Maria
McEwen Hyde,
1802-1891
(married to
Joseph Hyde)

Acknowledgments

Thanks to my wise and gentle husband, Robert Ames, who was the finest partner in the adventure of life and made it possible for me to make being a stay-at-home mom truly a fine profession.

Without the help of a group of talented "young people" I could not have brought this book into being. I am deeply indebted to assistants Jill Provan, Jan Willkom, and Joanie Sawyer. Kathryn Twinfeathers' skill with computers and excellent memory enabled me to continue working on manuscripts as my vision deteriorated. Nancy Stahler recorded appointments and got me to them on time. Her happy disposition kept my spirits light through every chore.

Three in a family of dear friends, Herbert and Kathryn Sanborn—Sandy and Kaye—and their son, Jim Sanborn, who has redefined sculpture in the art world, all opened wider the doors to art for our family and added luster to our lives in Washington.

I thank a learned trio of friends in Tucson: geologist and *Arizona Highways* photographer Peter Kresan, geologist Larry Gould, professional photographer Tad Nichols, and especially Pete for his technical advice and digitization of my paintings.

Nancy Wall, Pima Community College English professor, friend, and writers' group inspiration, really launched me into disciplined writing. Richard Brusca, former executive program director of Arizona-Sonora Desert Museum, gave me sound advice on where to go with my writing. Chris Szuter, former director of the University of Arizona Press, now at Arizona State University, positively encouraged me to complete my memoirs. Linda M. Brewer, Arizona-Sonora Desert Museum Press Manager, gave enthusiastic encouragement with editing advice.

The following resource people have been of priceless help:

Archivist Julia Randle, Bishop Payne Library and Archives at Virginia Theological Seminary, for her continued enthusiasm for my memoirs.

Doris Haag, Director of the Henry R. Winkler Center for the History of the Health Professions, University of Cincinnati Medical School Libraries, who recorded oral histories of the medical school professors, including a movie of the testimonial dinner on the occasion of Gustav Eckstcin's ninetieth birthday and the unveiling of his bust in recognition of his unique contribution to the College of Medicine.

Suzanne Maggard, reference/collections librarian, University of Cincinnati, Archives and Rare Books Library, who went to great lengths to provide invaluable information about Dr. Gustav Eckstein.

Katherine Collett, archives librarian, Hamilton College Library, who sent me a DVD of Eckstein's arrival for a visit to Alexander Woollcott's summer home.

Phillip Brooks for his interview of me for the Alexandria Historical Society, Inc.

The Office of Land Records, City of Fairfax, Fairfax County, Virginia, for their help in researching the history of the land on Seminary Hill, upon which we built our home.

Linda Federico, research librarian, The City of Fairfax Regional Library, Fairfax, Virginia.

To those physicians who have kept me lively long enough to complete *The Wayfarers*. They include cardiologists Dr. Ed Dick and Dr. Kathryn L. Bates; Dr. Marilyn Croghan, my oncologist; Dr. April Harris, my retinologist; Dr. Evan Kligman, my primary care physician; and Dr. Terry Valenzuela, Emergency Medicine, University of Arizona Medical Center.

Many people have touched my life and made it richer, and their influence is felt throughout these pages:

Tony Burgess, father of our grandson Beau, is a gifted scholar and an inspiring professor who makes teaching an art. Tony encouraged me to finish my memoirs and gave me "how to" books by other successful authors. He clarified for me new directions in writing.

John and Wendy Ames also encouraged me to complete *The Wayfarers* because they knew how important it is for the family and beyond.

Boyce McClung taught me to play the stand-up bass in the hope that learning a new skill would create new neurons firing in my brain essential for writing. He brought music again into our lives.

Helen Head Croft, my Mobile High School classmate and dear friend, and her son, Charles Croft, who has kept the two of us in touch when age made it difficult for us to do so.

Nancy Bishop kept me up-to-date on old friends in Alexandria and refreshed my memory of street names and locations.

Bill and Rosemary Edmonston welcomed us to Tucson and into their interesting lives. Their daughter, Betsy Banks, and her husband, Brian, have kept that friendship warm.

Tucson neighbors Janet and Bob Humphrey and their daughter, Courtney, who has been my friend from her childhood into her maturity.

Great Tucson neighbors Glory and Hector Campoy, who are kind and strong citizens and also share our love of art.

Sandy Wolf and Dave Dalton, Tucson neighbors, whose interest in studying the importance of bats offered many interesting conversations over informal meals.

Juanita Ahil, Native American elder, basket maker, and teacher, who broke down invisible cultural walls, always with a sense of humor.

The "Bookies," members of my Tucson book club, kept me reading current bestsellers when all I wanted to do was concentrate on my own writing:

Sally Cushman, with her feisty sense of humor, doesn't stand for any nonsense, cares a great deal about me and I about her.

Cathy Davin created course curricula to keep us studying in retirement, sharing her knowledge and love of short stories and poetry enthusiastically, which added great variety to my own creativity.

Other "Bookie" buddies include Janet Bideaux, Dot Crozier, Lera Gates, Nancy Hannan, Betty Lumia, Pat Martin, Elizabeth Ohm, Betty Rogers, and Norma Schnabel.

The teachers who influenced my life: Lockie Wingo, Marcell Tear, two of the three sisters D'Ornellis, and the teacher in Mobile who wrote and produced *The Queen of the Fairies*, making me love theater forever after.

In my college years, an interested professor, Arthur Postle, changed the direction of my life by insisting that I become a member of the University of Cincinnati Speakers Bureau.

Gustav Eckstein was my first employer and greatest mentor.

I acknowledge other dear relatives and friends through the years:

Susan Freund, our neighbor in Virginia, has also been my lawyer and friend in Tucson.

Betsy Tharp and Bob Zimmerman, Ohio friends who cheer me on in my writing and painting, have included me in many of their Southwest adventures.

Our congregation in Alexandria at Immanuel-Church-on-the-Hill, including Emily Bobbitt, my soft-spoken, Southern partner-in-crime at church, and her husband, Bill, who was in charge of grounds at the Episcopal High School; my dignified, gentle, Virginian friends, Vernie Knight and her husband, Buzzie, who was legal counsel for the National Archives; my friend Alberta Carten and her husband, Leo; my very British mentors, Johnny and DeeDee Walker; and my dear young pal, Julie Winterberg, and her husband, Ivan.

Jane Kroehl and family, who knew my son-in-law Michael Copass as a child, later moved to Tucson, becoming even closer to our family.

Bob's nephew Bill Baker and his wife, Wanda, kept us connected with Bob's family by visiting almost every year after we moved to the Southwest.

Rod Mondt, the most recent addition to the family as Muffin's partner, brings his personal warmth and experiences into lively conversation and brings out of me ever more memories to record.

My three daughters, Lucy, Martha, and Mary, and son-in-law, Dr. Mike, with their love and support, have brought *The Wayfarers* to fruition.

And now my publishing advisor Polly Letofsky at MyWord! Publishing, layout designer Andrea Costantine, and editor Donna Mazzitelli have made it all happen!

About the Author

Virginia Wade Ames (Born November 6, 1914)

Centenarian Virginia Wade Ames has led a life of creativity, using the arts to express her love of life, people, and beauty. While rearing her family, needle, thread, fabric, and food were her media. Friends and neighbors became the players on her stage as she and her husband choreographed social gatherings with unsung heroes, characters of the times, movers, shakers, and invisible makers of history.

With children educated and off on their own, she perfected her passions for silkscreen printing, watercolor, acrylic, and pastel painting. When a friend ran for office, her elegant paper hat-making events successfully threw his hat into the ring.

Ames is a cultural catalyst, not only bringing interesting people together but also seeing potentials for bringing about good—her work to get the Torpedo Factory Center for the Arts established in Alexandria is a prime example.

In her "retirement" to Arizona she has enriched lives with her artful teaching at the University of Arizona's lifelong learning SAGE/OLLI society. As macular degeneration began taking its visual toll on her artist's eye she turned her energies to word craft. At ninety-nine, she has four more manuscripts ready for publication and four great-grandchildren who will especially enjoy them. Her genteel wit and seasoned thoughts on how to treat each other can touch us all.

Made in the USA
San Bernardino, CA
29 September 2014